Minnesota's Lost Towns
Northern Edition

Minnesota's Lost Towns

Northern Edition

Rhonda Fochs

North Star Press of St. Cloud, In.
St. Cloud, Minnesota

Dedication

To my family:

In more ways than I can count,
I thank you for your belief,
your support and your help.

ISBN 978-0-87839-763-1

Printed in the United States of America.

Published by:
North Star Press of St. Cloud, Inc.
St. Cloud, Minnesota

www.northstarpress.com

Acknoweldgments

Without the assistance, help and support of many, many people and organizations, this book would not have been possible. Early historians, known and unknown, wrote local and family histories left for later generations and are an invaluable record of the times and people of the past. Their memories, letters, oral, and written histories are a treasure-trove of tales, anecdotes, and facts that would be lost without their foresight and their efforts to record them. Without their contributions we would be severely limited in our knowledge of the rich details of the past. It is a great debt, that I, that we, owe to those early historians.

I can't stress enough the importance of local historical societies and museums. These local repositories are true gems right in the midst of our local communities. With limited funds and resources, the staff and volunteers of these organizations preserve our past and ensure our future. I urge you to visit them, support them and perhaps even volunteer. Without them, and the people involved with them, we would be sorely lacking in our historical knowledge and legacy. This book could not have been written without them.

Libraries are another local treasure. Today's libraries provide a wide range of services delivered by knowledgeable and helpful staff. They make locating and accessing research materials a reality.

To those that allowed me the use of their photos, thank you. Your credits are listed by your photos.

Should I have inadvertently omitted anyone, my apologies. Any omission was purely unintentional. Again, thank you.

Aitkin County Historial Society
Aurora Public Library
Banning State Park, MNDNR
Becker County Historical Society
Beltrami County Historical Society
Blackduck History and Art Center
Buena Vista Ski Area and Logging Village
Carlton County Historical Society
Cass County Historical Society
Cass Lake Times
City of Buhl
City of Hibbing, Parks Department
City of Kinney
Clearwater County Historical Society
Cook County Historical Society
Crow Wing County Historical Society
Douglas County Historical Society
Douglas County City Public Works
Ely-Winton Historical Society
Grant County Historical Society
Gilbert Public Library
Great River Regional Library
Hibbing Historical Society
Hibbing Public Library
Historical and Cultural Society of Clay

County
History Museum of East Ottertail County
Hoyt Lakes Public Library
Iron Range Historical Society
Iron Range Research Center
Itasca County Historical Society
Kanabec History Center
Kittson County Historical Society
Koochiching County Engineering
Koochiching County Historical Society
Lake County Historical Society
Lakeland Public Television
Lake of the Woods County Historical
    Society
Lincoln Ladies Aid
Mahnomen County Historical Society
Minnesota Discovery Center
MNLINK Interlibrary Loan
Morrison County Historical Society
National Park Service, Voyageurs
    National Park
Norman County Historical Society
Northeast Minnesota Historical Center
Ottertail County GIS
Ottertail County Historical Society

Park Rapids Area Library
Pine County Historical Society
Red Lake County Historical Society
Roseau County Historical Society
Sandstone History and Art Center
Schroeder Area Historical Society
Staples Library
Virginia Area Historical Society
Wadena County Historical Society

Cindy Adams
Elizabeth Anderson
Nancy Anselment-Olson
Steve Backstrom
Janie Barthel
Lina Belar
Patty Benson
Kathy Bergan
Dori Betts
Sue Boehland
Glenn Browne
Tom Burke
Terry Burt
Paula Chapman
Audrey Chute

Jim Cordes
Catherine Crawford
Britt Dahl
Amy Degerstrom
Sandy Dennis
Kim Dillon
Sandy Drury
Corinne Dwyer
Seal Dwyer
Tamara Edevold
Andrew Filer
Nicole Foss
Suzan From
Renee Geving
Shirley Gilmore
Agnes Gilson
Diane Gjerstad
Doug Grindall
Heidi Haagenson
Lynda Hall
Shawn Hewitt
Kris Hiller
Marlys Hirst

Ren Holland
Megan Johnsen
Sue Jorgenson
Dan Karilus
Scott Knudson
Joanie Kramer
Connie LaFreniere
Dee Jay Lawrence
Al Lieffort
Bob Lemen
Barbara J. Livdahl
Julie Lueck
Roxanne Lundeen
Rachael Martin
Carrie McHugh
Patricia Maus
Barbara Milkovich
Nicole Miller
Frank J. Mitchell
Heather Monthei
Andrew Munsch
Nancy Nelson
Dale Nikula

Jackie Nurnberger
Allan Olson
Mark Peihl
Ellen Peters
LaVonne Peterson
Nancy Riesgraf
Mel Sando
Honor Schauland
Ann Skoglund
Susan Sowers
Gloria Stone
Margaret Sweet
Mary Theurer
Suzanne Thomas
John Thibert
Amy Troolin
Leo Trunt
Sharon Vogt
Mary Warner
Verne Weiss
Christopher Welter

Special thanks to Marlys Vollegraaf, for her way with words, her support, and her assistance.

Table of Contents

Introduction

Minnesota ghost towns are different. They are not the stuff of Hollywood movie sets nor the iconic "Wild West" images branded into our minds. They don't have the dusty tumble-weed strewn dirt streets lined with weather-beaten buildings. In the Midwest, our ghost towns are more the vanished villages, lost locations, abandoned communities, and relocated town sites variety. I call them "lost towns."

In northern Minnesota, with our abundant natural resources, there are a multitude of these places of the past. Generally based on a one-industry/resource economy and the service-oriented support businesses, such as banks, retail, saloons, and brothels, the communities thrived as long as the resources did. Once depleted, the industry owners moved to the next location, the supporting businesses failed, the residents moved on, and the village faded. They left few traces of their existence other than perhaps a wide spot along the highway, a clearing in the landscape, a crumbing foundation or two, decrepit weather-beaten buildings, and sometimes a cemetery and an old building or two.

I've long had an interest and personal connection to the notion of ghost towns. My grandparents homesteaded in eastern Montana in a town that would fade into history in the 1920s. My aunt owned land upon which a booming early 1900s Wisconsin logging town was located. The town was abandoned after tornado and fire, leaving few remains.

In the 1970s my mother moved to Hackensack, Minnesota and lived in a rustic basement cabin on Little Portage Lake. It was my first extended exposure to northern Minnesota and it took root—I live here full time and love it more each day.

To get to Mom's place you headed north out of Hackensack, turned west at the intersection of Highway 371 and Cass County Road 50. Every time we turned at the juncture, Mom would talk of a long-ago town that once sat there. While I had a fleeting fascination, I was young then and hadn't fully developed my love of history. I guess I didn't have enough of my own history to appreciate it as a whole. As years passed, I grew to treasure the past, eventually becoming a history teacher. But back then, I didn't listen as closely as I could have, should have. Not that Mom knew that much about the town, she just knew it used to be there and was intrigued by that fact.

Taconite Harbor on Minnesota's Lake Superior's North Shore also spurred my interest. Years after first visiting the lakeside community, I traveled back to the area and found Taconite Harbor gone. Lonely street lights and crumbling pavement marked the spot. This touched a chord in me. I wanted to know more about the community that was born, lived and died in my lifetime.

Moving to the Lincoln Lakes area many, many years ago, I became fascinated by the historic community of Lincoln and that, too, spurred my interest.

Many years and lots of history have been added to my life since those days. Last year, as I marked a mile-stone birthday, the big sixty, I decided to indulge my interest, pursue my passion and make it my mission to learn all I could. I vowed to locate, document and visit northern Minnesota places of the past, those places where lives were lived, children were raised, homes and businesses were created, and for various reasons were packed up and moved elsewhere.

This is the story of many of those towns.

What Is a Ghost Town?

With no clear-cut definition, determining what constitutes a ghost town is highly subjective, often a matter of degree and opinion.

Purists will define a ghost town—a true ghost town—as a town that has been completely abandoned. Others argue that a ghost town is any community that is a semblance, shadow (or "ghost") of what it used to be.

At its core, on a basic level, the most agreed upon definition would be that of a human settlement which has been abandoned. With an arbitrary definition in place it is possible to further classify ghost towns into categories or classes based on definitive characteristics.

The most common breakdowns and classes with Minnesota examples are:

CLASS A—Barren site, nature has reclaimed the land, no visible signs of former inhabitation (Lothrop)

CLASS B—Rubble, foundations, roofless buildings (Gravelville)

CLASS C—Standing abandoned buildings, no/rural population, hamlet, no viable organized community (Gull River)

CLASS D—Semi/Near Ghost town; many abandoned buildings, small resident population (Oylen)

CLASS E—Busy historic community; smaller than in boom days (Belle River)

CLASS F—Restored town, historically preserved status (Old Crow Wing, Buena Vista)

A seventh category could also be included:

CLASS G—Town joined or was absorbed by neighboring/ thriving city (Tyler Town)

Many communities, whatever their class, did leave behind tangible remains in the form of cemeteries. The hallowed grounds are a visible record of the times and lives of the town's inhabitants. Many regional areas also carry the former town's name.

Life-Cycle of a Ghost Town

Minnesota, with its abundance of natural resources, has a multitude of "places of the past," "used-to-be-towns," ghost or lost towns. Generally based on a one-resource, one industry economy, the population and all town activity was heavily dependent on that one factor. The town survived as long as the resource did. Once the resource was depleted, the industry and owners moved its workers and equipment to new locations and new opportunities.

The Michigan Chronoscope E-Press describes the process simply and effectively. After the owners and industry moved on, the supporting businesses (retail, banks, saloons, brothels, hotels) soon failed and the owners closed shop. Residents moved on to new lives, new jobs, new homes, and new communities. Some towns were dismantled, packed up, and shipped out and reassembled in new locations. Others were abandoned and reclaimed by nature. Many buildings were re-purposed and the towns left no physical remains except a cemetery or place name.

The earliest settlements first appeared along major transportation routes, primarily rivers. As time progressed, other transportation routes provided prime locations for a town, along tote roads or railroad lines. Others grew in haphazard patterns, when and where there was an opportunity. Native American villages were among the first communities. Though many were seasonal, there were some permanent villages. As settlers moved in, the communities became more permanent.

While each town or community was unique and had its own personality, there was a definite pattern to their life-cycles. The only variable was the rate of progression or pace at which a town moved through the cycle. Depending on the commodity or resource, this time frame could vary greatly.

Economists, sociologists and historians have labeled this a "boom-and-bust" economy. Models have been created that include definitive characteristics and stages of such an economy. Mining towns, particularly Western mining towns, were the examples most often used in setting the model. In large part, mining towns moved through the progression at a rapid pace. Moving at such an accelerated pace, it was possible to make observations that fit most of the towns that were products of a "boom and bust" economy. Michael Conlin, a business professor in Canada concisely lists the six stages of a "boom and bust" cycle in his book *Mining Heritage and Tourism*. The following are simplified modifications of his model as well as the process described by E-Press:

Stage One—Discovery and Growth
Resource is discovered and developed
Size of the workforce is capped by workforce required to exploit the resource,
Often dictated by size and type of resource

Stage Two—Production
Highest level of activity

Stage Three—Decline
Production begins to decline
Can be depletion of the resource or a decline in demand
Can also be that costs have escalated making it unprofitable
Decline may be rapid

Stage Four—Abandonment
Owners move equipment and workers to new locations, closing down current production
Supporting businesses fail/close shop
Residents move on

Stage Five—Decay
Town is either packed up or moved on
Buildings are left to decay

Stage Six—Disappearance of Evidence of Occupation
Everything moved on or reclaimed by nature

As the E-Press states, towns built on this model were doomed from the beginning to be ghost towns.

Ghost Town Code of Ethics

RESPECT PRIVATE PROPERTY—Many former town sites are now located on private property. Please respect all private property.

Do not trespass—do not enter private property without permission from the owner.

OBEY ALL POSTED SIGNS

Do not destroy, damage or deface any remains, buildings or structure.

Do not remove anything from the sites

Do not cause any disturbance to the foundations, vegetation or land.

Do not litter—Remove and properly dispose of any trash you take into the area.

Always be courteous, respectful and SAFE.

TREAD LIGHTLY—TAKE ONLY PHOTOS—LEAVE ONLY FOOTPRINTS.

Make as little impact on the environment as possible.

Honor the past and preserve it for the future.

By their very nature, ghost towns are subject to the ravages of time and the elements. Harsh winter weather and humid summers in Minnesota take their toll on the remnants of abandoned communities.

Vandalism as well as accidental or unintentional damage adds to the deterioration of the sites. It is our duty and responsibility to treat these historic sites with respect and to do all we can to preserve the integrity of the lost towns. Use common sense and follow this code of ethics.

Definitions

BLIND PIG:
A lower class establishment that sells illegal alcohol or illegally sells alcohol

BREAKWATER:
A structure for protecting a beach, harbor or shoreline

COFFERDAM:
A temporary watertight enclosure that is pumped dry to expose the bottom of a body of water so that construction may be undertaken

CORDUROY ROAD:
Eight-to-ten-foot logs plyed tightly together to make a swampy area passable. The logs would settle into the soft ground making a mat to drive on through swampy areas

DRAY:
A horse cart used for hauling

DRY GOODS:
Fabric, thread, clothing and related merchandise distinct from hardware or groceries

EGG CANDLING:
Using a bright light source to show details through the shell, such as an embryo

GROG:
Alcoholic drink, often mixed with water

LONG SIDING:
A section of track that allows a train to pull off to the side of a mainline, often for loading or unloading

RANGE LINE ROAD:
A road built by a dredge on a meridian or range line as the legal description used it

SACRISTY:
A room for keeping vestments, sacred vessels, records and other church furnishings

SPUR LINE:
A very short branch line—off of a railroad's main line; a secondary railway line which branches off a through route or main line

TOTE ROAD:
A temporary rough road

UNORGANIZED TOWNSHIP:
A township or other region of land without a formal government or governing body

WINDLASS:
A type of winch (hoist and pulley) used to raise and lower items, such as a bucket. Widely used on ships.

Aitkin County

Rebuilt schoolhouse 1926. (Courtesy of Leo Trunt/Aitkin County Historical Society. *rootsweb.ancestry.com*)

William Bain Homestead 1901. (Courtesy of Leo Trunt/Aitkin County Historical Society. *rootsweb.ancestry.com*)

ARTHYDE

1898-1954
Class A

From McGrath: North on Hwy 65/27 for 6½ miles. Right at County 2 for 8½ miles. Left at County 34/Kestrel Avenue for approximately 1½ miles

Homesteading 1890s Aitkin County required strong and determined settlers. As the Aitkin County Historical Society related in their 1991 *Aitkin County Heritage Book*, travel was difficult. The only transportation routes were rough temporary "tote roads"—built to supply the logging camps in the area.

Cheap land (eight to ten dollars an acre) and plentiful pine and hardwood forests lured many to the area. Though the land was fertile, there were rocks and stumps everywhere. Clearing it for farming was back-breaking work. The area was desolate and the isolation crippling. Fire was common and always a threat.

In 1898, the town of Millward began its existence on land donated by three local residents: Guy Thomsen, and brothers Arthur and Clyde Hutchins. The year 1909 brought great change to Millward. In the fall of that year the first railroad came through and to honor the brothers, the town changed its name to Arthyde, using portions of the brother's first names: ARTHur/clYDE.

The first store in Arthyde was built in 1912. Soon a sawmill, two other stores, and a school became part of the community. Never large, the population peaked at fifty. The post office was established in 1898 (as Millward) and was discontinued in 1954.

Little remains of Arthyde today (one structure remains standing). The Arthyde Stone House is now listed on the National Register of Historic Places. The one-and-one-half story bungalow-style house is almost entirely constructed of field stone, so common to the area. Built in 1922 as a private residence, it remains a private home today.

BAIN

CLASS A
1911-1944

From Aitkin: Northeast on Highway 169/210 for about 20.2 miles. Right (East) on County road 68 until the first curve. Between the first curve and where the road ends (old Soo Line Railroad tracks/bed) is where Bain was located (now part of Hill River State Forest).

Established in 1963, the Hill River State Forest, twenty miles south of Grand Rapids, Minnesota, encompasses a large portion of Aitkin County. Located within the forest boundaries are the sites of many of Aitkin County's lost towns, including Bain, Grayling, Rabey, and Shovel Lake.

Hill River State Forest is closely aligned with Aitkin County history and geography. Many of the former communities lend their names to Wildlife Management Areas (WMA), ATV trails and other forest features. Hilly, with a mixture of high ground islands and low marshlands, the area is much as it was in the late 1800s and early 1900s.

Millions of board feet of lumber were cut from the area. After the land was logged off, settlers moved in. Hoping to improve the area's farmland in the 1920s, ditches were dug to drain the land for cultivation. By the 1930s most farmers, tired of the never-ending struggle, gave up. Many of today's roads in the Hill River State Forest were constructed on those ditch banks.

Travel during those early days was primitive, rudimentary, and difficult on tote roads. Mary Bain Megarry, early resident, writes in her handwritten memoirs that the loggers had hewed out just enough room between the trees and brush for a wagon to scrape by. She also writes that there were chuckholes full of mud and more mud.

Bain Townsite 1920, after the fire. (Courtesy of Clifford Johnson/Leo Trunt. rootsweb.ancestry.com)

With such difficult conditions, progress in the area was slow. Mary recalls that every twelve or fifteen miles, people established places for loggers and lumberjacks to rest overnight and have their meals. A respite for the horses was provided as well. These overnight accommodations were often called "stations."

In 1901, Mary's father, mother and five siblings, all between the ages of three and sixteen, reached their Aitkin County homestead. This homestead would be located just west of what would become the community of Bain.

In 1909, the main line of Soo Railroad came through the area. Leo Trunt, Aitkin County historian tells in his book, *Beyond the Circle*, that it was customary for the railroad to build stations every five or six miles along the line. That distance was considered a reasonable journey for area farmers to travel in one day. Bain was selected to be one of the main line stations and the railroad named it in honor of William Bain, an early settler and prominent farmer.

As was also customary, the railroad built a depot in each station, as well as a section house, handcar house, passenger platform, train order signal, a well, and a two-seater outhouse.

Bain was platted on August 12, 1910. The post office was established in 1911. With all of the ingredients for a successful town in place, growth was rapid, and others came to the area seeking opportunity and prosperity. Soon Bain consisted of William Bain's hotel and boarding house, two stores, a livery business, and a one-room school. Bain was the trading place for a large area.

In October of 1918, Minnesota had been experiencing extremely dry weather over the past several months and years, as had much of central and north central Minnesota. Conditions peaked on October 11th and 12th with a rapid drop in humidity and high winds. In the dry conditions the area was a tinderbox. This coupled with the fact that the logging industry had left behind dry slash as they logged off the land. Those scraps were perfect kindling for wildfires. This fuel was also left lying around rail lines. Since train engines of that time gave off many sparks, fires were inevitable. Fire-fighting methods and equipment were primitive and crude if even available.

When fire did break out, it was impossible to outrun or escape the flames. Over thirty-eight communities perished in the fires, and parts of eight counties were destroyed. The fires ravaged the area from Aitkin on the west and Lake Superior on the east. The Minnesota Historical Society reports, over 450 people died, over 11,000 lost their homes, over 6,000 barns burned, forty-one school buildings were destroyed, and countless animals died. The fires would be known as the Cloquet-Moose Lake Fire, or the Great Fires of 1918.

Bain was one of the communities destroyed by the fires. Only the school house and one residence were spared. Two train engines were burned at Bain. The Palisade train took on all the people they could find and traveled in reverse all the way back to Palisade.

Both stores did rebuild and new additions to Bain would be a restaurant, shoe store, candy store, town hall, a freight service, and many new homes. Eventually the wood frame school was replaced with a modern brick building. Unusual for its time, the school taught grades one through ten.

A near neighbor to the west of Bain was White Elk. Organized in 1910 it would dissolve in 1938. White Elk was a farming community and was home to two schools, the Four Corners School and the White Elk School. White Elk would suffer greatly during the Great Depression and its population would diminish. There are still some farms and residents in the area.

Leo Trunt, area historian, writes that Bain was healthy in the 1920s but that it could not survive the Great Depression. In the early 1930s power was brought to the Bain area; however it was not until 1940 that the countryside get electricity. Telephone service came to the area in the 1930s as well.

The people of Bain were conservative and religious. Bain was known as a "dry town." However some folks relished a drink or two, so just outside of Bain, on the Southeast corner of Highway 169 and Bain Road, a few bars were built. One, Charlie's Place hosted live music, dances, and had a small store, bar, café, and an apartment in the rear. Changing hands many times, Charlie's burned in 1970.

Eventually the town faded away. In 1944 the post office was discontinued. Bain Township was dissolved in June of 1939. The Town Hall was sold and moved to Waukenaba Township where it is still in service. In 1942 the Hill City Trinity Lutheran Church was closed, followed by the school in 1950. The depot burned in 1955 and the remaining stores were torn down. Today only barren land marks the location of Bain.

GRAYLING

1897-1929

Class A

From McGregor: East on Highway 210 for approximately 2 miles. Right on 420th Street for approximately 1 mile. Grayling Cemetery on the right.

Originally known as Sandy River Crossing (in 1895), Grayling was located about halfway between McGregor and Tamarack. Like most area communities, its livelihood was logging and cord wood. Art Jensen remembered his mother often told him of how she could walk half a mile on just cord wood piles. Once the Soo Line Railroad came through, all of the wood was shipped by train to Cloquet or Duluth.

The Grayling community consisted of the railroad depot, a general store, hotel, and one other merchandise store. One of the stores, Borg's, was in business until 1930. It had been said that the famous golfer, Patty Berg (Borg) was a close relative to the Borgs in Grayling.

There was also a small school and church. The church was demolished in the early 1980s. The church bell is now proudly displayed at Grace Lutheran Log Church in McGregor.

Art adds an interesting note, during the drought of the 1930s, cattle were brought in to the area and were put to grazing in the swamp and lowlands of the Grayling area. They were herded by cowboys on horseback.

In the mid-1930s, the old Highway 2 was replaced by the present Highway 210. Little remains of the community except the cemetery and the area name of the nearby Grayling Marsh Wildlife Management Area.

HASSMAN

1911-1915

CLASS C

From Aitkin: North on U.S Highway 169 for 4 miles. At the intersection of US 169 and MN 210. The old store stands on the west side of the intersection.

There were big plans for Hassman. With all of the logging activity in the region, the town seemed a sure bet to grow and prosper. In 1911, the land was purchased and the town was platted complete with streets, avenues, and alleys.

According to Artis Orjala, the area had long been important to the logging industry. The nearby Rice and Mississippi rivers provided a vital transportation link.

Near the spot where the logs were gathered, a small community arose, consisting of a boarding house, two stores and a school. The original store was built in the 1920s. That store was later sold and moved just west of Aitkin where it was part of the original "40 Club." In 1937, the new owners built a larger home with a store and gas station. Sold again in 1963, the store is now closed. The school closed in 1963 as well. Artis reports that as of 1991, the school was serving as the Morrison Town Hall. A post office was established in March of 1914, but it lasted only thirteen months, discontinuing in April of 1915.

The high hopes for Hassman never materialized. In 1945, the town plat was vacated and the land was put to farmland.

The area is still bustling and a vital transportation link, now for automobiles. Located at the intersection of two major Minnesota highways, thousands of travelers make their way through the heart of Hassman every year. Most never notice the weathered store-front that marks the history of the area.

Hassman Store today. (Author's collection)

RABEY

1913-1941
CLASS A
APPROXIMATE LOCATION:
From Hill City:
East from Hill City on MN Highway 200 for 8½ miles. Just West of 250th Avenue and Rabey Road/Elliot Road intersection, where the ATV/Snowmobile trail crosses Highway 200.

Located in the far northern reaches of Aitkin County, just south of the Itasca County line, Rabey and the other railline settlements owed their existence to the Mississippi, Hill City and Western Railway Company.

Started in 1908, the railway opened the area for logging, freight shipping and the development of farms. Building the railroad was not an easy task. Even today, the area around Rabey is a quagmire, low-lying, marshy, and mostly swampland.

According to area historians Leo Trunt and Robert Lemen, building the railroad was arduous and torturous. Working entirely with ox, horse teams, and hand tools the work was slow and back-breaking. The swamplands had to be drained and dredged and the rails built upon a timber road bed. Mosquitoes, large and numerous, only added to the discomforts of the job. "Pea Soup" is how Lemen termed it.

The stability of the line was tenuous. The water-soaked land was at times unusable. Leo Trunt states that only forty-pound rails were used but soft spots along the rail line were always present, except in winter. It was decided early on that the heavier loads would have to be shipped in the winter, when the land was frozen and provided a solid base.

In 1909, a side track and depot was built at Rabey. Railcars would be used for many of the buildings in Rabey, at least in the beginning. A railcar served as a store until a more

Rabey Store. (Courtesy of Leo Trunt/Eileen Rasmussen Danson. rootsweb.ancestry.com

permanent one was built in 1913. Railcars were also used as a bunkhouse, cookhouse, and even a church.

The first school was also housed in a box car. A better school was built in 1915. The school also served many community functions as well, becoming a social center for the area. Church services, dances, and basket socials were held in the school

By the early 1910s things looked prosperous for Rabey. A post office was established in 1913. In the late 1910s folks from Rabey and Splithand formed the Rabey Telephone Company.

It wasn't long before more businesses joined Rabey. A store or two, with gas stations, a hotel, an eatery, and more. Baseball was also an important part of Rabey and other surrounding communities. Leo Trunt reports that in 1934, Rabey even had a sunshine committee, a sort of welcome club.

Never meant to be a long-term entity, the railroad pulled up its lines in 1935 and Rabey began its decline. The post office discontinued in 1941. In 1944, the State of Minnesota required an indoor well and plumbing in schools. With a dwindling population, it was deemed too expensive. The school closed. Buildings were sold and moved. In the late 1940s, a fire destroyed part of Rabey.

Ruth Township, where Rabey was located, could not afford to continue, so it was dissolved in 1937. In the 1950s the state of Minnesota made plans to improve Highway 200. The new plans called for the highway to go through the heart of Rabey. The remaining houses were purchased by the state and sold to those who would move them.

The last standing building was the potato warehouse. After years of harsh Minnesota winters, it caved in from the heavy snows and was burned so as not to pose a hazard.

There were several other communities that grew along the Rabey Line. Just to the east of Rabey was Seaver where a potato warehouse was built on the north side of the track. There were high hopes for Seaver, a petition for a post office was submitted, but denied.

West of Rabey there were several locations (spurs) that grew up in response to the advantages offered by the railroad. Robert Lemen tells of Pierceville, where a mill once was located. Next was Washburn where a mill and rural schools were situated. Two miles from Washburn was Martin Spur, named for brothers who had a mill and logging camp in the area. Adjacent to Martin Spur was Brauer.

Today, the area is primarily tax-forfeited land and an outdoor enthusiast's paradise. Hunting, snowmobiling and ATV trails abound. Still bearing the Rabey name, the Rabey Line ATV trail runs nineteen and a half miles through the Hill River and Savannah State Forests. Rabey once stood where the ATV trail crosses Highway 200, about halfway between Hill City and Jacobson.

SHOVEL LAKE

1910-1952
CLASS A
APPROXIMATE LOCATION:
From Hill City:
West on Minnesota Highway 200 for approximately 6 ½ miles. Turn left on Miller Road for 2 miles. Turn right on County Road 67 for ½ mile. Cemetery is on a hill on the north side of the County Road 67 near where the former Soo Line Railroad tracks cross the road.

Located in the far Northwest corner of Aitkin County, Shovel Lake was closer to Remer in Cass County and Grand Rapids in Itasca County than it was to Aitkin, which, depending on the season, could have been a three or four-day journey.

First inhabited by Native Americans, the Shovel Lake area was a prime wild ricing location. With an abundance of virgin timber forests and plentiful wild game, the area was soon noticed by lumber interests. With the area's rich resources, viable network of waterways, and easily accessible transportation routes, Shovel Lake would soon become an important shipping center in the late 1800s.

The logging drives began in the 1880s and continued until approximately 1911 at which time the Soo Line Railroad extended its Northern route through Shovel Lake. The settlers soon followed.

Fred Blaise, an area logger, saw the opportunity that the railroad provided and he and his partner built a lath sawmill just west of Shovel Lake. Known as "Spur 30" the railroad ran to the mill for loading.

Not only did the railroad provide shipping access for lumber it also greatly improved travel options in the area. Prior to the railroads, travel conditions were difficult. There was an old tote road that ran to Aitkin, but the journey was rough, rudimentary, long, and arduous. Even after the railroad was extended and settlement began, travel was still a major problem.

To illustrate, Leo Trunt shares the experience of Roscoe Reynolds. Roscoe was Shovel Lake's first postmaster and was also a prominent business owner. The first car in Shovel Lake was owned by Roscoe—a brand new, very large Studebaker. Roscoe would drive the car to Swatara, but due to lack of roads, the car had to be loaded onto a flat car and shipped by rail to Shovel Lake. Once it arrived in Shovel Lake, Roscoe

Ball Game at White Pine. (Courtesy of the Aitkin County Historical Society)

would jump in, drive around, navigating around all the stumps that were still in the streets of town. If he wanted to go anywhere other than the town proper, he had to load the car back onto the flat car and have it shipped back to Swatara, where he could once again drive it on the available roads.

When the railroad extended its line in 1910 through Shovel Lake it continued on to Remer and points west. The town of Shovel Lake was platted in 1910, incorporated in 1911, and a post office was established in October of 1912. The town grew quickly.

As was the custom at the time with the creation of a station, the railroad built a section house, water tank, well and windmill, pump house, depot and passenger platform, train order signal, and outhouse. A stockyard was also built with a shed, feed rack, and well. Lastly a mail crane was installed.

In addition to Roscoe's store, there was also another store, car repair garage, a blacksmith shop, restaurant, pool hall, barbershop, livery business, potato warehouse, bank, lumber yard, hotel, boarding house, and for a few years, a saloon. There was also a nearby peat factory. As Leo Trunt writes, the businesses changed hands many times throughout the history of the town.

Nearby, a large logging camp was located near Holy Water Lake. An article in the February 1923 *Aitkin Age* reported that approximately 600 men worked the camp. There were several other smaller mills, logging camps, and spurs in the area.

In 1912, the first schoolhouse was built. It lasted until 1925 when a brick school was erected. The newer building had two classrooms, a kitchen, a stage, and a fireplace. The school was often used as a community center.

Telephone service also soon was extended to the town.

Religion played an important role in the community. Though never having a large enough population to build churches of their own, services were held in the depot, school or in neighboring communities. There were also travelling missionaries and clerics.

Community involvement was a daily part of lives. Many organizations were formed. Community bands, 4-H, and farmer's unions were but a few.

Baseball was America's pastime and most small towns formed their own town teams. Shovel Lake did as well. The games were recreational yet competitive and the whole town would turn out for the games, accompanying picnics, and other activities.

The 1930s and the Great Depression were hard on all of America, but especially on small rural communities such as Shovel Lake. The timber resources were being depleted and the mills were closing. Farmers were experiencing economic difficulties and people began to leave town.

The Shovel Lake Bank was also experiencing difficulties. As Leo Trunt writes, the Shovel Lake Bank merged with the Swatara Bank moving their safe and facilities to that location. The bank lasted at Swatara for a few years but eventually merged with Remer.

Conditions continued to deteriorate. The school closed in 1942 and was sold shortly thereafter. The railroad depot closed and in 1943 the depot building was sold. The store closed in 1958. Many of the old buildings were moved and repurposed, many into homes elsewhere. The post office was discontinued in January of 1952. People moved on to new lives and new opportunities. Though there are still a few area residents and farmers in the area, Shovel Lake as a town ceased to exist.

Today Shovel Lake is in the heart of outdoor recreational activities. The old Soo Line Railroad bed now serves as an ATV and snowmobile trail. Shovel Lake is the center link of the three prong Soo Line North ATV Trail.

SOLANA

1910-1938
CLASS A
APPROXIMATE LOCATION:

From McGrath:
North on Highway 65 for approximately 6 miles (or 20 miles South of McGregor). Turn Right (East) on County Highway 2. Go South on Aitkin County Road 26. The ATV trail is across the road from the old town site.

Local folklore tells of a camp cook named Anna. Anna talked slow, moved slow, seems she did everything slow, and was nicknamed "Slow Anna." As the logging village north of McGrath grew, the town became known as Solana, which some pronounced "Slow Anna."

Eddie Tripp, in his 1991 reminisces of the community, also offers a less colorful, more conventional alternative to the town's naming. According to that version, the area name comes from a variation of an early surveyor's home town of Salinas, Kansas.

Solana was built as a support town and supply center for the area's (and some say Minnesota's) largest sawmill complex at White Pine, which was just a few miles away. Solana soon became a bustling center of activity. Everything and everybody was connected to the logging industry. There was some farming going on, but life depended on the timber and the railroad.

Growing quickly the town soon included a town hall, a railroad depot, a general store or two, a feed store, two hotels (one with a coffee shop), a section house, a blacksmith, a woodyard, and rental houses.

A school housing eight grades and serving approximately sixty students was built. Transportation to and from school was provided by three horse-drawn buses.

Solana did have its wild element. Wintertime brought the lumberjacks to town and with them came their drinking and fighting ways.

As the timber resources in the area dwindled, so did Solana. People began to drift away and leave town. Business was declining and many of the retailers folded. The depot closed and many of the buildings were moved and repurposed into homes around the area. The children were sent to McGrath for school. In 1938 the post office, established in 1910, was discontinued. Slowly, the town of Solana was no more.

Nothing remains of Solana. The Minnesota Department of Natural Resources states that in 1989, the Soo Line Railroad pulled up the main line tracks. Aitkin County purchased the rights-of-way and the old rail line would become the Soo Line Trail, which today runs 130 miles from Genola to Duluth. In addition to the ATVs and snowmobiles that frequent the area, the forest also offers hiking, hunting, and more.

SOLANA FOR SALE

In January of 2013, the historical town of Solana was listed for sale. Advertised on the popular website, Craigslist, the entire town or parcels of the town were available. The entirety of Solana was offered at $40,000, and that consisted of all twenty-four lots. The lots could be subdivided into twelve building lots at $5,000 each.

The description stated that there were no buildings in Solana and that the town site was surrounded by 112 sections (square miles) of public hunting land. The snowmobile and ATV trail is located across the road from the property.

Solana Depot. (Courtesy of the Aitkin County Historical Society)

VETERANSVILLE

1922-1927
CLASS A

APROXIMATE LOCATION:
From McGrath:
Northeasat on MN Hwy 27E/MN 65 N approximately 8 miles. Turn right on East White Pine Forest Road for approximately 1.9 miles.
From Solana-approximately 3 miles NW
Old railbed spur-Located within Solana State Forest

The communities of Veteransville and Silver Star in Aitkin County were part of an ambitious experiment by the federal government. Hoping to provide training and rehabilitation for disabled World War I veterans, the plan was well-intentioned, the goals idealistic and lofty, the implementation flawed, and the results unsuccessful.

The basics of the plan was to train the veterans and then provide them with the opportunity and the funds to get started in farming. Each veteran would get a small amount of money to purchase eighty acres in one of the colony locations.

Bill G. Reid did extensive research on the colonies located within Minnesota. According to Reid, in the winter of 1922, groups of disabled veterans traveled to Minnesota looking for suitable locations. However, winter is not the best time of the year to evaluate land conditions as the snow covers much of the terrain and the true layout of the land is not easily visible. Upon recommendations of the groups, several locations were chosen including Silver Star and Veteransville, in Aitkin County. Argonne Farms (twenty miles from Minneapolis), Onamia, and Moose Lake were the other primary choices. There were some trainees in scattered locations in Bemidji, Brainerd, Grand Rapids, and Aitkin. Reid's findings were published in the Summer 1965 issue of *Minnesota History*.

The numbers of veterans involved in the program were not large. Reid gave the count at fifteen in Silver Star and thirty-five in Veteransville. From the beginning, there were more disadvantages to the project than advantages.

As Reid illustrates, the first and major disadvantage was the fact that all but one of the colonies was located in cutover land in northern Minnesota. Early settlers and anyone familiar with the terrain of cutover land knows that clearing farmland in such a landscape is back-breaking, never-ending work, even for the most physically fit. The veterans were disabled and while spiritually fit, were not physically able to make the land into farms.

Other concerns were the poor soil conditions, small farm/land lot size, the relatively long development time frame

required to make the land profitable, and the veterans lack of farming skills.

Arriving in the winter of 1922, Silver Star and Veteransville were not what the men expected. Housed in dirty, cold, and frozen houses that had been built for the Solana fire victims, things did not bode well. As Martha Laswell from Silver Star remembers, once the snow melted, things were even worse. The veterans found muck and lowlands, not the fertile farmland they had hoped for. As Chester Robinson remembered, "stumps were everywhere, big, green and four rocks in between each stump." They had no farming equipment, nor little knowledge of how to farm. When the women arrived in early spring, they were devastated as well. There were no roads, only paths through the woods.

Few veterans stayed more than a few years and most, if not all, were gone by 1927, when the post office was discontinued in Veteransville. Silver Star never established a post office.

Each community had community halls, meetings, public speakers, dances, dinners, and school and church activities.

Today, little remains of the communities or of the experiment. The surrounding area is being reclaimed by nature. The Solana State Forest and other public lands offer recreational opportunities.

WHITE PINE

1909-1921
CLASS A

APROXIMATE LOCATION:
From McGrath:
Northeast on MN Hwy 27E/MN 65 N approximately 8 miles.
Turn right on East White Pine Forest Road for approximately 1.9 miles.
From Solana-approximately 3 miles NW
Old rail bed spur-Located within Solana State Forest

In the early days of Aitkin County, timber was king and everything revolved around the logging industry. In 1909, James McGrath built the largest local (some say Minnesota's largest) sawmilling operation in the area called White Pine.

White Pine was located just northwest of the support town of Solana. A three-mile spur rail line ran from Solana to White Pine. The sawmill complex consisted of a planning mill, drying kiln, company store, bunkhouse, cooking shack, blacksmith, horse barns, community hall, and a school. The post office was established in 1909.

Chester Robinson recalls that there were many nearby logging camps and that they furnished the sawmill with logs. Most

RHONDA FOCHS

The White Pine sawmill. (Courtesy of the Aitkin County Historical Society)

supplies were brought in by rail, but local citizens also sold logs, and fruits and vegetables to the camps. It was said that Mc-Grath forbade drinking in his camps. But moonshine was found and was also provided by locals.

The mill prospered for twelve years until a forest fire swept the area and the milling complex was destroyed. The Minnesota Department of Natural Resources estimates that over 1,200 people were put out of work by the fire. A newer, smaller sawmill was built but it was not successful.

In 1922, the federal government was looking for land to be used in a training/rehabilitation project for disabled World War I veterans. McGrath, himself a veteran, was able to negotiate the sale of 3,400 acres to the U.S. government.

The White Pine Post Office was discontinued in 1921. In 1922, the community and post office changed names and became Veteransville.

Today the White Pine area is part of the Solana State Forest. The old rail bed is now part of the forest system of trails.

The trail system is continuing to enlarge and many of the old trails are connecting with the main Soo Line ATV trails system. The area is also known for its hiking, hunting and other outdoor recreational opportunities.

11

Becker County

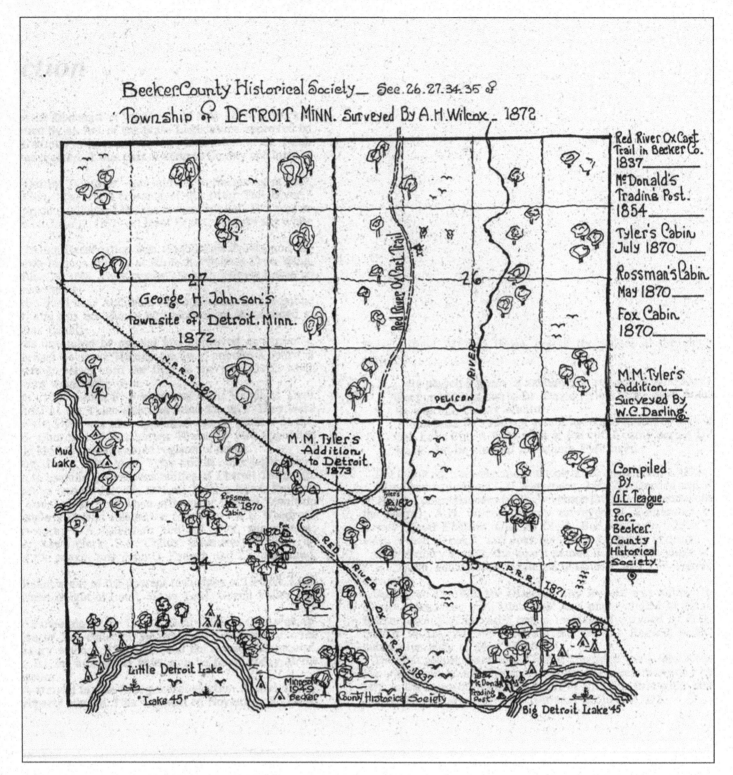

Tyler Town plat. (Courtesy of the Becker County Historical Society)

Tyler Town

1870–1878
CLASS G
APPROXIMATE LOCATION:
From Detroit Lakes:
Located within the City of Detroit Lakes. From US Highway 10 turn left on North Shore Drive. Continue on to where the Pelican River crosses the road and connects with Detroit Lake (just beyond the Holiday Inn)

Traveling westward, Merwin (Melvin) Tyler decided to stop and make camp for the night. Choosing a spot on the prairie near a winding river, he climbed out of his covered wagon and settled in for the evening. When Tyler awoke the next morning he was awed by the natural and scenic beauty that surrounded him, the glistening lake one-half mile in the distance, and the prairie lush with fragrant wildflowers. He knew, right then and there, that his journey westward was over. Right here, where the river connected with the lake, he knew he had found his paradise on earth. There was no need to travel any further. Here he would stay.

Most historical accounts (Teague and Prentice county histories) tell that Tyler built a small cabin and set about making this spot his home. A year later, in 1871, the Northern Pacific Railroad had reached his homestead. Tyler's cabin became a stopping place. With nowhere else for travelers to stay, Tyler's small cabin soon became the overnight stop for many. Now called Tyler's Hotel, an addition was made to the original cabin. Historical accounts tell of the railroad dropping mail off at Tyler's. The men would dump the mailbags on an empty bed; folks would sort through the heaps of mail and then take the mail addressed to them.

Others came and settled near Tyler's homestead and within a short time the area became known as Tyler Town. The Northern Pacific Railroad built a telegraph shack, which later served as a depot. A general store was soon built. The town seemed to prosper.

Late in 1871, two groups arrived in the area and recommended it to their members. One group leader, Civil War veteran Colonel George Johnston, wasn't impressed with Tyler Town. His choice was a town site a bit further west. As members arrived, they soon settled in the new location rather than in Tyler Town. It wasn't long before the residents in Tyler Town followed suit, packed up and moved west to the new site. Soon Tyler Town was deserted.

Eventually the new town site would become known as Detroit. Often confused with the other Detroit in Michigan, the name was modified and became Detroit Lakes, which it remains known as today.

Detroit Lakes continued to grow, its borders and boundaries ever increasing. It wasn't long before the original town site of Tyler Town was annexed becoming part of Detroit Lakes. The Becker County Historical Society states that many of Tyler Town's early streets, such as Frazee and Pioneer remained.

The Becker County Historical Society also writes that in 2008, Minnesota Highway 10 was re-routed to bypass Detroit Lakes. This led to the loss of the earliest street, Pioneer, which for over one hundred years had been the hub of Detroit Lakes. Today, Frazee Street East runs parallel to Minnesota Highway 10. The original Tyler Town site is on the east end of Detroit Lakes not far from the Detroit Lakes overlook just off of Highway 10. The area is still abundant in natural and scenic beauty, which is enjoyed by the residents and the thousands of travelers who flock to the area consider it a paradise.

Westbury

1904–1942
CLASS A
APPROXIMATE LOCATION:
From Detroit Lakes:
North on Highway 59 for approximately 3 miles. Just north of the Main Street side road and just south of 240th Avenue.

In the early 1900s the Soo Line Railroad extended its line from Glenwood, Minnesota, to Noyes, Minnesota (just shy of the Canadian border). As was the custom of the time, railroad stations were placed at intervals of approximately eight miles. The thinking being that eight miles was the optimum distance for freight shipments and to accommodate a farm-to-market network.

The first station north of Detroit Lakes was given the name Westbury. The Becker County Historical Society in its brief summary of Westbury reports that the railroad agent in Westbury was very busy. Not only did he supervise passenger travel and the waiting room, he also handled incoming freight, and the loading and unloading of supplies, as well as outgoing freight.

Farm related products where in abundance in the Westbury area. A local creamery produced butter and dairy products and was the economic institution for nearly 130 nearby farmers. Eggs were a staple commodity for trade and exchange at the co-op store. There was a grain elevator to handle the area's cereal crops (oat, wheat, barley and flax). The area was known for its potato crop and a co-op warehouse was built, to provide market shipping and to serve as a storage facility.

Westbury also included a section house, a blacksmith, a community hall, a cattle shipping facilities, a livery and a feed stable as well as a local bank. A town band provided musical entertainment.

As the times and economics changed, so did Westbury. Its post office, established in 1904 with the coming of the rail line was discontinued in 1942.

Westbury Cabin. (Courtesy of the Becker County Historical Society)

Beltrami County

Buena Vista store and post office. (Courtesy of the Beltrami County Historical Society)

Buena Vista School. (Courtesy of the Beltrami County Historical Society)

BUENA VISTA

1896-1912
CLASS F
APPROXIMATE LOCATION:
From Bemidji:
North on Highway 15 for 12 miles. Park at the Turtle Lake Town Hall and Picnic Area.

Nestled among the rolling hills, pines, lakes, and waterways, Buena Vista has always been a scenic paradise, sportsmen's haven, tourist retreat, historical treasure, and bustling hotspot.

Once the site of a turn-of-the-century boom town, Buena Vista's history is well-documented, colorful and, thanks to descendants of an early settler, the Dickenson family has created a living legacy. Four generations of the family, most recently, the children and grandchildren of logging pioneer Earle Dickenson, have not only lovingly and accurately preserved the past, they bring it alive. But more on that later.

First inhabited by Native Americans, Buena Vista has been at the center of things. Three important trails, the Red Lake/Leech Lake Trail, the Fosston Trail, and the Blackduck County Road, all intersect at this point. The heavily traveled land and water routes, were so important that the famed Hudson Bay Company established a trading post at the site in the mid-1800s.

Notable visitors to the region included the English cartographer David Thompson in 1798 and the colorful Italian explorer Count Giancomo Beltrami, for whom Beltrami County was named in 1823.

Dianne Dickenson, in her history of Buena Vista, writes that the Beltrami Expedition, including two guides and an interpreter, traversed the region looking for the source of the Mississippi River. Coming upon Lake Julia (which he named for his sweetheart back in Italy), Count Beltrami cited the lake as the northern source of the Mississippi. Later, Lake Itasca, the true source, would be discovered and credited to Henry Schoolcraft. After his excursion into northern Minnesota, Count Beltrami wrote extensively about his travels and findings.

Soon European settlers would move into the region. As the rich timber resources were discovered, the woods would fill with loggers, their equipment and their camps. Realizing that all of the homesteaders, loggers, and travelers would need supplies and services, a community grew.

The first resident in what would become Buena Vista was James Cyr, who settled on the site of the old Hudson Bay Trading Company. In 1896, George LaBrie, opened a store in Buena Vista and others followed.

That same year, John W. Speelman built the Summit House hotel on the south shore of Lake Julia. Taking note of the unique geographical feature of Buena Vista, its location on the Continental Divide (more accurately, the sub-continental divide), Spellman advertised that a raindrop falling on one side of the building would flow North into Hudson Bay and one falling on the other side would flow South into the Gulf of Mexico. Speelman's first Summit Hotel burned, but he built a second in 1904.

Within a year the town would burgeon. Buena Vista pioneer Ralph Dickenson in an interview conducted by the WPA in the late 1930s, recalled that at its height, Buena Vista was home to 250 people, not counting the hundreds of travelers and visitors. In addition to LaBrie's store and hotel and Speelman's hotel, there was a sawmill, several stores (St. Paul Cheap Cash Store, Dickenson's Mile Post Store, and two others), a school, church, post office (which was established in 1896), blacksmith, several saloons and other supply and service businesses.

According to area residents and historians, Madeline and William Sutherland, Buena Vista had hopes of becoming the Beltrami County seat. The land and $400 dollars were offered to build the courthouse. Bemidji won the election and become the county seat. Buena Vista, however, hosted the 1904 Beltrami County Fair.

Education was important to the residents. However, getting to and from school could be an adventure. In an article by area historian Hilda Rachey, former students shared their reminisces with her, stating that, in the winter, the students couldn't get home before dark, so they carried bells to ring to keep the wolves at bay.

Sold in bankruptcy, the Minneapolis, Red Lake, and Manitoba Railroad's new owners decided to build a much-hoped for rail extension from Bemidji to Nebish. The residents of Buena Vista were excited about the possibility of a rail line to their community. Their hopes were short-lived with the news that the rail line would bypass Buena Vista. The planned route was to run along the north end of Lake Julia through a new location to be called Puposky. History would prove it was the beginning of the end for the town of Buena Vista.

Some historians say that the end for Buena Vista would have happened in any case. As is true with most lost towns, the businesses of Buena Vista were supply and service—dependent on one industry, one economic base. While Buena Vista was not a logging town for the whole, once the timber resources were depleted, customers vanished. New communities along the rail line sprang up. Transportation improvement meant less travelers along the trails and Blackduck County Road. All of these factors worked against Buena Vista. Puposky never flourished and those rail lines were abandoned in 1938.

Back of Lake Julia Sanatorium. (Courtesy of Lakeland Public Television/Beltrami County Historical Society)

Buena Vista slowly faded. Some businesses operated for a while. In 1912, the post office was discontinued. According to the Sutherlands, by World War I, Buena Vista, as an active town, was no more. The buildings began to fall into disrepair, were burned or repurposed. Only the school house still stands, although it was moved from its original location. Now the Turtle Lake Town Hall, it sits just north of the old town site. The town hall is adjacent to an inviting picnic area and park named Beltrami Park, with shade trees, historical markers, hand water pump, and a community bulletin board that details the early history of the town. In 1996, the town site was listed on the National Register of Historic Places.

LAKE JULIA SANATORIUM

Considered part of the Buena Vista area, the Lake Julia Sanatorium was located just across Lake Julia. Built in 1915 at a cost of $55,000, the construction was financed by Beltrami, Hubbard, Koochiching, and later Itasca County. Nicknamed "The Sans," the sanatorium's first patient was in 1916.

Lake Julia Sanatorium. (Courtesy of Lakeland Public Television/Beltrami County Historical Society)

In the early 1900s, tuberculosis was a highly contagious disease. While it could affect any organ in the body, it primarily attacked the lungs. If left untreated it could be fatal. Since the bacteria that caused TB was transmitted by air, any prolonged exposure to an infected person would spread the disease. Thus there was a need to isolate those suffering from the disease. Sunshine, fresh air, rest, and recuperation were the standard treatments. Patients would experience extended stays at sana-

Doctor's residence, Lake Julia Sanitorium. (Courtesy of Lakeland Public Television/Beltrami County Historical Society)

toriums, often a year or longer. Dr. Jim Ghostly, son of Lake Julia Sanatorium's doctor, Mary Ghostly, recalled one young man that spent ten years at the sanatorium.

The Lake Julia Sanatorium was built on ninety acres of land which later grew to 120 acres, on the North side of Lake Julia. The two-story hospital could house approximately sixty patients. Large glass windows opened to the lake. Also on the site was a doctor's residence (log cabin), a greenhouse, gardens, an electricity generating plant, a dairy herd, and other animals. It was said that each bed had a head set, donated by two local newspapers, and each evening the patients could listen to radio broadcasts, music, and news. Since fresh air was believed to assist the cure, windows would be open year-round.

The sanatorium did have an impressive success rate, particularly if tuberculosis was diagnosed early. Much of that success rate can be attributed to Dr. Mary Ghostly. For twenty-four years, from 1929 to 1953, Dr. Ghostly was in charge of every facet of care at the sanatorium. Paid $100 a month, she was on call twenty-four hours a day. In addition she was in charge of all patient care, the entire medical staff, all support staff, the grounds and gardens, and was a single mother to two children. She was also a traveling doctor, visiting area schools and administering TB tests to all area students and staff.

Radiology was in its infancy during this time period. It was an area Dr. Ghostly excelled in. Her early diagnosis and skills at reading x-rays was legendary. Years later, as the science developed; radiology students would follow her standards.

In the 1940s, antibiotics would greatly eradicate the disease. The Lake Julia Sanatorium would close in 1953 and re-open in 1954 as a nursing home. In 1968, it would close for good.

The building, though in disrepair, is still standing on private property. Still a spot of scenic beauty, sunshine, fresh air, and quiet solitude the building stands majestically along the shores of Lake Julia. The property has changed hands many times. All that see the building agree that it would be an ideal resort or bed and breakfast, however, that has not yet happened.

The Beltrami County Historical Society has the original blueprints, several photos, artifacts, and a scale model built by Bemidji State University students. Stop by the History Museum and see the Lake Julia Sanatorium display, it will transport you back in time.

BUENA VISTA TODAY

On an unseasonably cool August day, packing a lunch and the dog, we headed up to visit Buena Vista. About twelve miles north of Bemidji, on Highway 15, you will be in Buena Vista. Highway 15, at this point, is the modern paved version of Buena Vista's main street. Rounding the bend, to the left (west) you will see a log-sided town hall and an inviting wayside rest known as Beltrami Park. The log town hall was originally the Buena Vista school. A hand water pump offers a cool drink and the shaded picnic shelter offers the perfect place for a peaceful lunch. Also in the park are some historical markers: a wooden

Buena Vista Today. (Author's collection)

also invited to tour the early town site, which is on the National Register of Historic Places.

We met up with Suzanne Thomas here. Suzanne is a current-generation Dickenson, descendants of an early Buena Vista settler and businessman. She is the daughter of Earle Dickenson, former Minnesota state legislator, lumberman, historian, and a founder of the ski area, logging village, and the Lumberjack Hall of Fame, of which he is an inductee. The Dickenson family are not only loving caretakers of Buena Vista's historical heritage but are creating a living legacy.

Area ski enthusiasts will be familiar with the Buena Vista Ski Area and Logging Village. The ski area is a full-service ski facility and features sixteen downhill runs, chairlifts, a tow-rope, tubing park, a three-story chalet with café, a full rental shop, ski shop, ski school, and cross-country skiing. Many winter events are hosted at the Ski Area and Logging Village.

At the base of the ski area sits the Buena Vista Logging Village. The view is panoramic as you drive into the village and it is akin to stepping back in time. A wanigan, a floating cook shanty for the logging camps, serves as an entry gate/ticket office. As we drove the dirt road, a recreated school house and church are the first buildings we saw. I learned that on summer Sundays, church services are held in the church. Special events such as weddings, private parties, reunions, and more can be arranged.

marker details the Continental Divide and a bronze plaque on a huge boulder telling of Count Beltrami's visit to the area. An informative bulletin board, sponsored by the Town Board, tells of the area's early settlers and early Buena Vista history. You are

Buena Vista Today. (Author's collection)

Main Street, Buena Vista

Leonard Dickinson Collection

Main Street is now County 15. The Summit Hotel
is in the left foreground, then the church, then the
schoolhouse. Dickinson's second store is on the
right; his second house is behind the store The old
road went directly down to Lake Julia.
The date is after 1912, when RFD began.

Buena Vista Main Street marker. (Author's collection)

The compound continues with original rail cars, vintage logging equipment, covered wagons, and the center attraction—the Lumberjack Hall of Fame, which is the approximately forty feet by sixty feet. Though re-created the rough hewn lumber building invokes another time, another place. The multi-purpose building is crafted of majestic pine and is filled with original artifacts, memorabilia, and photos. Reminiscent of an early logging camp dining hall, cook shanty, you can almost see the hungry jacks devouring their meat and potatoes. The walls are adorned with history, with one wall dedicated to the Hall of Fame inductees. New inductees are added every year.

Each fall the village hosts a Covered Wagon Rides Day. You can ride to the "top of the world" on the Continental Divide in a rustic canvas covered wagon. Usually the fall colors are at their peak and the view is spectacular. Self-guided walks to the top of the hill, music, food, crafts, and down home festivities complete the day.

On the first Saturday of February, the annual Logging Days is held. The 2013 celebration marked the thirtieth anniversary of the event. Demonstrations, contests, music, and other activities are held throughout the day, starting with a flapjack breakfast and ending with the newest inductees into the Lumberjack Hall of Fame.

After our visit to the ski area and logging village, we headed back to the old town site of Buena Vista. A mown grass pathway leads from the town hall to the streets of the long ago town. Walking among the shade trees and looking over the rolling hills and lakes it is easy to see what attracted those first settlers to the area. Information placards are placed at the sites of the early town structures. Each one details the building that once stood there and includes a vintage photo of the now vanished building. If you look closely enough you can make out a depression or two and a wayward piece of lumber that adds to the experience.

Visiting Buena Vista is about as close to visiting an old ghost town as is possible. Give yourself a treat and visit the area one day. Walk the streets of the old town, ski the slopes, ride the wagon to the top of the hill or take in Logging Days—you'll be glad you did.

Buena Vista Lumberjack Hall of Fame. (Author's collection)

FARLEY

1902-1915

CLASS A

APPROXIMATE LOCATION:
From Bemidji:
Northwest on U.S. Highway 71 for 12 miles. At the intersection of U.S. 71 and Turtle River Lake Road.

A roll of the dice, a toss of the coin, was done to decide the name of the community. It was an apt beginning for a town founded by gamblers at heart.

William Blakely, a newcomer to Minnesota, ran lumber camps in the 1890s. All of northern Minnesota, at this time, was lush forest, thick with millions of board feet of lumber, just for the taking. Never one to pass up an opportunity, Blakely learned that there was available forest land. Joining forces with Everett Farley, they bought up the logging contracts around Cass Lake and Turtle River. Farley had been a bookkeeper and by his own accounts, a creative bookkeeper, as well as a gambler.

Things went well for the duo until they started to deal with a couple of Turtle River men, who wanted more than Blakely and Farley were willing to give. Out of spite, or perhaps to avoid consequences, Blakely and Farley set up operations a mile north of Turtle River. The competition was on.

There are conflicting historical reports on Farley's growth. William Borden states that Farley grew more quickly than Turtle River. Another source states that Farley never seemed to develop as well as Turtle River. Blakely and Farley moved their headquarters to Farley.

While it lasted, Blakely and Farley was the largest lumber contractor in the area. With a contract for one hundred million board feet of lumber and over $100,000 of goods moving through their warehouse, no one else came close to the size of their operation. They employed nearly 2,000 men in their thirty logging camps. By comparison, other outfitters had six camps, at the most, with approximately 500 men working.

With such a large operation, Farley was a boom town. Soon home to eleven saloons (it is estimated that there was a saloon for every ten residents), Borden writes that Turtle River only had nine. Farley also had a newspaper (left-wing), one doctor and the only hospital north of Bemidji. Borden also writes that the doctor had the only x-ray machine in northern Minnesota.

Of the two towns, Farley had the first church. Services were provided by itinerant preachers, often called "sky pilots." One of the area's best-known, Frank Higgins, established a Presbyterian church in Farley.

The duo also owned a 115-foot, 450-passenger steamship docked at Cass Lake. Named the *Zetah May* it is said the ship's dance floor was forty feet by twenty feet. Special excursions and outings were held aboard the ship as well as by train, such as the Grand Opening of the Blakely Hotel. Built at a cost of $17,000, the hotel featured electricity and steam heat. Rooms were two dollars a night. Steak dinners followed by dancing into the wee hours of the morning were common.

Blakely and Farley lived the high life. Driving sleek carriages with dapper horses, fancy clothing and even fancier women, the good life would not last. In the next year, they would have only thirteen lumber camps. William Borden, in his essay "Looking for Farley" explains that the trouble was not in finding lumber, it was in their bookkeeper, McIver, who stole them blind. Blakely and Farley were also to blame. As Borden continues, Blakely and Farley did not pay good wages, did not have good cooks, a lumber camp necessity, and in the words of one lumberjack, "took things too cheap." Meaning they bought and sold timber too cheaply, eventually going bankrupt.

Just as Farley grew quickly, it would fade just as rapidly. In 1903, nearly half the buildings were empty. That year also saw a major train wreck. The newspaper reports read one dead, thirteen hurt, passengers hurled into broken glass and debris, ears torn off, scalps cut, and more. The next year the newspaper would stop publishing. Blakely became postmaster followed by his wife. The post office closed in 1915. The Blakely Hotel would burn that same year and nothing remained of Farley.

Highway 71 bisects the old town site. The old rail bed is now a recreational/snowmobile trail that parallels Highway 71. There are some new homes and residents in the area. Farley is still seen on some highway maps.

Farley 1912. (Courtesy of Beltrami County Historical Society)

FIRMAN

1902-1912
CLASS A
APPROXIMATE LOCATION:
From Kelliher:
West on County Road 36 for approximately 5 miles. Turn right on County Road 34 for approximately 2 miles

Families began to move into the Firman area between 1902 and 1903. By 1903 it was decided that a school was needed. Land was donated and the school was built of green timber. After it dried, there were large cracks in the floor. There were lots of lost pencils when dropped. There were no school buses. Students had to walk. The teacher would have a fire going in the wood stove placed in the middle of the room. Lunches were often frozen by the time the students walked to school, so they were put under the stove to thaw out by lunch time. Later another floor was built as well as a barn. Students could then ride horses to school or take a sled and cutter. There was a post office and general store.

FOWLDS

1906-1911
CLASS A
APPROXIMATE LOCATION:
From Bemidji:
North on U.S. 71 for approximately 5 miles. Turn right on MN 89 for approximately 14 miles. Turn right on County Road 603 for ½ mile.

Fowlds was a logging community built to support the Crookston Lumber Company's area operations. Built in an L-shape, the town consisted of a company store with post office, several saloons, boarding house and hotel, and across the tracks and into the woods, a red light district. When the lumber supply was depleted, the rails were pulled up, the houses and buildings were sold and moved, and the post office was discontinued, Fowlds, little by little, disappeared.

FOY

1903-1918
CLASS A
APPROXIMATE LOCATION:
From Kelliher:
West on County Road 36 for approximately 5 miles. Right on County Road 38 for approximately 5 miles. Right on County Road 23 for approximately 2 ½ miles. Left on Trails End Road NE.

Foy was located in Battle Township near the south shore of Upper Red Lake. Very little is known about Foy but one photo does exist.

Store post office and residence of John Foy. (Courtesy of LaVonne Peterson)

INEZ

1905-1919
CLASS A
APPROXIMATE LOCATION:
From Bemidji:
North on U.S. 71 for approximately 24 miles. Continue on to MN 72 for approximately 8 miles. Turn left on County 100 for 1 ½ miles.

Inex was supposed to be called Cormorant but one already existed, so it was decided to call the new community Inez. Little is known about the location. A post office was in existence from 1905 to 1919.

The Gunderson Store, Inez. (Courtesy of LaVonne Peterson)

QUIRING

1900-1936

CLASS A

APPROXIMATE LOCATION:
From Bemidji:
North on U.S. 71 for approximately 24 miles. Continue on to MN 72 for approximately 10 miles. Left on MN 1. Right on County Road 23 for ½ mile.

Quiring had a store, a post office, and three nearby schools. Arguments developed when trying to decide on a name for the community, when someone shouted out, "Be quiet and stop arguing." Thus the amalgamation Quiring came about and the new town took on the name.

Quiring Post Office. (Courtesy of LaVonne Peterson)

SHOTLEY

1903-1935

CLASS A

APPROXIMATE LOCATION:
South side of Upper Red Lake
From Kelliher:
North on MN 72 for 10 miles. Turn left on County 23 for 5 miles. Turn right on Rogers Road for ½ mile.

Christopher Rogers was a man with a plan. Sent to the area by his employer, the Booth Fish Company, he was to build a large fish warehouse near the shores of Upper Red Lake. The Canadian company and Rogers anticipated a large of amount of fish to be supplied by the area's Native Americans. Neither the warehouse nor the large supply of fish ever happened.

Rogers was a resourceful man, when the fish plans failed he had the thirty-seven acres platted into a town consisting of ten blocks. Named for the nearby Shotley Brook, the town was also known as Old Shotley, Shotley, and some maps even had the name Shorty. Soon the town became a "stopping place." Otto Berg, the town's first clerk, said not only was it a stopping place for the area's new settlers but also for the local lumberjacks, of which there were many.

Shotley was Roger's dream and he did all he could to expand the city. Berg recalls that Rogers even borrowed $6,000 from his sister in Chicago to build his family a large house. Rogers ran the saloon, his wife the hotel. Every extra penny went into adding more buildings.

Sensing opportunity, others soon came to Shotley, mostly by boat, to start their businesses. Soon there was a general store, two hotels, two saloons, a sawmill, and a shingle mill.

One day the postmaster went on an outing on Upper Red Lake. When he did not return that evening, a search was conducted. The boat oars were found the next day, his body the following month. He left behind a widow with five boys. Managing the hotel, serving as postmistress and raising five boys alone was not easy. A few years later she remarried.

In time, a school was established as well as a church. Most of the area's settlers were of Scandinavian descent and of the Lutheran denomination.

In 1963, the reminisces of Mrs. Julius Nyren (the widowed postmistress) were written. At the age of ninety-four she remembered that not only were there homesteaders in the area, but also many Native Americans from the nearby reservation. Many of the Natives traded in Shotley often staying overnight. Sometimes as many as thirty teepees would spring up overnight. Mrs. Nyren would remember how the Native Americans enjoyed her homemade bread. One time, tired of their demand for more bread, she told them that she didn't have any wood for her oven. The Native women disappeared and shortly returned with enough wood to last for several days.

Others remember how bad the mosquitoes were, saying they had to have smudge pots by their doors and cheese cloth covering their beds.

Today, Rogers Campground and RV Park occupies the old town site. Fishing, guide services, ice fishing in the winter, camping, groceries and supplies are all available. Even today Old Shotley is a "stopping place."

Carlton County

Forbay School built 1917. (Courtesy of the Carlton County Historical Society)

Forbay Community (Hydro Station is far left). (Courtesy of the Carlton County Historical Society)

FORBAY

1905-1960
CLASS A
APPROXIMATE LOCATION:
From Carlton:
East on MN Highway 210 past Jay Cooke State Park. Along the river near Thomson Hydro Plant.—Private Property

Automobile travel in the early 1900s was in its infancy, as was the automobile itself. With less than ten miles of paved roads in all of America in the early 1900s, travel conditions were rudimentary, rough, and nearly non-existent in some areas. The St. Louis River Valley west of Duluth, was one of those areas deemed inaccessible.

With plans to build an electricity generating plant, Great Northern Power (Minnesota Power's predecessor) knew they had to make accommodations for workers and for getting supplies in. Forbay was their solution.

Great Northern Power had workers at both their Fond du Lac and Thomson power plants. Minnesota Power historian Bill Beck writes that the company cleared land and laid track from Fond du Lac to the Thomson Hydro Station. It could then haul passengers and supplies. Passengers were transported by way of a gas trolley car. Gloria Murto, who grew up in Forbay, fondly wrote that she would always remember the small dark-green trolley type car. It held twelve passengers plus a driver. Wobbling from side to side, crossing the islets with rails on planks high above the water, was in her words, "scary."

Forbay was located on level land along the St. Louis River and adjacent to the hydro station. All accounts agree that the settle-

Forbay Residence. (Courtesy of the Carlton County Historical Society)

Forbay Picnic, 1914. (Courtesy of the Carlton County Historical Society)

Sandstone Retaining Walls (Forbay). (Courtesy of Kris Hiller, MNDNR)

Sandstone Culverts (Forbay) today. (Courtesy of Kris Hiller, MNDNR)

ment consisted of seven single-family homes, a superintendent's house, and a two-story wooden hotel (for single employees). Beck further describes the hotel as having eight double-sleeping rooms, a kitchen, sitting room and a family-style dining area. A flagpole sat in the center of the residences. During the winter months, a cleared area was flooded and used as a skating rink. There was a two-story school built in 1917. The upper floor was living quarters for the teacher and her husband. The school closed in 1931 and students were transported to nearby Esko.

The trolley car made its last run in 1949. Beck reports that it was later sold at scrap value ($500). The State of Minnesota, which had purchased the car from Minnesota Power, used the money to buy a Dodge one-ton truck with hydraulic plow. Both are now long gone.

In the 1950s, a wall of water washed out portions of the tracks and shortly after the railroad spur was retired. In the 1960s, Minnesota Power decided to get out of the rental housing business and decided to sell the houses. Once sold, the houses were moved out; many are still standing in nearby communities.

Little remains of Forbay. There are still some broken scraps of foundations and they are deteriorating and vanishing by the day. All remains are on Minnesota Power company land and are inaccessible. Within Jay Cooke State Park there are still some sandstone supports, culverts and railbeds scattered about. According to park naturalist Kris Hiller, these are remnants of the Lake Superior and Mississippi Railroad that also serviced Forbay and Minnesota Power. She states that these are far off the trails. However, as you drive through the park, you are driving on portions of the old railway.

June of 2012 again brought torrents of water down on the Forbay area and Jay Cooke State Park. Torrential rains wreaked havoc on the entire area. The famed Swinging Bridge at the park was swept away by the raging waters. Many parts of Highway 210 through the area were destroyed and are still impassable, particularly near the hdyro station. Mudslides covered the park's main parking lot, park employees had to abandon their cars and walk out. Slowly reparing the damage will take time, as will restoration.

31

IVERSON

1909–1927
CLASS A
APPROXIMATE LOCATION:
From Carlton:
West on MN Highway 210 for approximately 5½ miles.

Iverson Today. (Author's collection)

A close-knit, farming community, Iverson was located just west of Carlton, Minnesota, on the Northern Pacific main line. Originally called Pine Grove, the community was renamed Iverson, in honor of Ole Iverson—early settler, local farmer, railroad depot janitor, and owner of a small grocery store and later gas station. Iverson's place was always considered "the gathering place."

Other early settlers included the Denzler family of fourteen children from Germany. The first school in Iverson had only Denzlers as students.

Soon the town included a school, post office, general store, gas station, sawmill, and later a bar/restaurant. Religion was a strong influence and a church mission group was very active.

In her reminisces, Juella Sandvik Iverson, recalled that during the months of July and August (peak blueberry season), residents would watch as hundreds of folks from Duluth, Superior, and the surrounding area would arrive in Iverson, just to pick the blueberries. She said the train would even stop at different areas, about a mile apart, just so the pickers wouldn't have so far to walk.

For many years after the decline of Iverson as a town, the Iverson Inn would continue to be the local gathering place. It would later burn down.

Driving on Highway 210 today, you can see the area where Iverson once was located. A wide spot in the road and, at last look, a green highway sign noting Iverson and a few crumbling foundations are all that remains. There are a few area farmers and homes.

Iverson Today. (Author's collection)

Cass County

Cyphers today. (Author collection)

Cyphers today. (Author collection)

CYPHERS

1909-1933
CLASS A
APPROXIMATE LOCATION:
From Hackensack:
North on Highway 371 for approximately 6½ miles. Left on 60th Street NW for ½ mile

For a while, Cyphers was as far as you could go and getting anywhere else from there wasn't easy. Though only seven miles from Walker, before the railroad trestle bridge was built over Shingobee Island in 1896, it was a fifty-four mile trek through scenic but rough country. Mary Norton and her parents came to the area in 1912, when Mary was three. In a 1987 interview she recalled that when they arrived, there were no roads and they had to cut their way in to their property.

Mary tells that in the late 1890s, there were a lot of private sawyers in the area and several sawmills. After the lumber companies moved out, the homesteaders and settlers moved in and they needed local lumber. She states that the reason for the Cyphers town site was Pete Albert's big sawmill located on the shores of Cyphers Lake. In her words, they used to put the logs in the lake to soak them. The actual saws were on the second floor of the mill and were operated by steam engine. Adding to the advantages of location to Cyphers was the fact that the railroad long siding (an area to turn steam engines around) was nearby. The siding, a mile long, was the longest between Brainerd and Bemidji.

The naming of the community has an amusing history. Early resident and historian Peter (Tuck) Geving writes that because of the long siding, the community was sometimes called Long Siding. The area also had a boarding house that was frequented by visiting hunters, so Hunters was another early name. One day, one of those hunters couldn't remember the name of the town. The conductor was joking around with him. Finally the frustrated hunter blurted out, "Cyphers! I can't remember the name of the town." Peter says the name stuck.

In October of 1909, the post office was established and located in the Andrew Watts store. Mrs. Watts, who Mary termed a "catalog wife," couldn't take the hard north woods life or living in a tar paper shack any longer and left. Her husband, unable to manage the post office duties, sold the post office to the Nortons. In the mid-1930s, rural mail delivery was established and the one hundred people who used to pick up their mail in Cyphers now had home delivery. The Cyphers post office was discontinued in 1933. Eventually the post office ended up in the Nortons's garage and in the 1980s Mary donated it to the Cass County Historical Society Museum, where it is on display.

Cyphers experienced something that few communities in Minnesota have ever experienced—an earthquake. The *Cass County Pioneer* reported that on September 7, 1917, parts of Minnesota were shaken up. Areas affected were the Twin Cities, Wadena and Cass counties. There was minor damage in Staples and the newspaper reported that Cyphers reported the ground was shaking.

Rural mail delivery was the first of three crucial blows to the community of Cyphers. The Highway 200 construction was the second, while devastating effects of the Great Depression was the third. Soon Cyphers, as a town, ceased to exist and as Peter Geving states, nature is doing her best to hide any signs of the old town.

ELLIS

1890-1926
CLASS A
APPROXIMATE LOCATION:
From Motley:
North on Minnesota 64 for approximately 12 miles. Left on 80th Street SW for approximately 2 miles. Right on 79th Avenue. Northeast Corner of Intersection.

In one of its earliest editions, the newly-established *Cass County Pioneer* predicted a "prosperous future" for Ellis, stating the streets were broad and the lots large. The newspaper expected great things. So much so that they set up their printing facility in the town.

The editors go on, at great length, detailing the benefits of the area: healthy living with a nearby hospital, a soon-to-be-built cheese factory, which the newspaper says would be a great source of wealth to area farmers, a sawmill with a daily output capacity of 24,000 feet, and good farm land upon which has the opportunity to be self-sustaining. Less than five months later, the upstart newspaper would move its offices to nearby Esterdy.

Ellis was named for Joe Ellis. There are no records on Mr. Ellis's occupation or role in the city.

In its heyday, Ellis included a blacksmith, hotel, post office (1890 to 1926), a livery stable, sawmill, printing office, several residences, and a store. The store had several owners, later becoming the Odd Fellows Hall, which eventually burned down in the 1930s.

Ellis. (Courtesy of the Cass County Historical Society)

Two churches served the community, one being the Lutheran Church, which conducted services in Norwegian. In the 1950s, the church was moved to Leader where it is now known as Swan Valley Lutheran. The Bethel Presbyterian Church, the second church in Ellis, also moved to Leader becoming the Mennonite Church.

ESTERDY

1895-1910
CLASS A
APPROXIMATE LOCATION:
From Staples:
West on Airport road approximately 2 miles to County Road 30. Right on County Road 30 and continue to follow County 30 for 5 miles. Right on 96th Avenue SW for 1 mile. Continue onto 91st Aveune SW for approximately 2.3 miles. Continue onto 90th Street SW for 1/10th of a mile. Right. Old town site is on the right—Private Property.

In 1892, Dr. Van Sandine built a two-story log cabin hospital, which, according to the Cass County Historical Society, was the first hospital in the county. Dr. Van Sandine was known for his excellent care, and people came from miles away to be treated at his facility. The hospital was the only one in the area until, in 1900, Staples established a hospital and with advertising became the hospital of choice.

Settlers began coming to the area in 1893 and in 1895, when three prairie schooners (covered wagons) arrived from Iowa, they found a growing community. Located in the heart of logging country, the large settlement included a coal company, restaurant, two general stores, two hotels, a tailor, a lumber company, and the nearby hospital.

The *Cass County Pioneer* newspaper, having moved from Ellis, printed their newspapers in Esterdy from July to October of 1895. In October of that year, the newspaper moved to Walker where it published until 1962.

Little is known about the demise of the community.

GULL RIVER

1880-1895
CLASS C
APPROXIMATE LOCATION:
From Brainerd:
West on Highway 210 for approximately 6 miles. Just past the Gull River crossing.

Sometimes lost towns are right under our noses. For over twenty-five years I have driven past the two-story, weather-beaten, wooden structure on Highway 210, just west of Brainerd. I've often wondered what the story behind the house was, never imagining it to be a remnant of a true Minnesota ghost town. It was a casual remark by a Crow Wing County Historical Society volunteer that made me realize the connection and off I was to learn the story.

Built in 1867, that old building is the only structure still standing on its original foundation from the long-ago town of Gull River.

As the demand for lumber increased and the eastern supplies of it decreased, new sources of timber were sought. The virgin forests of northern Minnesota were coveted, and lumbermen flocked to the state. In the early years, access and transportation limitations kept the logging efforts to a minimum. Once the railroad came through, the logging of Minnesota's forest areas began at a fever pitch.

Sawmills were springing up all over northern Minnesota. The Gull River Lumber Company was one of the first, and the largest, in the Brainerd area. The partnership of the company, formed in 1879, included the Pillsbury family. Those familiar with Minnesota history will recognize that name as early businessmen and politicians.

An article in the September 11, 1880 *Brainerd Tribune* reported that within two years' time, the mill included a 154-foot-by-sixty-foot, two-story mill with a steam sawmill of thirty-six saws, two edgers, two trimmers, a slab and bolt saw, shingle machine (which could turn out over 40,000 shingles a day), a planer, tongue and groove machine making siding and flooring, a dry house (which dried over 30,000 feet a day), and an engine house that was approximately forty feet by forty-five feet. Driving by the area today it is hard to imagine such a large operation.

It wasn't long before a community arose around the mill and soon the population of Gull River was over 300, with some estimates as high as 500. Strictly a company town, the town also included a boarding house with room for eighty men, twenty-two residences, a company general store, a ma-

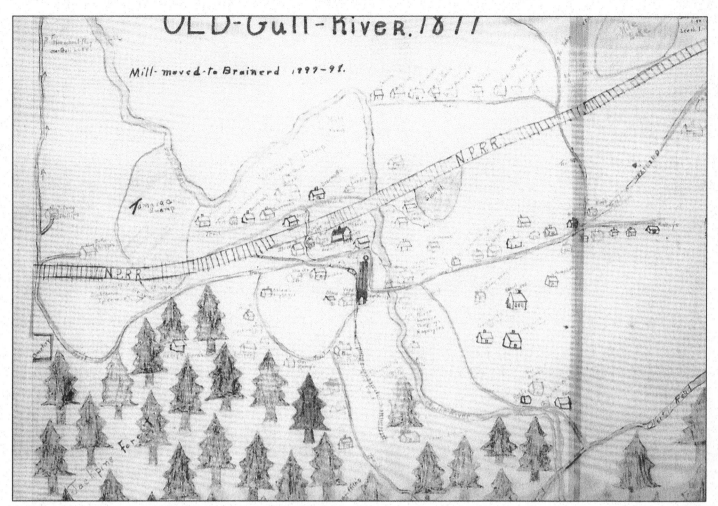

Gull River Map. (Courtesy of Crow Wing County Historical Society)

Chase and Pillsbury Office, Gull River 1879. (Courtesy of Crow Wing County Historical Society)

Vanished Village of Gull River. (Courtesy of Crow Wing County Historical Society)

chine shop, foundry, sash, door and blind factory, and a school with an expected enrollment of forty-two students.

The *Brainerd Tribune* made a bold prediction in that article. Estimating that there were over 250,000,000 board feet of lumber under the auspices of the Pillsbury Company, they stated that it would take at least twenty-five years to deplete the supply. Sadly the prediction would prove wrong.

Richard Wickmann, an area historian, details the demise of Gull River stating in his summary, "at its peak in 1879, just ten years later, the mill and the town of Gull River would no longer exist. Facing forces beyond their control, increased competition by lumber barons such as Weyerhauser and a dam on the Mississippi River in Brainerd that provided hydro power, plus financial incentives by Brainerd, all would combine to affect the end of the mill and the community."

A hand-drawn map, with details exists. It is in the files of both the Crow Wing County Historical Society and the Cass County Historical Society, as well as online. The map shows the layout of the mill and the village. It was drawn by the daughter of a resident of Gull River. The creator of the map stated that it was drawn for Jim Madden, who at the time was the owner of the nearby Madden's resort. At the time, Madden was planning his "Lumbertown U.S.A." exhibit.

Lumbertown U.S.A. was a replica of an 1870s logging village. Built in 1959, it was modeled after Knott's Berry Farm and filled with vintage antiques and artifacts. When closed, some of the buildings were moved to the Nisswa Pioneer Village in Nisswa.

The accuracy of that hand-drawn map was questioned. In the 1980s, a power line was proposed that would impact the Gull River area. An unknown study group was formed and additional research conducted. The group stated that they had several photographs and that these photos did not agree with the map. What these inaccuracies were was not disclosed. A revised map was drawn and overlaid onto the old map.

That 1983 report also stated that there was physical evidence of the village. In the early 1900s a dam that backed up the Gull River was constructed that was twenty-two feet high. Since the rail bridge at that point was six feet, much of the mill was underwater. It is said that area fishermen could see the mill foundations. However that was over thirty years ago and nature has reclaimed much of the physical evidence and archeological remnants that assisted in the making of the revised map.

Records state that the old schoolhouse was moved a half mile east across the field. There are conflicting reports on the status of the school. Some say it was torn down, others say it

Cunningham House, the only Gull River building remaining on its original foundation. (Author's collection)

Site of Gull River today. (Author's collection)

became part of a nearby resort. There is an old Gull River-era building still standing just across the field, where the school was reportedly moved. Its age would fit the time frame, however there is no positive identification of it being the school. Today it is used as a horse stable.

As for that majestic house on the north side of Highway 210, it has been determined to be the Cunningham house, home to Joseph and Mille Cunningham. The house stands tall as a testament to times long past. Nearby is the Gull River Cemetery where many of the pioneer settlers are buried. There are rural residences with many family ties back to the early families.

As I stood across the road to take a picture of the sentinel, I looked at a map and I could see that I was standing at the door of the old boarding house and overlooking the entire village. With imagination I could almost hear the activity.

LOTHROP

1894-1901
CLASS A
APPROXIMATE LOCATION:
From Hackensack:
North on Highway 371 for approximately 5 miles. Left at intersection of Highway 371 and Cass County 50. The town site was just to the south of the paved trail and gravel parking area.

In the 1970s, my mother moved to Hackensack, Minnesota, living in a rustic basement cabin on Portage Lake. To get to Mom's place you headed north out of Hackensack, turning west at the intersection of Highway 371 and Cass County Road 50. Every time we turned at that juncture, Mom would talk of a long-ago town that once sat there.

Today, as you turn at that juncture, you will find a small gravel parking lot along the paved path known as the Paul Bunyan Trail. Just south of that gravel lot, as well as under Highway 371, is where the town of Lothrop once sat. Little remains of the town. Longtime resident Mary Norton says that the trees have gotten so big that it would be hard to see any signs of Lothrop, even the roads.

Long before the 112-mile hiking and biking trail was ever envisioned, the railroad laid their double steel rails along the now paved route. Once the end of the line, Lothrop was platted in 1895 and named for a civil engineer and surveyor. Typical for railroad and logging towns of that era, Lothrop was a wild, rowdy end-of-the-line location. With nearly 2,000 lumberjacks and railroad men in the area, Lothrop became the

place of choice for spending the reported $100,000 paid in wages during the winter of 1895-1896. There were also family residents as the local newspaper reported on school Christmas programs. One account lists twenty-four family residences.

The town included a roundhouse, post office (1894 to 1901), several stores including a butcher shop, a bakery, a drug store, two general stores, two barber shops, three or four restaurants, a red-light district, and at least seven saloons. Mary Norton, a longtime resident and local historian, recalls that the red-light district had as many houses as there were taverns. Each had their own private place of business. Mary also recalled that the town of 1,000 was never laid out with a plan, the wood-frame houses were built in a hit-and-miss pattern.

Lothrop did have its own doctor, though some say, with questionable ethics. Various accounts state the doctor sold stuff to make people sick, and then could charge for the cure. If he was too late, he, as coroner, could pronounce them dead and sign the certificate.

While visiting with Renee Geving, the director of the Cass County Historical Society, she tells of Lothrop's colorful characters. Mustache Liz, termed a "left-over-lady-of-the-night," was aptly nicknamed. Mary Norton, whose family were early settlers in the area, recalled that Liz was not a large person and that she did have a lot of hair growth on her face. She used to wear an old man's hat and an apron that was longer than her dress. She walked with a stick that was shoulder tall.

Mustache Liz. (Courtesy of the Cass County Historical Society)

Mustache Liz's Cabin ca 1958. (Courtesy of *Mainly Logging*)

Folklore tells of a heated poker game, as often was the case in Lothrop. Red, having all of his worldly possessions in the jackpot knew he had a winning hand. With nothing else available to up his ante, Red threw Liz, whom he said he owned, into the pot. Alas, his hand was not as good as he thought and Denny McDowell won the entire jackpot, including Liz. Denny, feeling sorry for Liz, married her. Another version is that Denny tired of the ribbing he took because he was single so he decided to marry Liz. With World War I in full-swing, Denny was always being told he would be called up to serve because he had no wife. So he married Liz, even though he was too old to serve anyway. The two continued to live on the site of Lothrop for many years. Denny was killed while trying to rescue one of his pigs that had wandered onto the railroad tracks. Liz continued to live in the area until gangrene ravaged her body. She was moved to the hospital in Walker and eventually to the state hospital in Fergus Falls, which was a facility for the mentally ill. The custom was that anyone not able to care for themselves, was given a test. Since Liz could not read or write, she had little chance of passing any test and was confined to the hospital until her death in 1937.

Lothrop today. (Author's collection)

In its heyday, logging trains loaded with logs passed through Lothrop on their way to the mill in Brainerd, every fifteen to twenty minutes. It was said that over 150,000 feet of lumber was shipped every day and that expectations were to ship 150 million board feet.

Lothrop was short-lived. When the railroad line was extended north, and the Shingobee trestle built, the town died. By 1900, all that remained was the bordello, Mustache Liz, and a few residents.

MILDRED

1899-1954
CLASS A
APPROXIMATE LOCATION:
From Pine River:
North on Highway 371 for approximately 4 miles. Near the intersection of 14th Street SW.

Mildred has always been at the heart of things, to the community, the residents and most often the highways and byways that coursed along, around, and through it.

In its earliest days, it was on the Brainerd to Leech Lake tote road. During those times the early settlers wanted to call the community Cookston. The Postal Service declined that name, saying it too closely resembled Crookston. So, as an alternative, they chose "Mildred," which was the name of the daughter of the storekeeper, the store being the community's first place of business.

Established in the heart of logging country and along the well-traveled route, the town thrived. The loggers and the farmers of the area needed supplies and services and soon enterprising business owners came to the area. The town soon included a livery stable, sawmill, boarding house, hotel, photography shop, post office (1899), and a general store or two. Everything an early logging town could want or need.

Area historian Bill Burnson, in writing of Mildred, wrote that it had everything most early towns could want, and more. Unlike most other places, Mildred offered moral and cultural activities. They had literary and debating societies, a pioneer farmers club, good hunting and fishing, a town baseball team, a swimming school, a public school, and a strong religious base.

As the timber resources were depleted, Mildred still fared well due to its solid base of farming. That base not only kept Mildred strong, the town continued to grow despite the logging decline. Soon Mildred had to build a new school employing five teachers

Mildred was not without its problems. Twice the entire business district burned to the ground. In December of 1946, on a

Mildred Bible Chapel. (Author's collection)

Friday the 13th, the grocery store/post office and a vacant at-tached building burned and were a total loss. There were no in-juries and after the fire, the store's credit files and the post office records were saved. The *Walker Pilot* reported that the family and the post office were housed in a vacant room in the school.

In the early 1930s, Highway 19 (the predecessor to Hwy 371) was being re-routed between Pine River and Ten Mile Lake. It was determined that the entire town of Mildred had to be moved thirty-five feet. The logistics of doing so was problematic. Trying to satisfy both the owners and the state, the *Walker Pilot* detailed several of the concerns.

The store had warehouses and out buildings that had to be moved the entire thirty-five feet. The store warehouse was built of concrete with a cement foundation that would have to be demolished when moving the warehouse. The outbuildings had to be moved first, then the main building. The State of Minnesota was willing to reimburse the cost of moving plus some of the loss of business and retail.

One residence was a forty-acre plot that sat quite a distance back. While the buildings would not have to be moved, the landscaping would be destroyed. The trees, berries, fruits, and garden would be lost. In addition, the owners raised poultry, and the effect of being on the main road and the loss of a tran-quil lifestyle, for the owners and the chickens, was a major concern.

Mildred Cemetery. (Author's collection)

Mildred survived that highway displacement but not the next one. In 1970, Highway 371 improvements would route the newly-paved and widened road right through the center of town. Bill Burnson reported that the buildings were razed and burned, the signs removed and Mildred would be no more.

Today a few residences, a cemetery, and the Mildred Bible Chapel are in the area as well as hundreds of people still trav-eling through the heart of the community.

TOBIQUE

1912-1954
CLASS A
APPROXIMATE LOCATION:
From Remer:
Northeast on Cass County 4 for approximately 8 miles. Left on Tobique Road NE for approximately 1½ miles. Site is on NE side of Soo Line Trail North Route.

Early loggers and settlers knew the area as Roger's Spur. After 1910, when the Soo Line railroad came through, it would also be known as Tobique. With a logging camp between Remer and another west of Roger's Spur, the area was a centralized supply hub. Twice daily, mail would be shipped out and even though the trains were often late, Aloys

Tobique store. (Courtesy of the Cass County Historical Society)

Tobique School. (Courtesy of the Cass County Historical Society)

Warmert never missed getting the mail on the train. A post office was established in 1912.

In the beginning, the town didn't even have a depot. Later the railroad would bring in a boxcar complete with a stove and mail catcher, to be used as a depot. A small stockyard was also near the tracks. In 1954, the post office was discontinued.

WILKINSON

1910-1954
CLASS A
APPROXIMATE LOCATION:
From Walker:
North on Highway 371 for approximately 11½ miles. Near intersection of Highway 371 and Wilkenson Township #1.

Fifteen years ago, in July of 1998, the Wilkinson Store was closed. After over fifty-five years in business, Elizabeth (Libby) Kittilson had to call it quits. New state regulations required that her gas pumps and storage tanks had to be replaced. The cost of doing so was prohibitive, so Libby had no choice but to remove them. Without her gas she knew her business would drop off dramatically and so she made plans to close the store by spring. This was the end of Wilkinson

The town of Wilkinson sprang up along the Great Northern Railroad line in the early 1900s. It was the first station south of Cass Lake.

Not long after the 1903 Township Law was passed a group of citizens from Cass Lake and Bemidji declared their intentions to make final proof on 320 acres. The law permitted the entry of lands on the ceded Chippewa reservation, under certain conditions, for town site purposes. The town site was just outside national forest land and the western boundary of the former reservation.

Town boosters believed they had the makings for a logging headquarters with all of the logging camps in the area. The fertile farm land also attracted homesteaders and settlers and rapid growth seemed eminent.

Originally called Marcus, the name was changed to Wilkinson in 1910. Presumably the name was to honor Major Melville Wilkinson who was killed in the Battle of Sugar Point. That battle, in northern Cass County in 1898, is said to be the last Indian battle in the United States. In its earliest days, Marcus had only a section house and water tower.

Little else is known about the community. Records show a succession of postmasters from the post office that was established in 1910 and was discontinued in 1954.

For years the Wilkinson Store catered to vacationers, lake residents, and travelers. Folks were able to pick up most everything they needed, while at the cabin, including the news and happenings. With changing trends, folks started to bring their supplies with them or they made the trip to larger cities to pick up the things they needed.

Wilkinson is still the half-way point between Walker and Cass Lake. There is no longer a town nor a pit stop for travelers. You can still see that little store as you drive Highway 371, although it is no longer a store and is now private property.

Wilkinson store. (Courtesy of the Cass County HIstorical Society)

Clay County

Manitoba Junction today. (Courtesy of Andrew Filer)

Muskoda Today. (Courtesy of Andrew Filer)

MANITOBA JUNCTION

1910-1911
CLASS A
APPROXIMATE LOCATION:
From Hawley:
East on U.S. Highway 10 for approximately 2½ miles. Interstate #32 Exit. Left on Minnesota 32/260th Street South. Right on 28th Avenue North for approximately ½ mile.

Winnipeg Junction was a trouble spot with low, swampy, unstable land which caused shifting and twisting of the railroad tracks. Hoping to avoid the constant problems with the low land, the railroad planned to run a new mainline on higher ground, a mile to the north of Winnipeg Junction.

They planned to call this new location Manitoba Junction, as the line would run to Winnipeg, Manitoba. In spite of trying to avoid the swampy ground, the Northern Pacific still ended up locating Manitoba Junction in a slough that was difficult to get to. Today the BNSF maintains a junction there for its western branch, although today that line runs only twelve miles to Ulen.

Other than the railroad line, little exists at the old town site.

MUSKODA

1873-1930
CLASS A
APPROXIMATE LOCATION:
From Hawley:
West on U.S. Highway 10 for approximately 4½ miles. Left on 190th Street South (County Highway 23) for approximately 1 mile. Third left onto 12th Avenue South.

The steep grade of the area caused problems for the railroad in Muskoda. The community, originally located west of Hawley on a major north/south road, the railroad proposed a plan that would move Muskoda to a remote spot a few miles further west. As Mark Peihl, archivist at the Historical and Cultural Society of Clay County, notes, the residents were not happy. The new, remote location would make it difficult to ship their goods east. The proposal caused protest, and even included an order by the railroad to the depot agent to spy on his neighbors. Eventually, Mark writes, a quiet deal was reached, with the details never released to the public. Instead of moving the siding to the west, the Northern Pacific Railroad

Old Muskoda. (Courtesy of the Historical and Cultural Society of Clay County)

established New Muskoda back on the road, a mile south of its original location.

The town had a general store, grain elevator, potato warehouse, and a post office from 1873 to 1930. A great deal of sand and gravel was also shipped out of Muskoda. Muskoda did have a newspaper that published one issue and one issue only in 1877.

Nothing remains today of either Old or New Muskoda, except for the new siding. Mark Peihl writes that the abandoned grade is still visible in some fields and a housing development is on the old site.

STOCKWOOD

1895-1921
CLASS A
APPROXIMATE LOCATION:
From Glyndon:
East on Highway 10 for 4 miles.

As you drive through Clay County and the Red River Valley in northwestern Minnesota, you can see a series of ridges made up of sand and gravel. These ridges, known as beach ridges, are the shoreline of Lake Agassiz, the ancient glacial lake that once covered the area. These geological features caused all kinds of problems for the early railroad routes through the area.

From 1906 to 1909, the Northern Pacific Railroad changed its route through Clay County. Originally built directly on the existing grade, moving heavy east-bound trains over the ridges was problematic. To solve the problem, the Northern Pacific built a ramp at Stockwood that put the rail lines thirty feet in the air.

Mark Peihl, archivist at the Historical and Cultural Society of Clay County has done extensive research and writing on the Stockwood Fill, Clay County ghost towns, and the history of the railroads in Clay County. He writes that the people of Stockwood were not happy about the transportation system. To appease them, the railroad built a ramp to provide access to the tracks. A set of steps on either side was also built. A tiny depot sat at the top. The town of Stockwood was located in Riverton Township and consisted of the depot, a general store with the post office, a boarding house, implement dealership, school, and a few family residences.

There are no remains of the town. However, the ramp can still be seen from the air. The old school building is now the Riverton Town Hall.

Stockwood Fill. (Courtesy of the Historical and Cultural Society of Clay County)

Stockwood Depot. (Courtesy of the Historical and Cultural Society of Clay County)

WINNIPEG JUNCTION

1887-1910
CLASS A
APPROXIMATE LOCATION:
From Hawley:
East on U.S. Highway 10 for 2½ miles. Interstate #32 Exit towards Twin Valley/Rollag. Left onto Highway 32/260th Street South for one mile. Right on County 15/Junction Avenue for 7/10 mile.

With a population of approximately 250 people in 1905, Winnipeg Junction is one of Clay County's largest lost towns.

As in many other railroad towns at the turn of the twentieth century, the Northern Pacific Railroad had to work to avoid controversy in regards to its transportation routes. Wanting to abandon the town of Winnipeg Junction without protest, the railroad planned to build a new main line. Once the line was built, the plan was to reduce rail traffic through Winnipeg Junction to two trains daily—one east-bound the other west-bound. As Mark Peihl, archivist at the Historical and Cultural Society of Clay County, tells, that was the bare minimum of train traffic the railroad could maintain without having to start abandonment proceedings. The railroad, according to Mark, planned to leave the residents of Winnipeg Junction, many of them railroad workers, hung out to dry. Then, Northern Pacific could purchase their properties at bargain, low prices.

The residents were able to get an injunction with an admonition by the Railroad Commission telling the railroad that they strongly advised reaching a settlement with the residents. The railroad offered $25,000 to allow the Northern Pacific to abandon the route. The residents wanted $35,000. A compromise was reached at $30,000. The fee was for the right to abandon only, not for the real estate property.

In 1909, the remaining residents voted eight to two to dissolve the town. Within a few short years, little was left of the community that once included several stores, saloons, two restaurants, a bakery, grain elevator, and more. Many of the

Winnipeg Junction. (Courtesy of the Historical and Cultural Society of Clay County)

buildings were moved to other locations. The railroad tore up the tracks but left the main east/west grade through town, now Junction Avenue and County 115.

A few families are still in the area, and Mark says one building is still standing on its original location. He also shares that the old grade running to the north is still visible and that the Northern Pacific (now BNSF) old brick pumping station can be seen west of town on the bank of the Buffalo River.

Winnipeg Junction. (Courtesy of the Historical and Cultural Society of Clay County)

Winnipeg Junction today. (Courtesy of the Historical and Cultural Society of Clay County/Mark Peihl)

Clearwater County

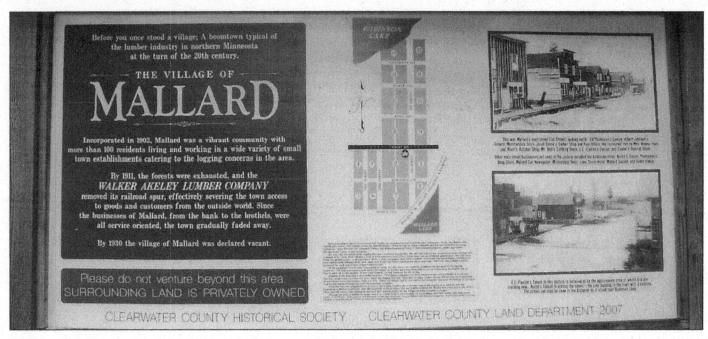

Mallard Town Site Marker. (Author's collection)

Streets of Mallard. (Courtesy of the Clearwater County Historical Society)

MALLARD

1902-1924
CLASS A/Marker
APROXIMATE LOCATION:
From Shevlin:
South on County Highway 2 for approximately 15½ miles.
Right on County Highway 37 for approximately 3 miles. Picnic shelter and historical marker will be on the left side of County 37.

Original Town Site of Mallard. (Author's collection)

YOU ARE HERE! The large historical sign with map and photos declares that, indeed, you are standing in downtown Mallard. The only thing separating you from Mallard in its heyday is about one hundred years.

With imagination and aided by the vintage photos, you can see the muddy dirt streets, wooden boardwalks, the three hotels, three saloons, bank, barber shop, two general stores, the drug store, town newspaper, butcher shop, shoe repair, restaurants, clothing store, livery barn, school and just over the hill to the west, the brothels.

Begun in 1901, as a rail head for the Red River Spur from Solway on the Great Northern route from Crookston to Bemidji, it didn't take long for the community to grow.

The town was platted in 1902-1903, shortly after the Walker-Akeley spur was completed. Construction began almost immediately with Sinker's general store being the first building to see construction. Shortly after the store was started, construction began on the town's first saloon. The Clearwater County Historical Society tells that those building the saloon must have been motivated as the saloon was completed before the store was finished.

In 1902, Sinker applied for and established Mallard's post office. Soon the first store outgrew its space, so Sinker built a second, larger store, calling this one the Pioneer Store. The original store became the barbershop. Quickly other buildings sprang up all over Mallard. Soon over one hundred residents called Mallard home. On Saturday nights, with the area loggers visiting Mallard, the town's population would swell to over 200.

Living in the heart of timber country and with all of Mallard's buildings being built of wood, the townspeople felt a need for fire-fighting equipment. Spending the huge amount of $3,500, the town purchased a hand-drawn fire engine. The engine was stored on the north side of Mallard Lake for easy access to the water supply. Olga Sandin and Norma Ressler, in their writing, describe the engine as having two handles on the front and a place in the back for two men to push. Norma and Olga called the engine a "white elephant."

Operated by a gas engine, in the cold winter, it would take an hour to get the engine heated up. Then it had to be filled with water and hand-drawn up the hill. By that time any hope of saving a building on fire was long gone, and the building would be burned to the ground. Olga states that it was never known to put out a fire. The rig did get used (on the Fourth of July) for water fights. The engine did pump water, just not when it was needed in a hurry.

The community had a school located near Robinson Lake to the north. The school district outlasted the town and the school building. The school building was moved in 1930 to Bagley where it served as a storage facility for the Bridgeman dairy. The last classes were held in 1941-1942 and the district dissolved in 1945.

For a short time, the town's newspaper, *The Mallard Call*, was the official newspaper of Clearwater County.

Mallard, the town and its businesses, was dependent on the timber resources in the area. When the logging camps were running strong, business was good. When the timber was depleted, the loggers moved on to the next location, and Mallard was left with no customers for its service-oriented economy.

The railroad spur was no longer needed. The railroad offered to rent the spur to the town at a cost of $1,300 per year. The residents declined, and the tracks were pulled up in 1911 and moved. With the largest source of their income gone, the businesses had no choice but to pack up and move on as well, lock, stock, and buildings. The post office was discontinued in 1924, and Mallard as a town was near the end. The last buildings left in the 1930s.

Mallard's sense of community did live on for decades. Reunions were held in 1989 and 1991 with good turnout. Histories have been written and the story of Mallard has been well-documented. The Clearwater County Historical Society has erected a historical marker at the old town site. The impressive venture includes a large placard that has vintage photos, maps, and a summary of the town. A covered picnic shelter invites folks to sit and enjoy the country setting. Along the fringes of the grassy hill are a few depressions but little else remains of the town. Private property surrounds the wayside rest.

Mallard Today. (Author's collection)

Mallard Today. (Author's collection)

MOOSE/MOOSE CORNERS

1892–1908
CLASS A
APPROXIMATE LOCATION:
From Shevlin:
South on County 2 for approximately 5½ miles. Left on 310th Street. Near intersection of Clearwater County 2 and County 29.

Traveling by oxen and hoping to find richer farm fields, newlyweds John and Bertha McCollum headed north from Sauk Centre. Joining the couple was Bertha's father, sister, and brother-in-law. Reaching northern Minnesota, they came upon the abundant timber forests and decided to go no further. Though the land was not the rich farmland John had wanted, he was persuaded this was the spot to make their home, and they all filed land claims.

Bertha's father, Darling Wheeler, started a saw mill, pumping water from the south end of his land to a homemade windmill. His sawmill was successful enough as to be able to offer work to other area settlers.

It wasn't long before the small settlement began to grow and soon there was a post office and a few stores. The community also had a small log schoolhouse. Serving the primary through eighth grade, there were about forty-five students.

Plans had been made for a rail spur to go to Moose. Hopes were dashed when the spur went a mile east.

Birdie McCollum Palm, born in Moose in 1897 recalled that times were hard. In a written memoir she said that even with the hard times, Moose was a happy place. Community gatherings were held at Thanksgiving and Christmas. She was especially fond of the skating and dancing outings, where groups of students and adults would walk to Shevlin to take part in the activities.

Moose. (Courtesy of the Clearwater County Historical Society)

In 1906, the McCollums moved to Oregon, the post office was discontinued, the timber resources depleted and the railroad tracks were pulled up. Moose, the town, no longer existed yet the township carries on the name.

WEME

1902–1912 (1960s)

CLASS A

APPROXIMATE LOCATION:
From Clearbrook:
East on Highway 92 for approximately 1½ miles. Right on 460th for 4 miles. Left on County 7 for 3 miles. Right on Township Road T-17 for 1/5 mile.

While the post office at Weme may have only lasted ten years, the community itself lasted for decades. In May 1896, part of the Red Lake Reservation was opened for homesteading. Since the area was blanketed with rich virgin timber and lumber was in great demand, sawmills were springing up all over the region. Within that first decade, most of the timber resources were harvested and the area converted from a logging to an agricultural base. It was this farming component that would define the community of Weme.

Open in the early 1900s, the Weme Store would serve the needs of the area residents until the 1960s when it would close for good. Started by Hans Weme, the store changed ownership many times over the years, even operating as a co-op venture for a time.

Catering to the ever-changing needs of area residents, the store provided all the services an agricultural community would need: general merchandise, farm machinery, sawmill, threshing machine, and feed meal. Years later, some of the younger residents would recall walking to the store for soda pop and candy. In later years, the store added building supplies, an electrical wiring service, and a trucking business.

Equally important to the town and its residents was the Eddy Co-op Creamery. Fully functional by 1907, the creamery was located on the bank of the Lost River, which allowed for clear spring water. The creamery provided butter, cream, milk, and a market for area farm products. Refrigeration, until 1939, was provided by ice blocks and an ice house. In 1939, electricity was available. For the first twenty years of the creamery, there was no market for buttermilk, so it was dumped into the sewer. Later it was sold as hog feed.

In the 1930s, the creamery also offered a machine shop and auto repair. A full line of gas station services was also available, including bulk tanks where a semi-trailer could load and unload. Home delivery of fuel and gas was an option. Farmers could purchase seed and feed at the creamery as well. The 1940s brought a first to the region—a meat locker.

In the 1950s, state regulations were more strict, the equipment was becoming obsolete and better roads provided more competition and sales outlets. Eventually it was decided to liquidate the creamery. The meat locker was sold to an area mink farmer. Nearly all of the other buildings were torn down, with only the creamery house standing in 1971.

The community also had a public school until 1942, when students were bused to nearby Clearbrook. Later the school building was sold, split into two sections, moved, and remodeled as private homes. Other activities included a debating team and a competitive town baseball team.

As previously mentioned the post office lasted only ten years. Established in 1902, it operated until 1912, when Clearbrook got its own post office and Weme became part of their rural mail delivery system.

Weme. (Courtesy of the Clearwater County Historical Society)

In 1997, only the foundation remained of the Weme store. Sitting among tall grass, weeds, dead trees, and brush, the community organized an effort to preserve the site and create a park. In 1998, Don and Shirley Lee donated the land on which the store once stood. Volunteers pitched in to clean up the debris, level the lot, and plant new grass. A concrete picnic pad was poured and a picnic table, flagpole, and flag added. The following year a covered picnic shelter was added. Funds were raised by selling raffle tickets for donated items, door-to-door ticket sales, and memorial donations. The effort to create the park and a lasting testimonial to the town was a community-wide effort just as things had always been back in Weme's earliest days.

WINSOR

1896-1910 Class C
APPROXIMATE LOCATION:
From Gonvick:
South on County Road 7 for approximately 1 mile. The lefse factory is the old Windsor School.

Long before the town of Winsor existed, this area had been of great importance to Native Americans. Here, along the well-traveled Red Lake Reservation trail, the Lost River is at its shallowest. This spot was known as the "Lost River Crossing." Large powwows took place here before and after Winsor. Nearby was a sacred burial site.

In May of 1896, the area was opened up to white settlers, and among the first was Hans Widness and his wife. Deciding that the area was the perfect place for a trading post, they built just that. They also established a post office in their store, which was later named Winsor Mercantile.

Soon other businesses followed, and before long the town had another general store, two lumberyards, a saw mill, confectionary, a blacksmith, a hotel, and a saloon. The saloon lasted just over a year. Records tell that the women voted it out. There is some question as to if the women actually voted or if they exerted pressure on those who voted.

There is also a question on the naming of the community. Some say that it was named after an assistant surveyor who had surveyed the area in 1890-1891. With no proof of that, others say the name is an anglicized version of Hans's surname.

The town also had a schoolhouse. Back in those days, a new school, in its first term, only had to meet for one month. William Watts, a twenty-battle Civil War veteran allowed the school the use of his home that first term, while he boarded elsewhere. The next year, the residents passed a bond for $800 for the purpose of building a new school. Not only would the school serve educational purposes, it also served as a community center and church.

It seemed Winsor was booming. In 1902 it was doing so well that the Fosston Telephone Company started to install telephone lines to the community. However, that came to a dead halt, when in 1910 the railroad decided to lay their track to the new town of Gonvick, rather than to Winsor. Winsor would not recover from the blow. The post office closed in 1910, and by 1911 most of the Winsor business district had moved elsewhere.

Winsor. (Courtesy of the Clearwater County Historical Society)

Still the residents built a new school in 1918. That building was used until 1949, when the district consolidated with Gonvick. The building stood empty for many years, until 1960 when former Winsor resident George Herberg bought it and opened up a lefse factory. Still going strong and still in the old school building, a bit of history lives on. When you are in the area, stop by, pick up some lefse and maybe, just maybe you can tour the historic building.

Winsor School. (Courtesy of Andrew Filer)

Winsor . (Courtesy of Andrew Filer)

Cook County

At right: St. Francis Xavier Church, Chippewa City. (Courtesy of the Cook County Historical Society)

Below: St. Francis Xavier Church, Chippewa City. (Courtesy of Bruce S.)

Chippewa City

1885-1936
CLASS C/F
APPROXIMATE LOCATION:
From Grand Marais:
North on U.S. Highway 61 for one mile.

It's the church! St. Francis Xavier Church, or the Chippewa Church as it was called, has always been the predominant feature of the community, both physically and spiritually. The church was such a part of life in Chippewa City, that nationally famed artist George Morrison, himself born and raised in Chippewa City, said that, "built on a rise above the lake, the church was a symbol of community and of our lives there."

For years, as far back as 1731, Jesuit missionaries had visited the North Shore of Minnesota on an intermittent and sporadic schedule. It wasn't until 1880, that Grand Marias had a regular priest. It was under this priest, Father Sprecht, that the church was constructed.

Before construction of the church, John Morrison would open his house for Mass and would often lead services when a priest wasn't available.

St. Francis Xavier was built in 1895 on land donated by community residents, the Fillsons. Funds to build the church were raised by conducting basket socials. Community members crafted baskets out of birch-bark and filled them with homemade baked goods. Area lumberjacks were the primary customers.

The church was built in a French style by an Ojibwe carpenter and measured approximately twenty-five feet by thirty feet. It also had a lean-to. Other sheds housed the priest's sled dogs and firewood. In 1896, a 225-pound bell was added, and in 1903, a sacristy. St. Francis Xavier was the only Catholic church in the area until one was constructed in Grand Marais in 1916. Mass continued to be held at St. Francis Xavier after 1916 but membership and Chippewa City's population began to decline. The last Mass at the Chippewa Church was held on Christmas Day 1936, with only one or two families in attendance.

The church was vacant until 1958 when local groups, such as the Lions and the Catholic Church, began a clean-up effort. The Cook County Historical Society declared the church an historic site that year. In 1984, the church was listed on the National Register of Historic Places. Ongoing grants from the Minnesota Historical Society and the Grand Portage Band of Chippewa continue to fund the restoration and maintenance. Summer tours of the church are offered.

Chippewa City reached its greatest population peak in the late 1880s. Employment opportunities, such as the building of the Grand Marais Harbor, maintained a growing population.

In 1907, a forest fire ravaged the area. Many homes were destroyed. Two government boats were stationed in Grand Marais, ready to provide a safe refuge for those fleeing the fire. Sailors from those boats saved the church from burning.

Staci Drouillard, in a Cook County Historical Society brochure, details the gradual demise of Chippewa City. Reasons included the 1918 flu epidemic, the Great Depression, and the loss of local employment, the expansion of Highway 61 in 1901, which cut through the community and the devastating 1907 forest fire. Another significant trend was the gradual change of land ownership from Native-owned to that of developers and businesses.

Today there are no original residents. The church, the cemetery, a few rapidly disappearing foundations and one home are the only visible remains of the village.

The cemetery is divided into two sections, the old to the east of the highway, the new to the west. Staci tells that for many years the cemetery was a tangle of tall grass and brush. The old traditional Ojibwe grave houses, wooden crosses, and other markers did not survive the elements. Still, the cemetery and church are sacred ground and symbolize the faith, strength, and history of the community.

Mineral Center

1918-1936
CLASS A
APPROXIMATE LOCATION:
From Grand Portage:
North on U.S. Highway 61 for 3 miles. Left on County 17/Mineral Center Road for four miles. Continue onto Highway 89 or Old Highway 61. 200 feet past intersection. Note: County 89/U.S, 61 is not maintained past this point.

Carrying everything on his back from Hovland, Malcolm Linnell was one of the first to settle in Mineral Center, or as it was known then, Reservation. Malcolm even carried his cook stove the fourteen-mile trek.

One year earlier, in 1909, Malcolm, his uncle and a few others from Black River Falls, Wisconsin, had visited the area. They had heard tales of the vast forests and of the wealth of mineral and fishing opportunities. Since the land was newly opened for homesteading, they wanted to check out the region. They were so impressed with what they saw that on their way back to Wisconsin, they stopped in Duluth and filed their homestead claims.

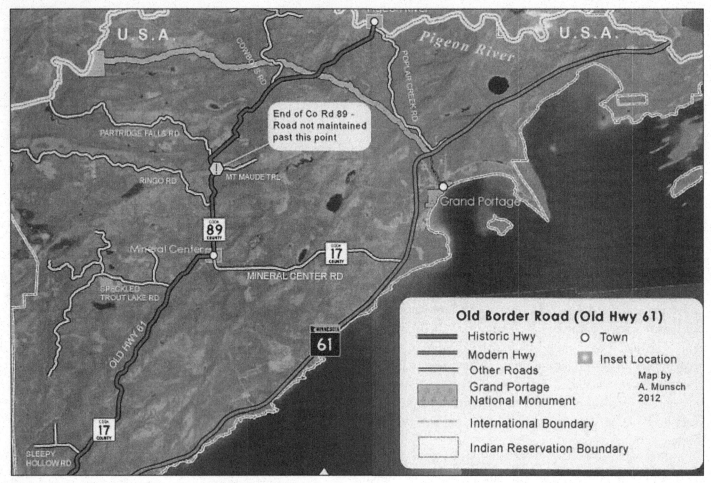

Mineral Center/Pigeon River Map. (Courtesy of Andrew Munsch)

Drouillards, 1940s. Mineral Center. (Courtesy of the Cook County Historical Society)

The following spring, in 1910, Malcolm and the others moved their families to Hovland. That summer they built their homesteads and settled their families in their new homes.

In 1918, a post office was established and the community was officially known as Mineral Center. In the summer, mail came by way of the steamer, *America*, to Hovland and from there over a trail to Mineral Center. In the winter, mail was delivered by horses and stage coach three times a week. The post office was located in the store.

Every fall before winter set in, storekeeper Peter Linnell would travel to the warehouse in Duluth to stock up on winter supplies. The groceries would arrive on the *America* in Hovland. The Linnell boys would meet the ship, pack up the goods on wagons pulled by three or four teams of horses and transport them to Mineral Center. In later years, they would meet the steamer in a Model T Ford truck.

In 1928, the *America* sank near Isle Royale. Her remains are visible a few feet below the surface and are a popular destination for scuba divers.

Forest fires swept through the area in 1908 and again in 1913, but Mineral Center did survive

More and more families joined the community, and by 1930 the population was 350. The need for a school became apparent, and soon the community had two schools. The first, Birchwood, was in operation from 1911 to 1937 before being torn down for salvaged lumber. Cloverdale school was open from 1928 to 1942. The Seventh Day Adventists also had a parochial school from 1922 to 1935. That building was later used as an Indian Curio Shop.

Mineral Center Road. (Courtesy of the Cook County Historical Society)

Mineral Center Road in Winter. (Courtesy of the Cook County Historical Society)

Mineral Center Road Today. (Courtesy of Andrew Munsch)

Gertrude Linnell recalled that the Birchwood School was white clapboard with two adjacent "his" and "hers" outhouses. A tall belfry with a huge brass bell sat on top of the building. Lanterns provided lighting as the school and the community did not have electricity.

In addition to the schools, the town included numerous homes, a store, garage, churches, and a cemetery. One former resident tells that his father was an area hunting guide and led many Twin Cities hunters on their quests. One of those hunters bagged a 402-pound white-tail deer. That deer still holds the nationally recognized record.

Records reveal little about the demise of Mineral Center. Statements as to the federal government purchasing the land, residents moving to other communities, and many buildings being torn down are the only reasons mentioned.

The cemetery is a visible reminder of the community. In 2010, descendants of Mineral Center residents cleaned up the cemetery and erected a wrought-iron gateway. In 2012, family members held a get-together at Grand Portage that featured a tour of old Mineral Center, presentations, programs, and memorabilia.

Andrew Munsch, on his historic Minnesota highways website writes that for a few years (mid-1960s), Mineral Center Road was used by U.S. 61 as a temporary connection between the old road to the Canadian border and the current U.S. Highway 61. Mineral Center Road (County 17) intersects County 89 or the Old U.S. 61. The old highway 61 is not maintained past that intersection.

NORTH CASCADE

1890-1920
CLASS A
APPROXIMATE LOCATION:
From Grand Marais:
North on U.S. Highway 61. Left on the Gunflint Trail for 4 miles. Left on County 48/Devil Track Road for 6 miles. Slight right on County 27/Ball Club Road. Continue to follow Ball Club Road. Left on Forest Route 153/The Grade. Forest Road 1286. South Shore of Cascade Lake—General vicinity only.

Originally a logging camp with a boarding house, North Cascade was the northern terminus of the Alger-Smith owned railroad. After World War I, the General Logging Company purchased the Alger-Smith interests and North Cascade became a substantial settlement.

With over a thousand loggers in the area, North Cascade became a central point. Consisting of a large warehouse (111 feet by forty feet), a roundhouse that could handle six locomotives, a sandhouse, a section house, a two-story boarding house, a store, two bunkhouses that could sleep one hundred, a school, a restaurant that could serve fifty diners, company headquarters, and even a hospital.

The Great Depression caused a decline and conditions never recovered enough to make large-scale operations profitable. A caretaker was on site until the early 1950s when his cabin was destroyed by fire.

In 1952, Minnesota historian, Julius F. Wolfe, Jr., traveled to North Cascade, driving on the old railroad right-of-way in an old car. He wrote that many of the remaining buildings were in disrepair. The ensuing sixty years since his visit have erased any traces of the settlement. Today the site is part of the Superior National Forest and is located only by general vicinity on the south shore of Cascade Lake.

Cabin North of Mineral Center Today. (Courtesy of Andrew Munsch)

PARKERSVILLE

1680-1860s
CLASS A
APPROXIMATE LOCATION:
On Grand Portage Reservation:
Across Hat Point from Grand Portage. American Side of the Pigeon River.

The lilacs still bloom in Parkersville. So do the English violets and other European exotic plants that Walter Parker planted there nearly 175 years ago. In addition to the flowering plants, Parker was also known for his potatoes and vegetables. The Native Americans traded fur in the winter, maple syrup in the spring, and berries by the bucketful in the summer.

In 1795, William Parks and a few others from the Northwest Fur Company operated a fur post at the location. Apparently there was a disagreement or disruption with the company and the men established a competitive post. Things were patched up in 1804 and this group moved back to company headquarters in Grand Portage.

The Parkers came to the site in 1837. In that same year, Parker opened a store and fur-trading post at the site, naming it after himself. Parker wasn't the first or the only one to create a community on the spot. Works Progress Administration records from the 1930s state that the Seventeenth Century explorer, Du Hlut, for whom Duluth is named, established a trading post at this site in 1680. It is not known how long he occupied the area.

As the WPA assumed, there had to be a settlement there, or Parker would not have constructed a store there. A post office, with Parker as postmaster was also established. Mail was delivered by boat in the summer and was transported from a point opposite Susie Island on a trail to Parkersville. In the winter, dog sleds carried the mail, often weighing more than a ton.

WPA records show that the Parkers had a big family—two boys and many girls. In order for his children to attend school, the Parkers moved to Ontonagon, Michigan, in the 1860s. Their twelve heads of cattle traveled in the boats with the family.

For a short time after the Parkers left, until 1876, a man named Jackson ran the post. Since no records tell of the site after that date, it is assumed it was deserted.

PIGEON RIVER

1916–1960s

CLASS C

APPROXIMATE LOCATION:
From Grand Portage:
North on U.S. 61 for approximately 2 miles. Left on Cook County 17/Mineral Center Road for about 5 miles. To Junction of County Road 17 and County 89 (Old Highway 61/Old Border Road). North for approximately 9 miles to Pigeon River.
Note: County 89/Old Border Road is not maintained past the junction of 17/89. Road is very rough and desolate.

Filling Station, Restaurant, Sextus City (Pigeon River). (Author's collection)

For nearly a century, international travelers have been crossing from Minnesota into Canada by way of a bridge over the Pigeon River. Today's nearly three hundred thousand vehicles travel Highway 61 NE past Grand Portage and on to Canada. This "new" route was opened in the mid-1960s and is the only one most folks remember. But long before this current route was in existence, way back in the early days of the twentieth century, there was another border crossing over the Pigeon River. This one was located thirteen miles inland from the present day boundary point.

Before 1917 and the bridge, the only way to cross the international boundary from Fort William to Port Arthur was by boat to Duluth. The Canadian Pigeon River Timber Company had logged the area and a rough logging road to the river's edge still existed. On the Minnesota side, officials worked to extend a road running north from Grand Marais to the river. With the two roads on opposite sides of the river, it was apparent that a bridge was needed.

The law stated that, since this was an international waterway, it could only be permanently bridged by a Joint Action of the U.S. and Canadian governments. Governments didn't work any more quickly in those days than they do now, so, realizing the futility of awaiting agreements between two govern-

Sextus City (Pigeon River). (Author's collection)

Sextus City/Pigeon River. (Author's collection)

ments, local groups decided to take the matter into their own hands. Disregarding all international law, Rotary clubs on both sides of the river began to raise funds to build the bridge. Engineering services were volunteered as was a great portion of the construction work. With approximately $6,000, the bridge was completed within a year.

Due to its less than legal origins, the bridge was immediately nicknamed the "Outlaw Bridge." When Prohibition became the law of the land, the moniker would become most appropriate.

Sextus Hotel ruins, Pigeon River today. (Courtesy of Andrew Munsch)

The Pigeon River Bridge, boundary between Canada and the United States. Fort William and Duluth Highway. (Author's collection)

Sextus Tourist Cabin Remains. (Courtesy of Andrew Munsch)

Travelers from both countries would attempt to smuggle alcohol across the border. Custom agents would confiscate the illegal bounty. Many a tear was shed as the agents then smashed the bottles along the rocky banks of the river and the liquid flowed downstream. For a time, Canada did not sell alcohol on Sundays. On those days, traffic to the Minnesota side of the river would be heavy with those looking for a Sunday drink.

A busy and active settlement developed at the border crossing, on both sides of the river, in both countries. Sextus City, later called Pigeon River, was the American community. Businesses grew almost overnight and business was brisk. Anything a traveler could want or need was available: food, gas, lodging, service, and a beer garden. Cathy Wurzer, in her "Tales of Highway 61" project reported that the bridges and the custom crossing closed from 11:00 P.M. until 7:00 A.M. the following morning. Those travelers who missed the open hours would spend the night in the hotel or in one of the twenty-three tourist cabins behind the hotel.

For thirteen years the Outlaw Bridge provided a way to cross the international waterway. In 1930, a new sanctioned

South Footings Pigeon River Bridge. (Courtesy of Andrew Munsch)

steel-truss bridge replaced the rickety wooden bridge. That International Bridge, as it was known, would remain until the new Highway 61 through Grand Portage was completed and a new border crossing installed.

Today, the settlement of Sextus City/Pigeon River is no more. Decaying tourist cabins sit behind the remaining ruins

Road Ends Here, Pigeon River. (Courtesy of Andrew Munsch)

of the Sextus Hotel. Footings along the river bank are still visible. The Old Highway 61 is now Cook County Road #89 and is no longer maintained past the juncture of County 89 and Cook County #17/Mineral Center Road. The road is desolate, full of potholes and crumbling pavement. As highway historian Andrew Munsch tells, it is still a public road but you'll see more deer than cars, if you see any cars at all, along its route.

TACONITE HARBOR

1953–1990
CLASS B
APPROXIMATE LOCATION:
From Schroeder:
South on U.S. Highway 61 for approximately 2½ miles. Left into Taconite Harbor Access/Safe Harbor. Old town site is immediately after entering the area.

Not all Minnesota ghost towns are the long-ago variety. Some are younger than I am, having lived their entire existence within the confines of my lifetime.

Early in 1953, Erie Mining embarked on a monumental task. The $300 million, multi-year endeavor would include the building of a taconite loading facility and power plant on the shores of Lake Superior in northern Minnesota.

Erie Mining was an early pioneer in taconite processing. As the Schroeder Area Historical Society summarized, the walnut-sized pellets were made of low-grade iron ore pressed into enhanced pellets. Taconite pellets are an economical way to enrich

low-grade iron ore. Pellets are also easier to ship and to use in the steel mill's blast furnaces. Produced seventy-five miles inland at Hoyt Lakes (another company developed town) the pellets would then be shipped by rail to the new facility at Taconite Harbor. From there they would be loaded into ore carriers and transported to steel mills on the Great Lakes waterways.

Lake Superior's northern shoreline is rugged and rocky with few natural harbors. In choosing a site for the facilities, Taconite Harbor, or Two Islands as the area was also called, met most of the criteria. With the two islands just to the east and only 1,500 feet from shore, it was determined that, with an added breakwater, this was the best place to locate the plant and loading dock.

The construction of the plant required the building of a cofferdam (a watertight barrier pumped dry that allows work below the water line), which held back the icy Lake Superior waters thirty-five feet deep for a distance of 2,000 feet. A concrete dock was built as well as a breakwater, each one of these structures being engineering feats of their own. In addition, a seventy-four-mile railroad had to be constructed, over rough terrain, to transport the pellets from Hoyt Lakes to Taconite Harbor.

North Shore residents were excited at the prospect of the taconite facility in their area. The construction would create much-needed jobs and boost the economy. While the jobs were a boost, the relocation of so many workers to the area initially put a strain on the housing situation, which was in short supply to begin with. To alleviate the problem, small eigth-foot by twenty-foot trailers were brought in, thirty to start with. Before long, there were 500 trailers on site and were called the Hovland Trailer Village. One resident recalled that they were small and cozy. Families with children were quite cramped, with one mother remembering that her children were small enough that three of them could fit crossways on one bed. A two-story steel building housed a grocery store, barbershop, and restaurant right on the grounds.

Once the harbor and plant were completed, twenty-four houses for the employees were brought in. The modest houses were located across from each other on a single street, between Highway 61 and the lake. The Schroeder Area Historical Society states that employees could purchase the houses for $400 down and $110 dollars per month. The homes had three or four bedrooms, with the foremen getting the houses with fireplaces.

Taconite Harbor was a true stereotypical 1950s suburban setting. Life was good for the residents, if one didn't mind living and socializing with the people one worked with. There were block parties, regular volleyball games, Little League, Cub Scouts, basketball and baseball, outdoor grilling, ice skating and sledding in the winter, and more. There was always something going on

Taconite Harbor. (Author's collection)

in the tight-knit community. No safer, nor more beautiful, place could be found. Nearby communities provided all the goods and services the residents could want or need.

The community residents did not have their own post office or schools. Mail came through Schroeder, and area schools provided educational opportunities. Elementary schools were located in Tofte and Lutsen with high-school-age students attending school in Grand Marais. The Schroeder Area Historical Society writes that the Tofte school stood on the Lake Superior Shore where today the Blue Fin Bay townhouses stand. Records show that at one time, there were seventy-four students in Taconite Harbor.

In the mid-1980s, the automobile industry was in decline as was the demand for iron ore. With the downsizing of the plant, many workers were out of jobs and moved elsewhere. The company bought up the vacated houses, renting them for a time at a cost of $150 to $180 per month. The *Minneapolis Star* reported that the houses were a viable alternative for folks who worked in the region and couldn't afford the area's pricey properties. The Taconite Harbor homes were low-cost homes with a million dollar view.

As time progressed, the mining company decided that providing sewer, water, and municipal services was too expensive. They no longer wanted to be landlords. The remaining resi-

Trailers Taconite Harbor 1950s. (Author's collection)

Taconite Harbor Homes. (Courtesy of the Schroeder Area Historical Society)

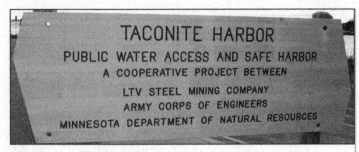

Taconite Harbor Safe Harbor/Boat Landing. (Author's collection)

dents were given the option of purchasing their homes and moving them, but few took that option. In late 1989, the houses were put up for bid. Purchased by developers, the last house left Taconite Harbor in 1990.

With the loss of the Taconite Harbor residents, nearby communities were hugely impacted. It was estimated that the residents of the company town made up a third of the population of the Schroeder community and the financial loss alone was a blow to the region.

The mining company had plans to put a storage dump for dolomite and limestone on the old town site. Environmentalists objected, and that plan was abandoned. In June of 2001, the last taconite pellets were shipped out of Taconite Harbor and the plant closed.

The demise of the town and the relocated homes was noted by newspapers as far away as Los Angeles, California.

Today, the area still has that million dollar view. The site is easily accessible—just east off of Highway 61 on the Lake Su-

perior side. It is well marked with a State of Minnesota marker for the boat area and safe harbor. As you exit Highway 61, the winding trail's first open space is the old town site. Look closely and you will see broken blacktop, lonely lampposts, trees and shrubs that were planted by the residents and other traces of the community. Park the car, stretch your legs, and look to see what other remnants are still visible. It is both serene and a bit eerie. One newspaper called it something out of the *Twilight Zone*.

Travel further down the blacktopped road and you will come upon a nice display of vintage equipment, even a huge taconite boulder. There are interpretive signs for the displays. Wind down the road a bit further, and you will be on the shores of Lake Superior and at the Taconite Harbor boat launch, breakwater, and rugged shoreline. The scenery is amazing—there are restrooms, boulders to climb and sit upon, and the old processing plant and loading area. The facilities dominate the landscape and can be seen for miles in all directions. The area surrounding the plant is restricted, but the view is open to all.

Recently, the University of Minnesota's Center for Landscape Change did an analysis of the Taconite Harbor/Two Island site. Stating that Minnesota Power owns a large tract of the land and is exploring options, a site analysis was done as well as a design plan. The plan calls for a Village Square with retail and recreational options. No mention is made as to the viability or probability of the proposal becoming reality. Perhaps Taconite Harbor will live again, as it does in memory.

Taconite Harbor today. (Author's collection)

Crow Wing County

One-half of the Beaulieu House, Old Crow Wing, Crow Wing State Park. (Author's collection)

Main Street Boardwalk and a self-guided tour, Old Crow Wing, Crow Wing State Park. (Author's collection)

One-half of the Beaulieu House, Old Crow Wing, Crow Wing State Park. (Author's collection)

BARROWS

1911-1918/1921-1924
CLASS C
APPROXIMATE LOCATION:
From Brainerd:
South on Business Highway 371 for 3 miles. Barrows is on the west side of Highway 371.

Early tests revealed large amounts of iron ore five miles southwest of Brainerd. The discovery led to the drilling of Barrows Mine, named for an early promoter of the area. The venture initiated a boom to the area and as the hopes and dreams grew, so did the new community of Barrows. Newspapers of the time reported on the rapid growth of the town that soon included several stores, three hotels, a saloon or two, a post office, town hall, bank, church, pool hall, meat market, restaurant, and weekly newspaper. Main street was busy and real estate lots were the hot commodity.

The growing population soon necessitated a school and a two-story one was promptly built. One of the early teachers, Mae Staples, taught grades one through eight and coached two boys' basketball teams and one girls' team. An early resident, Gladys Nichols-Anderson wrote that Barrows was an ideal small town to live in.

Other early residents tell of bootleg alcohol. A triple murder occurred in the community in 1923. A twenty-two-year-old man killed his wife's father and grandparents. The crime was believed to have been brought on by moonshine whiskey. He believed them to be unduly influencing his wife to leave him.

As quickly as Barrows grew, so did it end. The short-lived mine was closed shortly after it opened. Nichols-Anderson and others recalled that "quicksand" was the reason for the mine's demise. The thin soil would sift into the mine, causing cave-ins and other problems. With the closure of the mine, the towns fate was also sealed. Many of the houses were sold for as little as twenty-five dollars and moved to nearby Brainerd and other locations. The school fell into disrepair.

In June of 2006, a wildfire swept through the old town site. Two homes, the abandoned school and over 700 acres were destroyed. Driving through Barrows today you can see that the trees and vegetation are rebounding. The former town site does have a community feel to it—the Crow Wing Township Hall, a Barrows park, and several residences are in the area.

BORSZAK

1909-1910
CLASS A
APPROXIMATE LOCATION:
From Brainerd:
From the junction of Highway 210 and Highway 371. North on Highway 371 for 11½ miles. Right (east) on County 13 for 2 miles to town of Lake Hubert. Left on Clark Lake Dam Road, which runs parallel to the Railroad (now a trail). Borszak was on a spur above the station at Lake Hubart next to Borszak Lake (now dried up).

Hoping to make life better for underpaid garment workers in Chicago, Borszak, himself an immigrant textile worker, planned a community for his fellow Russian-Jewish colleagues. Setting up a silk factory and village in 1909 to 1910, Borszak built a house for himself, a tiny store, and a large structure to house the sewing machines his workers would use. The building was never completed. Borszak ran out of money and was unable to attract any investors. The house was later sold and the sewing machines shipped back to Chicago. Borszak Lake dried up and the platted streets reverted to forest.

LENNOX

1889-1900s
CLASS A
APPROXIMATE LOCATION:
From Brainerd:
From the junction of Highway 210 and Highway 371. Highway 371 South for 15 miles to Fort Ripley. Lennox was ½ mile from Fort Ripley.

Near the geographic center of Minnesota, approximately half a mile south of Fort Ripley, sat the settlement of Lennox. Established as a flag stop on the Northern Pacific Railroad line, the stop was originally called Albion. The name was later changed to Lenox to honor an early treasurer of the railroad. As the station was built, so were two stores, one with a post office. In 1915, the spelling changed to Lennox and the settlement began to decline. The station was discontinued in 1946. One store was torn down, the other became a private residence.

MANGANESE

1912-1924

CLASS C

APPROXIMATE LOCATION:
From Brainerd:
Highway 210 East for 14 miles to Ironton. Left on Irene Avenue and go 0.2 miles. Right to stay on County Highway 30 for 3.9 miles. Left and go 0.6 miles to the site of Manganese.

The once busy streets are now tree-lined pathways barely discernible to most but visible on some aerial photos. Most that lived in or remember Manganese are gone, but at one time the thriving town was home to six hundred people.

Platted in 1911, the town was built by the Duluth Land and Timber Company on an eighty-acre site. Four mines were located within the village. Also included in the busy town was the village hall, a railroad depot, grocery store, bank, livery stable, water tower, and a new $10,000 hotel with dining room constructed by Fitger Brewing of Duluth. As Gene Foote, a former resident recalled in a 1985 article, there were also many pool halls and a blind pig, an illegal liquor business run by a woman out of her home.

As mining declined, so did Manganese. Gene Foote remembered that in the 1930s, a house a day would leave town. The railroad tracks were pulled up in the 1930s as well. The last residents left town in 1955. The remaining buildings were torn down or moved. Gene's parents, some of the first to move into town, were among the last to leave.

When asked about the town's demise, Gene Foote said that the area soil was clay, which was unstable, causing wells to collapse. Gene would visit the townsite for years after the town was gone, reminiscing about the remains and remnants that were still visible. Today, nature has reclaimed the old town site.

Manganese. (Shawn Hewitt Collection)

OLD CROW WING

1848-1871

CLASS F

APPROXIMATE LOCATION:
From Brainerd:
Business Highway 371 South for approximately 11 miles.
Right at State Park Road for ½ miles.

Spanning nearly 300 years of human history, the site of today's Crow Wing State Park, located at the confluence of the Mississippi and Crow Wing rivers, has seen a lot. The region has been an eyewitness to a major Native American battle, fur traders, the Red River Oxcart Trails, the growth and demise of a rowdy frontier town, a murder, and the creation of a state park. Adding to the cultural and historical aspects of the site, the natural and scenic beauty makes the region very special.

First inhabited by Native Americans, the area prior to 1768, had been home to the Dakotas. Territorial conflicts and skirmishes with the Ojibwe culminated in a bloody two-day riverside battle. Father Voight, in his history of the region, writes that the Battle of 1768 was of national significance. The defeat of the Dakota forced them to leave their homeland and settle in the Minnesota River Valley, opening the lakes region to the Ojibwe.

The early 1800s saw the American and Northwest Fur Companies establishing trading posts at the site. After the fur trade, the oxcarts came. A major stopping point along the Red River Oxcart Trail, the carts forded the Mississippi near the confluence. By 1848, with the canoe and land traffic, the village of Crow Wing was burgeoning. The Minnesota DNR park brochure states that at its peak, the town was 700 strong. For over a century, Crow Wing was the northernmost settlement of Europeans on the Mississippi River. The town's make up was predominately Ojibwe, and was known as the Ojibwe Capital of Minnesota. In 1852, Father Pierz built a Catholic mission at the site, followed in 1860 by an Episcopalian mission and a few years later, a Lutheran one.

Names familiar to Minnesota history frequented the village: historian William Warren, future Governor Henry Rice, fur trading brothers Allen and William Morrison, pioneer trader William Aitkin, missionary Henry Whipple, Ojibwe Chief Hole-in-the-Day, Mission priest Father Pierz, and others.

By the mid-1860s, the town reached its population peak and included thirty buildings: two hotels, several boarding houses, at least two saloons, two stores, a blacksmith, two churches and cemeteries, a post office, a fort, and stockades with several wigwams around the perimeter. Main street was

Father Pierz Chapel, Old Crow Wing, Crow Wing State Park. (Author's collection)

a wooden boardwalk along the river, with most of the town's buildings facing it.

Clem Beaulieu, an early trader with French and Native ancestry built a palatial home in the town. Built in the Greek Revival style, the two-story home was twenty-five feet by thirty-one feet and considered the town's finest.

Crow Wing also had a school, the only one north of Sauk Rapids. Voight writes that when Crow Wing County was established in 1857, the school was designated a district school. When more school districts developed, the Crow Wing School was District 1.

Crow Wing village was the county seat of Crow Wing County from 1857 until 1871 when the seat was transferred to Brainerd.

In 1871, a young girl, Helen McArthur, who lived two miles from the village, disappeared on her way home from the town. It was at first believed she ran away but several years later some bones were found. Since Helen had one leg shorter than the other, they identified the bones as hers. Two Native Americans were charged and arrested. Angry citizens abducted the suspects from the Brained jail and took them back to Crow Wing, where they were hung.

For decades Crow Wing was a bustling, thriving town. It took only a few short years for it to be deserted. Father Voight cites two main reasons for the town's demise. The first reasons were the fact that Native Americans were being removed to reservations. Crow Wing's natives were moved to the White Earth Indian Reservation. Secondly, the railroad's choice to bypass Crow Wing, in favor of Brainerd, was the historic town's death knell.

Clem Beaulieu was certain that the railroad would cross the Mississippi at Crow Wing. Looking to make a fortune, he invested heavily in the region's land. In 1871, the Northern Pacific Railroad balked at the high prices Beaulieu wanted and chose

Brainerd, and Beaulieu's dreams came to a halt. Beaulieu, himself part Native, moved to White Earth where he died in poverty. His palatial home was split in two, and in 1880 his nephews loaded the home on oxcarts and moved it away.

Voight writes that the Catholic church was removed in 1915 with some of the altar and furnishings going to the St. Mathias parish. The Catholic cemetery was in ruins as was the other town cemetery. Many bodies were removed. Within eight years the town was a ghost town.

For years, concerned individuals had been advocating the preservation of the historic town site. When it was learned that there were plans to sell the Catholic Church property and build a night club on the site, it became evident that immediate action had to be taken. Bishop Bartholeme of St. Cloud purchased the ninety-three-acre parcel in 1952. The Minnesota Legislature appropriated funds, with a stipulation for matching funds, for the purpose of creating a state park. The acreage, except for the land where the church and cemetery stood, was turned over to the State of Minnesota. The church land is within the confines of the state park but is owned by the Diocese of Duluth. Over the years, additional land has been acquired and today the park is just over 3,000 acres.

Roy W. Meyer, state park historian, writes that the park had two primary purposes: to provide public recreation and to protect the old Crow Wing town site. The entire park was listed on the National Register of Historic Places in 1970. Extensive re-

Old Crow Wing Marker, Crow Wing State Park. (Author's collection)

search was done to identify and mark important historical sites including the Ojibwe rifle pits and the Overlook, the three mission churches, the oxcart trail (the park contains some of the only visible ruts still remaining), the school, the buildings and homes, as well as other locations. The Overlook was the high ground on which the Ojibwe warriors could see the Mississippi for miles upstream. Interpretive signs have been located throughout the park and maps highlight trails and significant stops.

Clem Beaulieu's house, or half of his house, was brought back to the park with plans to restore it to its natural state. The house is considered the oldest standing structure north of St. Anthony Falls. It sits on the hill overlooking the river as it did 150 years ago.

The park has recreated the wood boardwalk and visitors can stroll the old town site on a self-guided walking tour that highlights the town's history and structures. Overnight camping, a picnic shelter, and other amenities make the journey back in history worth the trip.

WOODROW

1915–1931
CLASS A
APPROXIMATE LOCATION:
From Brainerd:
Highway 210 East for 6 miles. Right (south) onto County Road 25 NE and go 1½ miles. Left (east) on Woodrow Road NE for just under a mile. Village site is on your left at the junction with 55th Avenue NE (Dullum Road).

The Dullums, married for just three days, arrived in Crow Wing County in 1914 and set about making a life in Woodrow, the mining boom town named for then president Woodrow Wilson. One of the first things the couple did was purchase land and build a two-story, twenty-

Main Street, Woodrow, ca. 1914. (Shawn Hewitt collection)

four-foot-by-sixty-foot hotel, operating it as a boarding house for up to forty-two mine workers at a time. The mine, originally called the Wilcox and later the Omaha, had a total production of nearly three hundred tons of iron ore in its short five-year life span. Mrs. Dullum (first name not known), with the help of a hired girl worked eighteen-hour days, cooking meals, packing dinner pails for men working all three shifts, cleaning, and caring for her own three children.

In addition to the Dullum's boarding house, Woodrow included two general stores, a restaurant, post office, and another boarding house. For a short time, the Dullums had a general store with a pool hall in the basement.

When the mine closed in 1919, the town literally dried up as well. Times were hard and while most of the town moved away or abandoned homes, the Dullums stayed. Doing what they could to make a living, they farmed, sold butter, and for a while Mrs. Dullum, a former teacher, became a substitute teacher to make ends meet.

In 1969, the *Brainerd Dispatch* did a feature article on Mrs. Dullum. At the age of eighty-eight, she was living alone in the original boarding house they had built fifty-five years earlier. She was as self-reliant as ever. Little is left of Woodrow, a few decaying and crumbling foundations, and a new home here and there. Today, there is a road named in honor of the Dullums.

Douglas County

Belle River creamery. (Courtesy of the Douglas County Historical Society)

Belle River Store, 1924. (Courtesy of the Douglas County Historical Society)

Belle River Store, 1924. (Courtesy of the Douglas County Historical Society)

Interior Belle River Store, 1924. (Courtesy of the Douglas County Historical Society)

Belle River today. (Author's collection)

BELLE RIVER

1885-1906
CLASS C
APPROXIMATE LOCATION:
From Miltona:
Northeast on County Road 14 for approximately 2½ miles.
Slight right to County Road 3. County Road 3 for approximately 4 miles. Left to keep on County 3. On the right hand
side of the road will be St. Nicholas Catholic Church.

Belle River. (Author's collection)

For nearly one hundred years, St. Nicholas Catholic Church has stood sentinel over the region. Built to replace the original 1871 church that burned in 1915, the Gothic-style church was completed in 1916. The church cemetery is located on the site of that original church. Able to seat 800 people, in 1916 membership was 106 families.

A small community developed just west of the church. First named Riverside because of its location on the banks of the Long Prairie River, the name was changed, by vote, to Belle River. Support businesses for the area farmers included a cooperative creamery, post office, and general store known as the Belle River store. The store operated until the owner's death in 1975.

Today, little remains of the town, though there are a few buildings. The stately church is still active and vibrant with a strong membership.

Belle River. (Author's collection)

St. Nicholas Catholic Church. (Author's collection)

Spruce Center Dam. (Courtesy of the Douglas County Historical Society)

CHIPPEWA

1861-1869

CLASS A

APPROXIMATE LOCATION:
From Brandon:
North on County 16 for 3 miles. Top of the hill—village site is on private property. Edgefield Cemetery is just down the road.

On a hilltop just north of present day Brandon, Chippewa was a station on the stage coach route from St. Cloud to Fort Abercrombie (near Brecken-ridge) in the 1850s. The stage route ran along a military road built by the government for troops in 1859. Early settler Henry Gager manned the station until 1862, when the Sioux Upris-ing forced Gager and other settlers out of the area.

Area historian Duane V. Peterson writes that stage stations were known to be caches of whiskey, and Chippewa was said to be one of the best.

During that conflict, there was a stockade at Chippewa (Fort Chippewa), and once the soldiers were there to provide protection, most of the settlers returned. Soon others came, and Chippewa was the center of activity. A town site was laid

out, and the town included two stores, a hotel, blacksmith, and post office.

In late 1879, the railroad reached west from Alexandria and ran three miles south of Chippewa. Chippewa's businesses began to move near the railroad. Soon the area near the tracks would grow and prosper and Chippewa would cease to exist. The new community would be named Brandon, in honor of Stephan A. Douglas, whose birthplace was Brandon, Ver-mont. Douglas County was named for Stephan A. Douglas.

SPRUCE CENTER

1885-1905

CLASS A

APPROXIMATE LOCATION:
From Miltona:
NE on County Raod 14 for approximately 2½ miles. Left on County Road 3 for 1½ miles. Right on Spruce Center. Drive for 1/3 miles.

On their way from Belle River to North Dakota, the Merickel brothers stopped to water their horses and to have lunch. The brothers were on their way to help with the 1879 wheat harvest. Lloyd Engstrom, in a 1991 interview, recalled his visit with Arthur Merickel, one of the

Spruce Center, early 1900s. (Courtesy of the Douglas County Historical Society)

SPRUCE HILL

1870–1894
CLASS F
APPROXIMATE LOCATION:
From Miltona:
Northeast on County Road 14 to Spruce Hill Park Road
(County 105). North ¾ mile.

brothers. Arthur said that, as he and his brother were eating their lunch, they looked over the land. With a rushing creek flowing through the property, they decided that this was the ideal spot for a new business or a flour mill.

Excited about the prospects, they turned around and went back to Belle River to discuss it with their father. Agreeing with his sons, plans were made. The next year they put in a dam, and a flour mill was built and put into operation. For over sixty-five years (until the 1950s), that mill provided food and grain for dairy cattle.

The post office was established in 1885. On the application, Hannah Foote gave the name Scriven, also known as Spruce Center. Joy, five miles to the north and Belle River, six miles to the south, were listed as the nearest post offices. Scriven appears to have been a family name. Hannah's explanation for the Spruce Center name was that the town was in the center of spruce, birch, and aspen, thus Spruce Center.

In the late 1880s, the land was surveyed and platted. The plat shows four blocks with twenty-eight lots each. Each lot was fifty feet by forty feet by one hundred-forty feet. Lloyd Engstrom tells that Spruce Center offered a unique service—a water pump in the middle of the road. Many owners and teamsters watered their horses there.

Another unique feature of Spruce Center was that the residents built their houses facing Main Street, then raised their barns and granaries on farms they operated from the backs of their homes.

Around 1900, Spruce Center also had a profitable bee keeper who sold the hives. In those days, it was believed bee stings could cure arthritis.

The post office was discontinued in 1905, though records indicate the community continued on for several years. Lloyd Engstrom's interview stated that the mill operated until the 1950s. Today there are a few residences and a nearby bait farm.

Purchasing 160 acres in a pre-1870 government auction, George Gordon, his mother and his brothers, were the first to see the possibilities of Spruce Hill.

Relocating from other parts of Douglas County to the property at Spruce Hill, the Gordons first built a family home. Their next venture was to build a dam on Spruce Creek and to construct and operate a saw mill. Area homesteaders and settlers were pleased to finally have a mill in the area.

From the beginning, the mill was plagued by natural disasters: flash floods, dam washouts, the loss of timber flooding downstream and, in 1879, a tornado that destroyed the upper story of the mill, leaving it in ruins.

In 1880, the local newspaper reported that the Gordons had received an offer of $5,000 for their mill and that the family was going to accept. The community was saddened at the loss of the pioneering family. The town continued on but was in need of a store. The Gordons did not have a store but they had carried some merchandise. A year later, the newspaper again put out a call for a store. Six months after that plea, they reported that Mrs. Young had opened a store. From all accounts Mary Young was an energetic woman who ran the store until she married in 1890. Together, she and her husband lived in and ran the store until the town's demise

The bridge over the Spruce Creek continued to be a problem. Township records state that in 1903 the bridge had to be replaced. In 1923, the road and the bridge were vacated.

Gene Sibell, in his "Saga of Spruce Hill, Part II" wrote that the growth of nearby Spruce Center was the primary reason for the decline and demise of Spruce Hill. Spruce Center offered a central location, a wider variety of businesses and a good east/west road running through the town.

Ada Johnson, a resident of the former town and a talented artist, has preserved Spruce Hill history in her artwork. Capturing long-ago Spruce Hill, she has created detailed hand-drawn maps and pastoral paintings. Many of these special pieces are on display at the Douglas County Historical Society and in homes of collectors in the area.

In 1955 the State of Minnesota sold the land on which Spruce Hill once sat. Years later, in 1973, the property was sold to Douglas County. It is now the Spruce Hill County

SPRUCE CENTER MILL
ADULTS left to right Rena Nelson, Hilda Gustafso
August Nelson, Charley Gustafson.
CHILDREN: Myrtle, Marie and Clarice Nelson

Spruce Center. (Courtesy of the Douglas County Historical Society)

School District 66 Foundation. (Author's collection)

Park. The park is 110 acres in North East Douglas County and it includes the old town site of Spruce Hill. Plans are to develop an interpretive history of the village.

Visiting the park, the creek flows lazily through the countryside. Two picnic shelters offer a welcome respite. The wide walking paths meander along the creek side. As the field opens up, you are in Spruce Hill. Markers are placed where the buildings once stood. Depressions are clearly visible. Some building foundations remain.

Originally in a log cabin just north of the present church, the Spruce Hill Lutheran Church stood. Built in 1884, the current wood-frame building is viable and active. A few area farmers left bequests from their estates, and with donations the church upkeep is funded. Services are held only on special occasions: Christmas, Easter, mid-summer, as well as funerals and weddings. The nearby cemetery is restored and well-maintained.

Residents from the area will still state that they are from Spruce Hill. Though the village itself, no longer remains, the active church, the county park, and a sense of history keep the village alive.

Spruce Hill Store site today. (Author's collection)

Grant County

Hereford Store. (Courtesy of the Shawn Hewitt Collection)

Aastad. (Courtesy of the Grant County Historical Scociety)

Herford Store. (Courtesy of the Grant County Historical Society)

Hereford Cemetery Marker. (Courtesy of Roger Strand)

Hereford Cemetery. (Courtesy of Roger Strand)

AASTAD TOWNSITE

1881-1905

CLASS C

APPROXIMATE LOCATION:
From Ashby:
West on County Road 26 for approximately 5½ miles. Continue onto County Road 26/100th Street for approximately 5½ miles. Left at County 15 Intersection. The Rock Prairie Church is the east edge of where Aastad would have been.

Since its construction in 1873, the Rock Prairie Lutheran Church has been the prominent feature of Aastad. It still is.

Organized and built by the early Norwegian settlers, from Marshall, Iowa, early services were conducted in Norwegian. Many of those settlers set up and ran businesses for a while. They included a general store, a restaurant for a year, a post office, three different blacksmiths, a feed mill, a cheese factory, and a creamery.

One homesteader, in 1882, hired two brothers to help him dig a well. Using picks, shovels, and a windlass (a hoist and pulley system) they dug thirty feet down. At that point, one of the brothers collapsed. The other brother went down to investigate, and he too was overcome and killed by the noxious fumes. Attempting to recover the bodies safely, a lantern was lowered. Once the flame stayed lit, they retrieved the bodies.

As in most of the Grant County places of the past, the demise of Aastad came about due to the lack or railroad services or discontinuance of the railroad line.

Today, the Rock Prairie Church still dominates the landscape. It stands at what would have been the eastern edge of Aastad.

HEREFORD VILLAGE

1887-1939

CLASS A

APPROXIMATE LOCATION:
From Wendell:
West on MN 55 for 2½ miles. Left on 280th Avenue for 1½ miles. Just west of County Road 41 and ½ mile south of 280th Street.

Set amongst the cornfields, the rural countryside pastures and adjacent to the pioneer cemetery, stands a historical marker commemorating the village of Hereford. Erected by members of the Church of God, which functioned from 1907 to 1938, the majestic granite marker is a testament to the town and its early settlers.

As the marker and historical records summarize, the town was located on a short-lived line of the Great Northern Railroad. Named for the breed of cattle that once grazed the lush land, the community was rural in every aspect.

The village consisted of a section house, two elevators, a coal shed, a blacksmith, a general store, a post office (1888 to 1923), a lumberyard, a stockyard, a depot, a school and a church. The Wahpeton Gravel Company had a block factory in the Hereford gravel pit.

As the village began to decline, the store was torn down—one elevator was moved to Norcross, the section house was moved to Wendell, and the depot to Erdahl. In 1939, the rest of the buildings were sold. The school was moved several miles from town in the 1940s. The land was later purchased in an estate sale.

All that remains today is the marker and the cemetery.

POMME DE TERRE

1868-1902

CLASS C

APPROXIMATE LOCATION:
From Elbow Lake:
Northeast of Elbow Lake on County Road 4 for 7½ miles. Brick school house and cemetery just east of the river crossing.

The rural tranquility of the area belies its colorful and tumultuous past.

As early as 1823, long lines of ox-carts rumbled their way over the landscape. Traveling from Pembina to St. Paul, the caravans carried furs to market and returned with trade goods and supplies.

In the mid-1850s, the Minnesota Stage Company created a route from St. Cloud to points west and north. Selecting a scenic knoll overlooking a small lake, Minnesota historian William Goetzinger writes that Pomme de Terre became an overnight stopping place along the three-day journey from St. Cloud to Fort Abercrombie. A rudimentary station house was built to accommodate the guests. Business was brisk and without incident, until the summer of 1862.

Rumors had long been circulating about the possibility of a Dakota uprising. August of 1862, spurred by late annuity payments and fueled by unsympathetic, even arrogant, bureaucrats, the situation escalated, and the rumors became fact. Within days no place on the Minnesota frontier was safe. Settlers fled their homes and sought refuge in numbers and fortifications.

Pomme de Terre. (Courtesy of the Grant County Historical Society)

Fort Abercrombie was under siege as were other outposts. Skirmishes flared up everywhere and continued for weeks. Pomme de Terre was at the center of the tensions. Minnesota author Candace Simar has written a four-book series about Fort Abercrombie, based on the uprising and its effects on the frontier. The second in the series is titled *Pomme de Terre*. Her fictionalized accounts are historically accurate and are backed by solid research. Bringing the people, the places, and the times to life, they provide a personal perspective to the uprising as well as to the people and places affected.

Pomme de Terre, the village, was located one mile west of the station and fort and was platted in 1874. Centered around a grist mill on the Pomme de Terre River, Grant County's first village grew quickly, soon consisting of two stores, two blacksmiths, a grain elevator, a hotel, a saloon, a school, and the mill. The mill, one of the first in the northwest, operated at a capacity of one-hundred-twenty-five barrels of flour a day. Long lines waited to get their grain ground. The mill and elevator were destroyed by fire in 1887.

Efforts to name the village as the county seat in 1873 failed when Elbow Lake was chosen. That decision would begin the decline of Pomme de Terre. The railroad's decision to route its line through Ashby would seal the fate of the town. Many buildings were moved to Ashby and soon the only physical remains would be the brick school house, now a town hall and the adjacent pioneer cemetery.

Pomme de Terre cemetery and town hall (the former school). (Courtesy of T. Burt)

THORSBORG

1888-1930s
CLASS A
APPROXIMATE LOCATION:
From Elbow Lake:
3 miles East on County Road 79. County Road 21 to the South. On the East side of County 21—a mile South of State Highway 79.

Once a rail station on the Great Northern Railroad, Thorsborg was an important grain center. Regional grain was hauled to the town and was then loaded, by wheelbarrow, onto the rail cars.

Thorsborg Depot. (Courtesy of the Grant County Historical Society)

The community had a post office from 1888 to 1890 and included a general store, grain warehouse, and a school. Built at a cost of $300, the school was constructed on land donated by Knut Knutson. Operating until 1937, the building was later moved to Elbow Lake where it became a private residence. The store later relocated to Erdahl. Today there is nothing left at the site. There is a minimum maintenance road one-half-mile south of Highway 79. Going east on this road to where it crosses the river there is a view, looking south, of where the old railroad crossed the river.

WEST ELBOW LAKE/CANESTORP

1873-1883
CLASS A
APPROXIMATE LOCATION:
From Elbow Lake:
West on Division Street W (County 1) for 1 mile. Cross the railroad tracks and this is the general area. The town was just off of County 1 south of the railroad tracks.

Since its construction, the elevator has dominated the landscape of West Elbow Lake. Long after the village ceased to exist, the elevator remained standing until destroyed by fire in 1990.

Not only did the elevator dominate the landscape, everyday life was heavily influenced by grain and grain farming. West Elbow Lake, also known as Canestorp, was a rural farming community. Early settler Olaf Olofsson, upon arriving in the area, changed his name to Ole Canestorp, a variation of his home village in Sweden, Kananstorp. The community adopted the name to honor Ole, who came to the area in 1871. Ole would later serve as probate judge, county treasurer, and state senator.

The village was a station on the branch of the Great Northern Railroad. Stage coach services linked the community to Elbow Lake and other locations. In addition to the elevator, there was also a lumberyard, a stockyard, a store, and a school. Rail service to Elbow Lake was discontinued and the village ceased to exist.

West Elbow elevator. (Courtesy of the Grant County Hiistorical Scoeity)

Hubbard County

Farris Collage. (Courtesy of Frank J. Mitchell/Hubbard County Historical Society)

FARRIS

1898–1915

CLASS A

APPROXIMATE LOCATION:
From Cass Lake:
West on U.S. 2 for approximately 3 miles. Left on Tower Road for 1½ miles. Tower Road curves to the south and becomes 315th Avenue. 1/3 miles on 315th Avenue.

In the late 1890s, the Great Northern Railroad expanded its line into northern Minnesota. First extended from Park Rapids to Akeley and then to Walker and on to Cass Lake. Farris was the first station west of Cass Lake on the Eastern Railway branch line.

In 1897, Farris merged with the nearby town of Graceland. They kept the name Farris for the newly formed community, though they did install a new city council. The official newspaper was the *Graceland Enterprise*.

An April edition of the *Hubbard County Clipper* carried a large ad that offered lots for sale in the new town site of Farris. The following week, the Hubbard County surveyor posted a warning in the newspaper, stating that the town site had not been legally platted and filed. He also informed readers that he would prosecute the parties involved to the full extent of the law.

Hubbard County historian Frank J. Mitchell reported on a proposal by the Farris Town Site Company. With the dream of creating a huge resort area, the hope was to dig a canal from Little Midge Lake to Wolf Lake. Since Wolf Lake had a natural connection to other lakes and the Mississippi River the plan seemed to be a great idea. The expected cost would have been $500 to $700. There are no records to indicate if this was ever attempted or completed.

Frank J. Mitchell also writes that Hubbard County's first murder took place near Farris. In May of 1911, the disappearance of Peter Neste was reported. The sheriff and other county officials sent out to investigate found a partially burned body under some brush. The body was that of Peter Neste, the missing man. Upon further investigation they learned that Neste's daughter described an argument between her husband and her father and that her husband had killed her father with an axe.

The old town site is now a Farden Township park and features a ball field, basketball court, tennis court, restrooms, and a picnic shelter.

Farris School. (Courtesy of Frank J. Mitchell/Hubbard County Historical Society)

GRACELAND

1897–1898

CLASS A

APPROXIMATE LOCATION: 2 miles from Farris

Elvis wasn't the only one to have a Graceland. Hubbard County had one, also. Established in the late 1890s, Hubbard County's Graceland was two miles west of Farris. Presumably named for the local storekeeper, Grace, his store was the only one in the area and business was brisk. Before long, Graceland had a two-story school, two saloons, a butcher shop, barber shop, and a newspaper office. Hauling his printing press over the Steamboat Landing Road, William Penner set up shop and called his newspaper *The Graceland Express*.

Frank J. Mitchell, Hubbard County historian, writes that in April of 1898, the *Walker Pilot* reported that Graceland was ready to incorporate. Graceland had a population larger than Walker had when it incorporated. Eventually Graceland would incorporate, not as Graceland, but as Farris. Just two miles from Farris, the two towns would become one, with the citizens keeping the newly joined community's name as Farris. The post office, which began in Graceland, also took the name Farris. The Graceland postmaster took over the reins of the joint community.

Farris 1900-1905. (Courtesy of the Hubbard County Historical Society)

Itasca County

Cooley. (Courtesy of the Iron Range Historical Society)

Cooley

1900–1974

CLASS A

APPROXIMATE LOCATION:
From Nashwauk:
South on Highway 169 for approximately 1½ mile.

Early loggers arrived in the 1880s and just twenty years later the region had been logged off, the timber supply depleted. But the area's riches were still abundant. By 1900, it was known that rich deposits of iron ore lay just below the surface of the ground. The problem was in getting the ore out. Local historian Leo Trunt wrote that the problem was resolved once the Great Northern Railroad extended their line through the Cooley area in 1908.

The earliest mine, the Hawkins, was opened by the International Harvester Company in 1902. Two miles down the road a washing plant was built in 1911. These early mining ventures would open up exploration and more mines, including the Butler Brothers mines in Cooley.

Because of poor transportation, it was more practical to have the workers housed near the mines. Alan Stone, a Cooley resident, recalled that, when Cooley first began (and since all of the workers were men), the first housing units were primarily boarding houses. As time went on, the men demanded that their families be brought over from Europe. Small company homes were built and rented to the families. Most of these homes were located on the east side of Highway 169.

Cooley was actually two locations, known as First Cooley and Second Cooley. Residents remember that houses were the only structures in Second Cooley. First Cooley was closest to Nashwauk and Second was a half mile to the southwest towards Pengilly.

The largest building in Cooley was a clubhouse for the men. Company meetings as well as other functions were held there. Alan Stone remembered that Santa Claus would visit the clubhouse every year, and he had a large bag of candy and a shiny silver dime for each child.

Cooley also had a post office, a company store, a volunteer fire department, but no school. It was cheaper to transport students to surrounding school districts than to build and staff a school of their own.

Mines in the region practiced open pit or surface mining. While open strip mining could be and was dangerous, the Butler Brothers had many safety rules in place, more so than at other mines. The Butler Brothers were innovators in mining. They were the first to use trucks to haul the ore out in-stead of trains. They were also among the first to work with low-grade iron ore. The Butler Brothers were also remembered as being benevolent. When men lost their jobs during the Great Depression, the Butlers looked for ways to keep the men working. Leo Trunt wrote of one instance when a water line had to be dug. Rather than using machines, which would have been faster, the men hand-dug the ditch, which kept the men working.

The women of Cooley were a bit non-traditional. Several of the homes in Cooley were built by women, who were skilled carpenters. During the Second World War, the women went to work and were employed at the mines doing everything from filling rail cars to running the belt control panel.

Most workers and residents recalled that life was good in Cooley. Nearby lakes offered fishing, swimming and other recreational opportunities. There were bowling leagues, golf tournaments, bingo, bridge games, and more. There was also a ladies club and activities for the whole family.

As mining changed, so did Cooley. Washing plants were no longer needed nor used. The Harrison Washing Plant in Cooley was dismantled in 1969. A new Butler Taconite plant was built in 1967 and hopes were high for the future. Those hopes were short-lived as mining again faced hard times in the 1980s. One of the parent companies of the Butler Taconite Plant went bankrupt, and the plant was closed and torn down in 1983.

Cooley's population gradually declined and had only thirty-three people in 1970. The land was needed for the new taconite plant and railroad facilities. Houses were moved out of Cooley, some to nearby Swan Lake and others to neighboring communities. The town was dissolved in 1974. Old-timers say that when Highway 169 was changed around 1970, there were no traces of Cooley left behind.

Kanabec County

Brunswick Blacksmith Shop. (Courtesy of the Kanabec History Center)

Grass Lake Church. (Courtesy of the Kanabec History Center)

BRUNSWICK

1860-1918/1927-1934
CLASS A
APPROXIMATE LOCATION:
From Mora:
MN 23W/MN 65S for 6 miles. Left on MN 70E for one mile.

Three times is the charm, or so the saying goes. Brunswick, Kanabec County's first county seat and site of the first county court house, had three locations in its history. While the third and last location was the largest, the town would become a place of the past.

Brunswick's first location was established shortly after 1858, at Millet Rapids on the Snake River. The small community included a post office, store, logging headquarters, and a few other buildings.

Moving a mile upstream in 1864, the town again moved in 1869 to a site on Highway 70, just east of Minnesota 65. With a sawmill, hotel, store, post office, bank, two churches, the first county court house, and a school, the third site was not only the largest, but the longest lasting of the three locations.

The railroad reached nearby Mora in 1882 and as Mora grew, Brunswick declined. Mora would become the county seat, and eventually Brunswick faded away. Today there are farms and residences in the area.

GRASS LAKE

1878-1904
CLASS C
APPROXIMATE LOCATION:
From Mora:
MN 23/65 South for 6 miles. Left onto MN 70E for 6½ miles. Right onto County 43 for ½ miles.

Kanabec County's first church, the Swedish Mission Church in Grass Lake, still stands. The 1898 building replaced an earlier one that burned in 1894. Known as the Grass Lake Church, it is the only building left in the long ago town of Grass Lake in Southeastern Kanabec County.

Swedish settlers had been in the area since the 1870s, and in 1872 established Grass Lake. Before long the small community on the stage route included a blacksmith, two general stores (one with a post office), a feed mill, butcher shop, hotel, sorghum mill, two churches, a livery stable, and a half-way house. The half-way house was where immigrants stayed until

they could move to their land. A school was also located in the town and operated from 1875 to 1954.

In the late 1890s, Grass Lake's population was approximately 200 and the town was strongly being considered as a station along the new railroad route. The Kanebec History Center writes that negotiations between an area landowner and the railroad were progressing until a Grasston businessman and landowner came forward and offered his land, free of charge, to the railroad. As could be expected, Grasston was chosen as the site for the station. That decision would spell the end for Grass Lake. The town faded. Over time all the structures, except for the Grass Lake Church were destroyed or moved. In 2001, the last remnants of the school were torn down.

Last used in the 1960s, the Grass Lake Church had also deteriorated and was in disrepair. Hoping to preserve the church and the last vestige of the town, the Kanabec History Center hoped to move the building to their museum in Mora. However, costs were so prohibitive it was beyond their financial means.

A community group formed the Friends of the Grass Lake Church. In conjunction with the History Center, the group held informational and planning meetings, raised funds and began to restore the structurally sound building. The volunteer group has replaced the roof, repaired water damage, restored or replaced doors, and much more. Grounds work is also a part of the preservation. The 115-year-old building, complete with original pews, is owned by the Kanabec History Center and is available to host special events, weddings, reunions, and more. The History Center also sponsors several events at the church. The cemetery is also preserved and can be toured. The Kanabec History Center urges you to bring bug repellent when you visit.

WARMAN

1907-1920
CLASS C
APPROXIMATE LOCATION:
From Mora:
MN Highway 65 N for 13 miles.

When homesteader Gust Westman noticed granite outcroppings on his land, he knew he had to tell his friend Samuel Warman. Samuel owned several granite and marble shops in the Lakeville, Minnesota, area and was always on the lookout for new granite reserves and opportunities. According to Warman's son, B.D., in a taped interview, his father liked what he saw. Moving his family to the area, Samuel with several partners, purchased 400 acres and formed the Warman Creek Granite Company. Two years later, Samuel Warman would run out of money. The company reorganized, without him, and became the Pike-Horning Granite Company.

Warman had homestead rights to forty acres of land. Planning to start a new quarry, Samuel and his wife platted out the town of Warman Creek. A 1907 announcement touted 142-foot-by-fifty-foot lots, sixteen-foot alleys, and eighty-foot streets. Grandiose plans included a railroad spur to help transport the enormous granite blocks, a hotel, a general store, several homes, and a granite polishing works. This time around the quarry would be powered by horses, not steam.

The rival granite company, didn't like the idea of the town being called Warman, so a few months after the incorporation of Warman Creek, the Pike-Horning Granite Company platted another town, just east and across the road, naming their town North Mora. Eventually the two towns became known simply as Warman, dropping the Creek part of the name and never adopting the North Mora name. It included a general store/ post office, a blacksmith, a hotel, and eight houses.

The granite was said to be of higher quality than that of the renowned granite of Vermont. But B.D. Warman states that hair seams throughout the granite made the area granite worthless. Still, the granite quarries operated for many years and was producing a distinctive "Warman Granite."

Samuel Warman was killed in a 1909 quarry accident. Operating a capstone, a revolving cylinder with a vertical axis for winding cable, the capstone broke and fatally injured Samuel.

Warman area schools were ahead of their times. B.D. states that his father, appalled by the first one-room school, convinced the area residents to consolidate. By doing so, state aid, accredidation, and the opportunity for better teachers would be available. The Warman Creek Granite Company donated land for the school. In 1908, a new four-room schoolhouse was built, consolidating three districts. A former teacher stated that the school had running water, indoor toilets, steam heat, a janitor, and living quarters for the teachers. The building housed

grades one through eight and had two teachers. Community events, dances, basket socials, Sunday school and town meetings were held in the building. School buses provided student transportation. B.D. Warman describes the buses as having heavy waterproof canvas covers and were horse-drawn with sled runners in the winter. The seats were twelve-foot long benches. A wood stove provided heat.

An unnamed teacher recalled that in the winter of 1916-1917, seventy students had to spend the night in the school. When school had started that morning, there was no snow. However, throughout the day the snow began and continued to fall, intensifying with time. By the end of the school day, it was snowing so heavily that it was unsafe for family or students to venture out into the blizzard. Feeding the children bisquits, the students, bundled in their coats, slept on the school room floor. The next morning, after the two-foot snowfall, the children were able to go home.

The anticipated rail spur never materialized and eventually Warman would fade away. In 1966, after nearly sixty years in business, several owners, and buildings, the Warman Store closed. Today, a green highway sign marks the region. The Solid Rock Christian Church, the only structure left in the town, is active and housed in a vintage building.

Warman. (Courtesy of the Kanabec History Center)

Warman Creek. (Courtesy of the Shawn Hewitt Collection)

Warman. (Courtesy of Amy Rea)

Kittson County

Caribou Store. (Courtesy of the Kittson County Historical Society)

Caribou Today. (Courtesy of Andrew Filer)

CARIBOU

1905–1919

CLASS A

APPROXIMATE LOCATION:
From Hallock:
MN 75 east for 13 miles. Left on County Road 15 for 6 miles. Right on County Road 4 for 17½ miles. Right to stay on County 4 for 1 mile. Left onto County 53 for 1/5 mile.

With a name like Caribou, one would think the hunting would be good. According to the Kittson County Historical Society, the area has always been good for hunting—it still is. The Historical Society writes that the medical pioneer Mayo brothers had a hunting cabin on the Roseau River as did railroad tycoon James J. Hill of the Great Northern Railroad.

Settled primarily by Ukrainian immigrants, Caribou is just one mile south of the Canadian border. Back in those early days, the border wasn't there, at least not physically. During those first years, homesteaders settled on both sides of the river which was, in reality, the border, and they traveled freely back and forth between the two countries.

A Kittson County Historical Society newsletter states that the border was more established in 1909, marked by iron posts, which are supposedly still there. The border was not patrolled, so travel was still free and without issues. That changed in 1930, when boundary laws were more strictly enforced. At that point, international travelers had to pass through customs to enter either country.

Prior to 1904, when a store in Caribou opened, all supplies had to be purchased in Hallock, thirty-five miles away. A post office was established in 1905, lasting fourteen years until it was discontinued in 1919. Two churches also called Caribou home, the Wilbur Mission Chapel (also known as Grandma Bailey's Sunday School) and St. Michael's Ukranian Orthodox Church. The Wilber Mission Chapel was built in 1911 and

served as a community center for years until it was razed in 1991. St. Michael's, built in 1905, was constructed by builders from the Ukraine. Still standing today, it is now listed on the National Register of Historic Places.

In addition to St. Michael's Church and cemetery, a few cattle farmers and residences are in the area.

ENOK

1896-1907

CLASS C

APPROXIMATE LOCATION:
From Hallock:
South on U.S. 75 for 9½ miles. Left on County Road 7 for 7 miles. Left on County Road 2 for ½ mile.

In the early 1890s, a general store was built in the newly-settled area that would become Enok. A few years later, in 1896, a post office was established. Cindy Adams of the Kittson County Historical Society writes that in the early days, mail came from Kennedy by horse, buggy, and sleigh. She adds that the postmasters received money for stamps sold. Since postage in those days was two cents for stamps and postcards were a penny, not much income was made from selling postage.

Joining the store and post office, was a blacksmith shop, a feed store, and the Farmer's Cooperative Creamery Association. In 1921 the creamery was destroyed by a wind storm.

The store went through a succession of owners. In 1911, the store was enlarged, modernized, and renamed "The Golden

St. Nicholas (St. Michael's) Church, Caribou. (Courtesy of Andrew Filer)

Enok Today. (Courtesy of Andrew Filer)

Enok Today. (Courtesy of Andrew Filer)

Rule Store." According to Phil Lundell, an area resident, the town had an impressive choir, the Enok Choral Society. Approximately twenty young women and twenty young men made up the group. They took their choir responsibilities seriously. With limited transportation, getting to choir practice was often by foot. As Phil Lundell recalls, many had to walk three or four miles, often in heavy snow and bitterly cold temperatures.

Today, the community is rural with a few nearby residences and older buildings standing.

NORTHCOTE

1880-1974

CLASS C

APPROXIMATE LOCATION:
From Hallock:
U.S. 75 North for 5½ miles. At intersection of U.S. 75 and County Road 4.

Surrounded by fertile farmland, Northcote was a thriving agricultural center as well as a railroad town. Settled in the late 1880s as Alice, the name was changed to Northcote in 1881. The town was named after English statesman and financier Sir Henry Stafford Northcote (1818 to 1887). While having no direct ties to the community, speculation is that Sir Northcote had financial interests in railroad tycoon and Great Northern Railroad founder James J. Hill's land interests and projects in the region.

Northcote Front Seat. (Courtesy of Glenn Browne)

Happy Halloween! Northcote. (Courtesy of Glenn Browne)

Northcote grew rapidly. Since farming was such an integral part of the community, several businesses were established to meet the local farmer's abundant grain production. Four elevators were built and kept busy. A farm implement and machinery dealership soon joined the burgeoning town. Other businesses included a hardware store, grocery store, general store, a few blacksmiths, a pool hall, a machine shop, a livery, one hotel, restaurants, and a bank.

Deciding that education was important, the Northcote School District #4 was organized in the earliest days of the community. In those first years there were forty-nine students between the ages of five and twenty-one. The Kittson County Historical Society writes that there were two school terms a year: one from September to late June, the other from March to early July. Sixty-six books filled the library. The Northcote School closed in 1929, and students were bussed to Hallock.

Also vitally important to the residents was church. A Presbyterian Church was built in 1899. At one time there was a Ladies Aid Society and a church group for young people.

As owner of the Great Northern Railroad, James J. Hill owned vast amounts of land in the region. In the late 1880s, Hill gave his son Walter a large tract of property to set up an experimental farm, called Hill Farm. Scott Clow, in writing of Hill Farm, stated that, at the time, the farm was the largest farm in the United States.

Employing many people, with as many as 250 seasonal employees, the bonanza farm consisted of many large buildings at an estimated cost of half a million dollars. There were cattle barns, hay barns, horse barns, silage barns, blacksmith shops, and more. Clow also writes that the largest silos in the world were at the farm. A slaughter house butchered beef for the farm's use. The first steam-powered engines and caterpillars did the heavy work such as plowing. With nearly unlimited financial resources, the Hill Farm imported bulls from Europe. There were also four elevators, ice houses, dry tank, smoke house, water tower that provided the whole farm with running water, boarding house, and twelve cottages for employees.

John Bergh, Hill Farm historian, writes that the most significant building was the $49,000 dollar home Walter built for himself. Clow adds that the large mansion was built in part to host elaborate hunting parties. It was said, Walter did not load his own rifle on those hunts, hiring men to load and re-load so as not to waste his time. Walter stayed on the farm for five years, but, having a wild side, he moved on to other pursuits. After Hill's departure, the farm changed hands many times, and eventually was divided up into smaller parcels and sold.

Northcote Today. (Courtesy of Andrew Filer)

Northcote Today. (Courtesy of Glenn Browne)

Northcote 1948. (Courtesy of the Kittson County Historical Society)

Northcote was bypassed by the new railroad in the area. That, combined with better roads and the availability of automobiles, signaled the town's end. There are still a few houses in the town, some residences, others are abandoned.

NOYES

Window dressing. (Courtesy of Glenn Browne)

Northcote Today. (Courtesy of Andrew Filer)

1927-1990

CLASS C

APPROXIMATE LOCATION:
From Hallock:
U.S. 75 North for 20 miles.

Long before the village of Noyes was established the area had been an important center for international travel. When the St. Paul and Pacific Railroad (predecessor to the Great Northern Railroad) built a line through the area in the late 1870s, a vital transportation link was initiated. Connecting lines in Winnipeg and other Canadian cities opened up new markets.

Originally the U.S. Customs office operated out of the nearby community of St. Vincent. A competing railroad, the Minneapolis, St. Paul, and Sault St. Marie (Soo) constructed a line to Canada through the region in 1904, and the village of Noyes was established the following year. The customs office was relocated to the new community, which was named after the local U.S. Customs agent.

Though always a small community, the international traffic, primarily rail, kept the town busy and gave it a cosmopolitan feel. The village soon included several businesses including a restaurant, oil station, stores, post office, and a dance pavilion. The Kittson County Historical Society writes that the pavilion was a popular destination. People from all over the region, even from hundreds of miles away, came for the well-known big bands that regularly played the dance hall. Another reason for the pavilion's popularity was that, at the time, Prohibition was the law of the land, at least in the United States. Yet beer and liquor could easily be obtained at Emerson, Canada, just across the border from Noyes.

For the first several years, the U.S. Customs office at Noyes was housed in the Great Northern Railroad Depot. The depot

location was especially fitting as most of the international traffic was by rail. In 1923, the depot burned to the ground and was rebuilt in 1924. That same year, 1924, the U.S. Border Patrol was established, and crossing the border then meant an official crossing stop. A granite obelisk marker was erected at the border in 1929. The following year a Customs and Immigration building was built. Minnesota Highway 6, later known as U.S. 75 was routed through the town of Noyes.

A few years later, a roadside parking area was built. The Minnesota Department of Transportation stated that the project was designed to create a small rest area directly across from the U.S. border station. The wayside was part of a large project that included paving U.S. 75 and widening the highway to six lanes between the station and the wayside. A scenic park was planned that included a triangular shape with trees and shrubs and over 2,000 plantings. Walks and a monument formed a border for the flower beds. Tables, benches, picnic fireplaces, and a flagpole flying both Canadian and U.S. flags were features of the park. In 1997, MN DOT did a clean-up of the park including cleaning and repairing the stone work, planting new flowers and installing an interpretive marker to the 2.3-acre site.

Over the years, the railroad depot was modernized with improvements such as lighting, heat, and toilets being added. Heavily damaged by a flood in 1966, a new depot, using wood from the old depot, was built in 1967.

In 2003, Canada closed its port of entry to the U.S. through Noyes, and in 2006, the U.S. followed suit. All international traffic was diverted through nearby Pembina. Post September 11, 2001, security concerns designated U.S. borders as restricted territory. Fieldworkers inspecting the Noyes facility were allowed limited access only to examine the area. Workers noted that the wayside seemed preserved. The original parking area access and traffic island had been removed. Due to homeland security issues, MN DOT reports that visitors are no longer allowed to stop at the wayside rest. Nor can vis-

Noyes Post Office. (Courtesy of John Gallagher, Post Mark Collectors Club)

Noyes. (Courtesy of Andrew Filer)

itors stop on the highway shoulders near the site and no photos are allowed. The bridge crossing into Canada is closed.

As for Noyes, the town, Glenn Browne, area historian and photographer, writes that the town is gone and only three houses remain.

caused the banks to fail, an elevator and store burned, and other buildings were moved and were repurposed into homes and garages.

Today the town is gone. A few buildings remain and a few residents are in the area.

ORLEANS

1883–1974
CLASS C
APPROXIMATE LOCATION:
From Hallock:
U.S. County Road 1 North for 10 miles. Left for ½ mile.

Orleans may not have been big but it was an important trading center. Settled as Boulder in 1897 and established as Orleans in 1904 when the Soo Line Railroad came through the county, the community was based on a farming foundation. Home to four grain elevators, the town also included two banks, a lumberyard, two stores, a blacksmith or two, restaurants, a hotel, and a school. When one of the stores burned to the ground, another was brought to Orleans on log rollers.

In recalling what had happened to Orleans, the Kittson County Historical Society writes that the Great Depression

ROBBIN

1892–1933
CLASS C
APPROXIMATE LOCATION:
From Hallock:
U.S. 75 South for 14½ miles. Right on County 11 West for 11½ miles.

Traveling west to North Dakota on State Highway 11 in far northwestern Minnesota one passes through the used-to-be town of Robbin. The gateway community was originally railroad property that was later divided and sold to early settlers in the early 1900s.

One of the first, and last, buildings in the town was the Robbin Store. Known as the "Friendly Store," one could buy groceries, meats, and just about anything needed. The store was built in approximately 1900, operated through the 1930s and 1940s, and was torn down in the mid-1980s. A post office operated from 1892 until 1933 when rural free delivery was adopted. For a while a rural telephone exchange served the area until region-wide consolidation. Robbin had its own band and baseball team. A Woodsman Lodge was active in the area.

Glenn Browne, area historian and photographer, writes that Robbin, the town, is gone. A few houses remain. The old bridge was recently torn down and replaced by a new, larger one across the Red River to Drayton, North Dakota.

Orleans Today. (Courtesy of Andrew Filer)

Orleans Today. (Courtesy of Andrew Filer)

Orleans Today. (Courtesy of Andrew Filer)

Koochiching County

Main Street Craigville. (Courtesy of Russell Lee/Library of Congress)

Saturday Night in a Saloon (Cheers). (Courtesy of Russell Lee/Library of Congress)

Steam Baths are Very Popular Among Lumberjacks. (Courtesy of Russell Lee/Library of Congress)

Present Method of Transporting Logs. (Courtesy of Russell Lee/Library of Congress)

Gemmel. (Shawn Hewitt Collection)

CRAIGVILLE

1915-1952

CLASS A

APPROXIMATE LOCATION:
From Marcell:
MN 38 North for 11½ miles. Follow MN 38N for 7 miles.
Continue onto Highway 5 for 5 miles.

Craig. (Shawn Hewitt Collection)

Main Street Craigville. (Courtesy of Russell Lee/Library of Congress)

Watch closely to the opening credits of the iconic NBC comedy series *Cheers* and you will see a vintage photo from Craigville. Colorized for the *Cheers* montage, the photo, titled "Saturday Night at the Saloon" shows two men at the bar having a drink with a woman, cigarette in hand. Another woman standing behind the bar is ready to chug her drink down. That photograph, also featured in Ken Burns's *Prohibition* documentary, was taken by Russell Lee in 1937 as part of the Farm Security Administration's (FSA) goal to assist poor farmers. The best known part of the FSA's work is the over 75,000 vivid, stark, black-and-white photos taken in those years. The Lee photograph used by *Cheers* is apropos for the television series set in a Boston bar. Equally so, it is representative of Craigville, a rowdy-frontier logging town that thrived on gambling, saloons, bordellos, and a Saturday night crowd of up to 5,000 area lumbermen.

The town, not platted until 1924, had been established much earlier, first in Itasca County in 1915, and later transferred to Koochiching County in 1918. Benhard Rajala, in his history of the regions logging era, *TIM-BERRR*, described Craigville as a one-sided street. The thirty-plus buildings were nearly all "blind pigs," businesses that sold rotgut liquor, gambling joints, bordellos, and dens of inequity. Among those disreputable businesses were the more legitimate establishments: a few general stores, a railroad depot as Craigville was on the Minneapolis and Rainy River Railroad, two hotels with restaurants, sawmill, lumber camps, and Finnish baths for those few times the loggers wanted to clean up.

Lawlessness was the norm. The nearest law enforcement was in International Falls, a two-day journey. Occasionally a deputy from Big Fork, eleven miles away, would venture to Craigville to assist. Regardless, Craigville was home to unscrupulous rogues and scoundrels, only too happy to relieve a logger of his pay or gambling winnings. Drunkenness made the taking all the easier. Many a time, a missing lumberjack, often homeless with no family, would be found floating in the river. Rajala relates the tale of two young school boys dallying by the river. The boys noticed a basketball floating in the river. As it drifted nearer they snagged it, only to learn it wasn't a basketball, but the back of a man's head.

Card sharks and cheating were common. The underlying factor in the seamy side to life in Craigville was the liquor. Prohibition made things worse, as Rajala wrote. A tough town got tougher. Already outside of the law, a little moonshine and illegal alcohol didn't bother anyone. Once in a while a federal officer, termed a "revenuer" would try to clean Craigville up, but to no avail.

Eventually the timber was depleted, the railroad pulled up, and the town was slowly abandoned and faded away. In the late 1970s a few dilapidated buildings still stood—a store or tavern or two. Today no remnants of the wild hell-raising town remain. It lives on only in the tales told and the photos that bring it to life.

GEMMELL

1905-1974

CLASS C

APPROXIMATE LOCATION:
From Northome:
U.S. 71 North for 10½ miles. Right on County Road 12 for 1/5 mile.

Known as "The Cedar Capital of the World" and with the purported "largest cedar yard in the world," Gemmell was timber country.

Early homesteaders had settled in the area at the turn of the century, but it wasn't until the arrival of the railroad in 1905 that Gemmell took root. First called Stoner, the name was later changed to Gemmell in honor of W.H. Gemmell, the first road-master of the Minnesota and International Railway (M&I). The ready timber supply, the railroads and the growing town all gave rise to the promise of jobs and oppor-

Children Playing in Front of a Saloon, Gemmel. (Courtesy of Russell Lee/Library of Congress)

Dwellings, Gemmel. (Courtesy of Russell Lee/Library of Congress)

Post Office, Gemmel. (Courtesy of Russell Lee/Library of Congress)

tunity. Before long, Gemmell had a population surge of 2,000 and included a full complement of businesses to fill the community's needs, including seventeen hotels, an ice cream parlor, at least four restaurants, several stores, a gas station, a host of saloons, more than ten sawmills, and a church.

The first school classes were held in the spring of 1907. The Koochiching County Historical Society in their *Northome Bicentennial Book* wrote that those first classes were held in an abandoned building. A log table and twenty-one kitchen chairs made up the furnishings. Classes were later conducted in a large room over a saloon until a new two-room schoolhouse was built in 1908. Later a brick building was constructed.

Fire was an ever-present danger. Several sources report a major fire, date unknown, that destroyed many mills, camps, and other businesses. Many left the area after the fire. The timber supply dwindled and was eventually depleted. As the timber would go, so would the town. Businesses shut down or moved away. The residents left, and soon Gemmell became just a spot along Highway 71, a place of the past.

RAINY LAKE CITY

1894-1900

CLASS F

APPROXIMATE LOCATION:
Little American Island in Voyageurs National Park, International Falls, Minnesota.

Rumors of gold in Northern Minnesota were persistent. Early geological explorations in the 1850s had published reports of rocks near Vermillion Lake containing numerous veins of quartz. It was widely known that such veins often included traces of other minerals, including gold. The discovery was enough to send hordes of prospectors and miners to the region in 1868. The dreams were short-lived. No gold was found.

Still, the rumors persisted. In 1893, while camping on Little American Island, a diligent prospector spotted a vein of quartz with potential. Digging out a sample, crushing the rock and working it out, he found a few small gold flakes. The rush was on, this time on a larger, more frenzied scale. Prospectors flocked to the island as did those looking to make their fortunes by selling supplies to the gold-seekers. Others supplied liquor, women, and gambling. All had dreams of striking it rich. Mining companies jostled for the best locations. Overnight the pristine wilderness gave way to a crude civilization.

Incorporated in 1894, the Koochiching County Historical Society records show that the town was to have seven east/west

Rainy Lake City Saloon. (Voyageur's National Park)

Minnesota Avenue Today, Rainy Lake City. (Voyageur's National Park)

avenues and four north/south streets with 1,045 lots platted. Within a short time several merchants came, including a lumberyard, bank, furniture store, numerous hotels, bakery, eight dry goods stores, restaurants, a newspaper, livery, a post office, school, and at least seventeen saloons. There was also a doctor of sorts—his training consisting of serving as an apprentice in the Civil War. Nearly all of the businesses were located in tents, at least in the early days. With time, wooden buildings would be constructed.

Rainy Lake City was a rough and tumble frontier town. It looked every bit the stereotypical image of a "Wild West" town. Colorful characters, rogues, scoundrels, saloon girls, card sharks, and gamblers were part of the cast. Rowdiness and shenanigans took place day and night. The necessities of life were in short supply and cost a pretty penny when they could be found. Health and sanitary conditions were abysmal, at best. Some sources write of typhoid outbreaks occurring from time to time.

David E. Perry, author of *Gold Town to Bust Town*, writes that as families began to join their men in Rainy Lake City, improvements were made to the rambunctious town. Schools were built, sidewalks were constructed, a city jail was authorized and built, and ordinances were enacted to curtail public drunkenness and city use of firearms as well as disorderly conduct.

The gold deposits were difficult to get to and expensive to mine. Transportation costs were prohibitive and the discovery of gold in the Klondike made Rainy Lake City a place of the past. By 1901, the boom would bust, and Rainy Lake City would live only in the history of the region.

The remnants of Rainy Lake City and the mines are now within the confines of Voyageurs National Park near International Falls. Boat excursions to Little American Island are offered where it is possible to see bits and pieces of the town and the prospecting. A park brochure highlights the history of the region's gold rush and even includes a mini-scavenger hunt. Plans are slated to develop the town site into an interpretive center using a Prohibition-era saloon as the shelter for the historical exhibits.

Caution is urged, the brochure states, as falling into a mine shaft could result in serious injury.

Lake County

Cramer Road, Cramer. (Courtesy of the Cook County Historical Society)

Forest Center Aerial. (Courtesy of the Ely-Winton Historical Society)

CRAMER

1911-1917
CLASS A
APPROXIMATE LOCATION:
From Finland:
North on MN 1 West for ½ mile. Right onto Cramer Road for 11½ miles. Junction of Lake County 7 and Lake County 8.

Arriving in the rugged country in the early 1900s, John Cramer, from Pennsylvania, liked what he saw and homesteaded a quarter section on a lake that would later be named Cramer Homestead Lake. John Cramer was a teacher by trade. Each day he would walk from his homestead to the Maple School where he taught while proving up his claim. In 1910, the Alger-Smith logging railroad reached mile post 62, which meant it was sixty-two miles from Knife River. Realizing the need, John bought land near the railroad and built a store. The new settlement was given John Cramer's name and he served as first postmaster.

At mile post 63, a small settlement also developed and was called Case. Water and coal facilities and several branch lines ran west from Case. In 1913, John Cramer sold his store and it continued to operate until Alger-Smith ceased their operations in the early 1920s. Cramer had a railroad depot, store, post office, school, and other railroad buildings. And was an important shipping point. The chief commodities being shipped were ties, poles, logs, and herring. The cold winters provided free refrigeration for the fish. Early resident Bob Silver wrote in his memoirs that the most interesting cargo he saw was a 1919 Pan Motor car. The car, made in St. Cloud was one of only 800 produced, so seeing one was a memorable event, especially in the north woods.

In 1913, Cramer Township was organized but with the coming of the Great Depression, values were so low that the township was dissolved in 1932. Cramer did have schools in the area. After Alger-Smith ceased operations many residents left. For many years some of Cramer's buildings were used as hunting cabins.

FOREST CENTER

1949-1965
CLASS B—HISTORICAL MARKER
APPROXIMATE LOCATION:
From Ely:
MN East for 19 miles. Left on Forest Route 1461 for ½ mile. Slight left onto Forest Route 173 for 2 miles. Right to stay on Forest Route 173 Tomahawk Road for 15 miles.

When the 2011 Pagami Fire roared across the Boundary Waters Canoe Area Wilderness (BWCAW) near Ely in its 145-square-mile swath, it swept over the former town site of Forest Center. Abandoned for nearly fifty years, the town's footprint was nearly obliterated as nature reclaimed the forest floor. So much so, that former residents Ferdinand and Pat Thums, when revisiting the town a few years ago, writes Hugh E. Bishop in his Lake County history, that they had trouble recognizing anything other than a big rock that marked the old sawmill site. If not for an orange marker placed on a neighbor's tree years ago, they might not have located their old home site. The inferno erased all of the regrowth that had occurred over the past fifty years.

In the 1940s, Central Wisconsin's Tomahawk Kraft Paper (later renamed Tomahawk Timber) was awarded timber rights to 150,000 acres within the Superior National Forest. According to area historian, David Kees, that translated to a ten-mile by sixty-mile cut area. That was a lot of timber to harvest. TKP had logging camps in the area, and as Hugh E. Bishop wrote, after operating large traditional camps, TKP decided to establish a community for employees and their families.

Located on the shores of Lake Isabella, about forty miles from Ely, the area was remote and still is. Yet out of that wilderness, a close-knit community was forged. The company town included fifty-three homes, coffee shop, non-denominational church as well as a Lutheran Church for which the company had donated materials, a post office, electrical generating plant, water system, laundry, swimming beach, and a school. A road system ran throughout the village.

Social life was active with the whole community participating. From the many photos I've seen of the town, I could have grown up there. Forest Center was a 1950s suburbia, northwoods style. The recreation center hosted dances, roller skating, wedding receptions, and other community events. There were Fourth of July children's parades, baseball, crafts, picnics, swimming, bike riding and winter sledding. The homes were fully modern with large flower and vegetable gardens and even white picket fences. The school was also a center of activity.

Forest Center Homes. (Courtesy of the Ely-Winton Historical Society)

Tomahawk Timber Company Store, Forest Center. (Courtesy of the Ely-Winton Historical Society)

Early Forest Center School. (Courtesy of the Ely-Winton Historical Society)

Forest Center Marker. (Courtesy of Heather Monthei)

Forest Center. (Courtesy of Heather Monthei)

Grades one through eight were taught there, but the high school students were transported first to Ely and then later to Silver Bay.

By 1964, even though the timber resources were still strong, the company was shutting down operations. The BWCA was being established and since the timber harvest was conducted within the BWCA, speculation gave that as the reason for the company's abrupt demise.

Forest Center. (Courtesy of Heather Monthei)

118

Many of Forest Center's buildings were moved to other communities. Others were demolished. The town site was cleared and replanted. Today, there is little left at Forest Center. Nature reclaimed the town site and camouflaged the building sites. The Pagami Fire did expose some vestiges of the community removing some of the thick underbrush and showing a few crumbling foundations and pieces of asphalt flooring. Already the forest is regrowing and again erasing any remains.

ILLGEN CITY

1924–1950s
CLASS C
APPROXIMATE LOCATION:
From Silver Bay:
Northeast on MN 61 North for 5 miles. At intersection of MN 61 and MN 1.

Carving a settlement out of the wilderness requires hardwork, ingenuity, innovation, and vision. Rudolph and Mary Illgen had those in abundance and then some. Following a family tragedy, the death of their son, Bernard, the couple and their two daughters moved from Iowa, purchasing land in northeastern Minnesota. According to a 1958 feature article on the Illgens in the *Silver Bay News*, the couple had planned to go into scientific farming but soon found themselves in business. It was said Mary made the best ice cream and people came from miles around to sample it. Being at Beaver Crossing on the Alger-Smith logging railroad line, the crews started boarding with the Illgens. One thing lead to another, and soon the Illgens were serving food, offering boarding rooms, and selling gas in the first one-gallon gas pump in the region.

Rudy had a lot of firsts, including the first electric plant in the area and the first radio broadcast. By hooking up the radio to the telephone and calling all the party-line members, the radio broadcast was heard by all. Rudy was instrumental in establishing the first school in the region.

There was a rumor that a new road was going to be constructed along Lake Superior up the North Shore. Rudy was convinced this road would prove to be instrumental in the development of the North Shore region, even writing a book called *Silver Avenue*. Realizing the need and the potential, the Illgens purchased land from 3M. This land would become Illgen City.

With big plans and not much money, Rudy and Mary set about building a new hotel digging the basement by hand with shovels. Named the Aztek, Cathy Wurzer tells in her *Tales of the Road* that the hotel had a dozen rooms, a dining room, a lobby, and a fifty-foot hand carved mahogany bar. It even had lights powered by a Mack truck power plant. Said to be the finest hotel for miles around, local folklore has Al Capone visiting while on one of his many jaunts/vacations from the heat of Chicago. Another lodging option was the Illgen Cabinola Tourist Park. The cabinola was a combination cabin and travel trailer. The design was patented by Rudy. Thirty cabinolas were built and named for states in the union.

World War II would cause a decline in Illgen City's businesses. Gas rationing severely limited auto travel and employees were hard to find, so the hotel and other businesses closed. The Whispering Pines Motel was built in 1956. The Aztek burned in 1958. The Cabinolas were sold to make way for the new Highway 61. The Whispering Pines Motel still stands, though it was severely damaged by fire in 2009. The motel's driveway is the old Highway 61. One of the original cabinolas, newly remodeled, is now the motel's Honeymoon Cabin. Travelers can't miss Illgen City even today. Just north of Silver Bay, a green highway sign marks the location. To the left is the Whispering Pines Motel. Stop in and spend the night in a truly historic building the old cabinola, now Honeymoon Cabin.

Illgen City. (Author's collection)

Whispering Pines Motel, Illgen City. (Author's collection)

Illgen City Travel Service. (Author's collection)

sales to pay for heating and supplies. A school was started in 1951, and grades one through eight were taught to approximately fifty students. In those early years, high-school age students had to board in Ely, fifty miles away. When the Silver Bay school started, Agnes's husband, Doyle was the bus driver. The bus trip transporting Sawbill Landing students and students from nearby Forest Center was sixty miles one way.

The Boundary Waters Canoe Area (BWCA) was created in 1965. Agnes states that people in the portal zone were moved out. The school burned in 1964, the rails were removed in 1970, and Sawbill Landing ceased to be. Little remains. In August of 2011, there was a Sawbill Landing class reunion where Agnes and her friends were able to reminisce and share stories and hugs.

SAWBILL LANDING

1949-1965

CLASS A—BARREN LAND

APPROXIMATE LOCATION:

From Isabella:

East on Minnesota 1 East for 400 feet. Continue onto Forest Route 172/Wanless Road for 1 mile. Left on Forest Route 369/Trappers Lake Road for 4 miles. Right onto Forest Route 367 for 3½ miles. Right towards Forest Route 174/Dumbell Road for 1 miles. Left onto Forest Route 174/Dumbell Road for 2.8 miles. Right onto Forest Route 173. Junction of Sawbill Landing Road and Dumbell Road.

Traditionally, logging had been done in camps, and in 1940 there were at least seven logging camps in northeastern Minnesota and Lake County. As the railroad reached the wilderness, staging or landing areas were created. Here the timber would be taken by truck to the railroad lines and shipped out. Rather than living in logging camps, several families became independent jobbers and chose to start their own town near the landing. Sawbill Landing was that town.

Agnes Gilson, an early resident, remembers that there was a café, grocery store, gas station, post office, and at least a dozen homes. The only phone at the time was at the landing. No one had home phones. Electricity was supplied by a light power plant. Agnes said you couldn't plug anything too heavy in but it was great having lights.

A Sunday School with a once-a-month visiting preacher was located in a building donated by a logging company. According to an article by Linda Lamb, the building had once been a bunk house and mess hall for prisoners of war. Linda also writes that the school was the center of activity for the community. Dinners, dances, and summer softball were great fun and also served as fund-raisers. Residents hosted rummage

SECTION 30

1883-1923

CLASS A

APPROXIMATE LOCATION:

From Winton:

South on MN 169 South for one mile. Left on Kawishiwi Trail/Section 30 Road for 1 mile.

Ownership of Section 30, the mine, and the surrounding area was complicated. The 2,180 acres was laid claim by every option available, legal and illegal. Possession was upheld by shotgun. Eventually court proceedings, according to area historian Milt Stenland, lasted fifteen years (1886 to 1902), cost more than a million dollars, and was finally decided by the U.S. Supreme Court. The Section 30 litigation would be the most complicated and longest legal mining case in the history of northern Minnesota. The court ruled Eaton and Merritt (one of the seven Merritt Brothers who later discovered the Mesabi Range) were the landowners.

Once ownership was determined mining began in earnest. Traditional mining methods were used and involved underground mine shaft drilling with skilled workers bringing the ore up. Later, open pit mining methods would be used. After much work and excavation, the first train load (thirty cars carrying fifty tons of ore each) left the Section 30 mine in June of 1910.

In the early mining days it was common practice to have the miners live close to the mines. Workers built, bought, or rented homes owned by the mining company in the mine area, called "locations." The locations, towns, and communities were generally self-contained and had all the amenities and necessities workers would need. Depending on the size of the location, the amenities would vary in availability and variety.

As that first load of ore left Section 30, the community was

Section 30. (Courtesy of Ely-Winton Historical Society)

flourishing. Home to hotels, boarding houses, a hospital, a dance hall, community center, grocery store, silent movie theater, pool hall, and the miners' homes, the town was home to hundreds. Everyone shopped Oppel's Store. It was a cross between a country store and fore-runner of the modern shopping center. Former resident Aune Bobence recalled the best part of the store was the large penny-candy counter. The store was so busy that eight clerks, a bookkeeper, and two butchers were kept busy full time. M. Oppel delivered groceries by horse and

Section 30, 1960s. (Courtesy of the Iron Range Historical Society)

wagon, later by auto. Nearby Native Americans traded at the store. A wooden boardwalk ran from Section 30 to nearby Winton. Residents would walk to Winton for church and Winton residents came to Section 30 for work or to shop at Oppel's.

The large population necessitated a school. In 1910, there were two teachers and sixty-five students. In 1913, a larger school was built. The two-story building had a basement with a heating and ventilation plant, four classrooms on the first floor and living quarters for the principal and his family as well as rooms for the teachers. In 1920, there were 120 students and five teachers. After the mine closed, the population and number of students declined. The 1950s saw students bussed to Ely, and in 1969 the school closed. Used as a town hall, museum and deputy sheriff's office, the building was razed in 1979. Class reunions were held at least until 2008.

Relatively short-lived, the mine lasted just fourteen years. In 1923, when the mine closed, many moved on to new locations and lives. Hoping the mine would re-open, some stayed. The community remained active for many years. Some residences remain in the area, and for a while some foundations were visible. For the most part, however, the area is being reclaimed by nature.

Lake of the Woods County

Bankton School site. (Courtesy of Marlys Hirst)

Bankton Town Hall. (Courtesy of the Lake of the Woods Historical Society)

Faunce Fire Tower. (Courtesy of Andrew Filer)

BANKTON

1915-1932
CLASS A
APPROXIMATE LOCATION:
From Williams:
CSAH 2 for 3½ miles. Straight left onto Wilderness Avenue
1/4 mile. Continue on CSAH 2 for 3½ miles. Continue on
County Road 2 SW/Rangeline Road SW/for 2 miles.

Within the boundaries of Minnesota's Beltrami Island State Forest lie several Lake of the Woods County early communities. Settled in the early 1900s, most were drawn to the area by the prospect of free homestead land. In order to gain title to the property, settlers had to "prove up." This involved paying a filing fee, building a dwelling, and living on the land for a specified time.

Homesteading was hard work, and often life was on the subsistence level. Survival depended on utilizing the resources of the area: hunting, trapping, logging, out of the area fall harvest work, and farming the marginal land. The soil (sandy, loamy, swampy, and surrounded by peat bogs, which the early Native Americans called muskeg) made things difficult. The area's abundant blueberries supplemented the sparse food stocks, and for many, there might not have been any food were it not for blueberries.

Bankton had a post office from 1915 to 1932, a school and community hall. The eight-sided hall was always in use hosting dances and other community get-togethers. Records show that at one time, over forty families lived along the present-day Bankton Forest Road. In 1935, the federal Resettlement Program relocated the residents, many of them settling in other parts of Lake of the Woods County.

Today, the Bankton Forest Road is designated as the Homesteaders Historic Drive. A Lake of the Woods County Tourism brochure details the drive stating that open areas along the route are the fields left by the early settlers. Many of the homesteads are marked with a willow tree or lilacs planted by those early residents. Two cemeteries remain and are marked, as is the old townsite, on the state forest map. Informational signs mark some of the locations, where some building remains are visible but physical evidence is quickly being reclaimed by nature.

CEDAR SPUR

1909-1917
CLASS A
APPROXIMATE LOCATION:
From Williams:
East on MN 11 for 2½ miles. Left at County 98/12th Street NW
for 1/5 mile.

As its name implies, Cedar Spur was a timber-rich rail town. As Wally Mason and Marlys Hirst wrote in their history of Cedar Spur, the Canadian government, in its goal of opening markets in their prairie provinces, built a railroad from Winnipeg to Thunder Bay. The rail line also served to make settlement in the northern reaches of Minnesota more accessible. Towns sprang up all along the rail route. Cedar Spur was one of them.

The newly established community had everything it needed to grow quickly. A readily available timber supply, to be used for building homesteads and for income, combined with freight and shipping options provided ample growth potential.

Mason and Hirst also write that homesteads in the area had unique shapes. The Homestead Act allowed for four forty-acre parcels with the stipulation that the parcels be adjoining. The young homesteaders chose the richest farmland and the highest ground for their claims. Since the prime land was not always in a square pattern, many geometrical-shaped homesteads were established including z-shaped, t-shaped, or row pattern.

With all of its rich timber, logging and wood products were big business. Other businesses would soon follow—a store and post office were established in 1909. For a short time there was also a confectionary store. A church, cemetery, and school soon were part of the community. Prospects looked good for the town.

All the timber, while good for business and settlers, also had a downside. The cut timber, the wood shavings, and scraps made fire a constant concern. In the fall of 1910, the area was a tinder-box. Reports tell of a few small fires burning in the slashed regions south and west of Cedar Spur. Locomotives often sparked fires. Whatever the cause, the fires flared, eventually engulfing the entire area in a fire-storm. Everything in its path was destroyed.

In a Lake of the Woods County history, Mason and Hirst tell of the school teacher who had been watching the smoke-filled sky all day. When flames were sighted, she quickly ushered the students out. Five minutes later the school was consumed by fire. She led the children to a nearby homesteader's cabin, where they spent the night, being reunited with their families the next day.

The County Historical Society's website lists the grim statistics: forty-three people were killed in the fire, over 400,000 acres were scorched, homesteads were destroyed, and the communities of Pitt, Graceton, Williams, and Cedar Spur lay in ruins.

Some buildings were able to be saved, others rebuilt. The fire cleared the land and once the remaining timber was harvested, the area became agricultural.

The dwindling timber supply and improved transportation methods signaled the end of the Cedar Spur. The depot was moved to Saskatchewan in 1923, and the school closed in 1929. The post office was discontinued in 1917 with the advent of rural free delivery. Soon Cedar Spur ceased to exist.

FAUNCE

1917-1938

CLASS A

APPROXIMATE LOCATION:
From Williams:
CSAH 2 for 3½. Straight left onto Wilderness Avenue 1/4 mile. Continue onto CSAH 2 for two miles. Continue onto County 2 SW/ Rangeline Road SW for two miles. Continue straight onto Faunce Forest Road for 4½ miles. Left onto Santa Anna Forest Road and Faunce would be to the right.

People still flock to the Faunce area. Some come for the blueberries that grow along the country roads and throughout the jack-pine forests, wherever the tall pines let in enough sunlight for the berries to flourish. The lush berries are at their peak from early July through the end of August. Early settlers depended on the berries for survival. As area pioneer Ernie Peterson wrote in his reminisces, the berries would be sold and what didn't sell was canned, often 300 to 400 quarts a season. The berries were so important that Peterson said, they were often the difference between eating and not eating.

Others come for the recreational opportunities, hunting, four-wheeling, snowmobiling, and more. Faunce Campground is located at the site of Faunce, and provides visitors an overnight lodging option. A nearby CCC Camp is still standing and offers a historical perspective as does the CCC fire tower built in the 1930s that is still standing.

As blueberries are still important today, the Lake of Woods Tourism office advertises the designated "Blueberry Pickers Scenic Drive." The route takes you through the heart of Beltrami Island State Forest, through the heart of the region's early settlements including Faunce.

Situated atop an ancient sandbank of the glacial Lake Agas-

siz, Faunce, named for an area school superintendent, is approximately twelve miles south of Williams, Minnesota. Like other towns in the area, most of the early settlers had been drawn to the area by the prospect of free land. Homesteaders could claim 160 acres, pay a filing fee, build a home, and make a life. Making that life was often hard, back-breaking work.

The region is sandy, swampy, and a peat bog, sometimes known by the local term, muskeg. It wasn't until the early twentieth century, after a massive dredging effort created ditches for roadbeds to be built upon, that the area became accessible. As part of that dredging project, area landowners were assessed one dollar per acre, meaning each landowner owed taxes of $160. As Ernie Peterson wrote, at the time that sum was an insurmountable obstacle—families could live a year on that amount. Eventually many would be forced to leave the area.

Consisting of several families the community also had a store and post office, livery stables, a few other businesses, and a school. The school and the store were located in several locations within the community. The post office operated from 1817 until 1938.

Carla Hagen, a Minnesota author whose family was from the region, wrote a fictionalized account of life in the community during the 1930s. The story is backed with solid research, historical accuracy, captivating characters and a setting so realistic you can taste the blueberries. Titled *Hand Me Down My Walking Cane*, the book brings the times, the place, and the people to life, so much so it is hard to know where reality left off and fiction set in.

In the late 1930s, New Deal policies and the Resettlement Administration would relocate the families and hasten the end of Faunce as a town and settlement. The Beltrami Island State Forest embodies Faunce as well as other area settlements. The maps are marked with the old names, signs still indicate the

Faunce Store. (Courtesy of the Lake of the Woods Historical Society)

Faunce Ridge Road. (Courtesy of Marlys Hirst)

locations, and visitors still visit the area. The fire tower still stands, scenic drives take one through the regions, and camping, hunting, and other pursuits abound.

HIWOOD

1918–1936

CLASS A

APPROXIMATE LOCATION:
From Warroad:
South on County Road 5 for eleven miles. Continue onto 540th Avenue for two miles. Right on Dick's Parkway SW for 5½ miles. Left on Hiwood Forest Road for one mile. Left.

It took awhile for settlers to claim their homesteads in the marshy, boggy land in Lake of the Woods County forest areas. The saturated soil first had to be ditched and drained. Once access to the lands was completed, the area grew quickly. Before long nearly every parcel was claimed. Soon communities developed out of the wilderness. Hiwood was one of them.

A post office was established in 1918 as was a store and a school. The Hiwood School was built entirely with volunteer labor. Life was hard and living was often on a subsistence level. When Roosevelt's New Deal programs came into effect, the Resettlement Administration relocated the residents in the late 1930s. The post office was discontinued in 1936, and the store was closed and moved to near Warroad.

Today, Hiwood is state forest land and just miles from the Red Lake Wildlife Management headquarters.

Hiwood Post Office. (Courtesy of the Lake of the Woods Historical Society)

Mahnomen County

Duane. (Courtesy of the Mahnomen County Historical Society)

DUANE

1904-1924

CLASS A

APPROXIMATE LOCATION:

From Mahnomen:

North on Highway 59 for 8 miles to Bejou. Turn right on CSAH #1, also known as 140th Street and continue 10 miles to the intersection of #1 and #3 (also known as 240th Street). Cemetery is ¼ mile north of intersection.

The life story of Reverend Duane F. Porter reads like a dime novel. Born in 1850 in a log cabin located in the wilderness of Minnesota, Porter's mother was Chippewa, his father white. As a young man, he led the rough and tumble life of a logger among the drinking, fighting, and rowdy men found in logging camps.

According to family and folklore, Porter, in 1884, after awakening in a road-side ditch after a drunken stupor, was converted. He went on to become the longest-serving pastor in the Methodist Church of anyone in Minnesota history. For over sixty years, Porter ministered to the Chippewa at White Earth Reservation and during the years of 1905 to 1918 in Duane.

Porter documented his long service at White Earth. His notes are archived by the Methodist Church Conference in Minneapolis, Minnesota. The story of Duane and of Reverend Porter are so intertwined that the telling of one story is the telling of the other.

As Reverend Porter wrote, his mission work at Duane all began with his decision to build his people a church. After much prayer, he petitioned for the land and was awarded eighty acres for religious purposes, upon which the community of Duane would be built. The church also awarded an additional eighty acres at Pine Bend.

The next concern was to secure lumber for the church and buildings. That winter, Porter himself, hauled the lumber the thirty-two miles from the Government mill to Duane. A post office was established in 1904, and for a while Porter served as the postmaster.

Unable to support himself and his family, Porter was also on salary with the Indian agency working with the Removal Indians, helping them with their allotments. Traveling most of the week, Porter would return to Duane each weekend and preach on Sunday.

Porter, in 1908, was successful in getting a government-built school in Duane, which was also named for Porter, the Portersville Day School.

In 1909, Porter surveyed a twelve-mile road from Fosston which opened up Duane. The road would later become a state highway.

Gradually the Indian community dwindled. Porter blamed the 1906 Clapp Amendment, which allowed the sale of Indian-owned land. According to some reports, over ninety percent of land on the White Earth Reservation was sold. Porter wrote that the sale of Indian land resulted in paralyzing the Indian. That coupled with the policy of enrolling native children in off-reservation schools would cause irreparable damages to the native population and Duane.

As Duane declined, Porter advised those who had sold their land to go to the eighty-acre church allotment in Pine Bend, twelve miles east of Duane.

The final blow to Duane was the government decision that all Indians had to live on their own allotments. The people scattered and the mission was abandoned. The post office dissolved in 1924. Reverend Porter relocated to Pine Bend. Duane, as a town, ceased to exist.

Duane covered a wide region. The school was a mile south of the #1 and #3 intersection. The cemetery is located about a quarter-mile north of that same intersection and is located on private property. A lone building is said to be standing still, just after the intersection, among the trees, also on private property.

Duane Post Office. (Courtesy of the Mahnomen County Historical Society)

Mille Lacs County

Great Northern Railroad Depot, Princeton MN, made of Brickton brick. (Photo use by GNU Free Documentation License)

BRICKTON

1889-1929

Class A

APPROXIMATE LOCATION:

From Princeton:

North on U.S. 169 for 2½ miles. Marker is on the East side of U.S. 169 (it looks as if it is in someone's front yard). There is an RV Dealership on the West side of U.S. 169.

Even today, the numbers are staggering. 20,000,000 bricks a year, requiring fifty trainloads of forty-seven to fifty cars each to transport the yearly production output. Five brickyards running at full steam, each employing forty to fifty workers. Eight-hundred-million bricks produced in a thirty-six-year production run.

Brickton, approximately two and one-half miles north of Princeton, sits on a rich deposit of clay, which was long known to exist. As William S. Oakes remembers, it wasn't until 1886, when the railroad provided access to the area and transportation opportunities that the industry developed and flourished. An added bonus for the industry was the abundant timber resources of the area. The trees, mostly low-grade and not fit for lumber, made excellent firewood and the brickyards needed large quantities of cordwood to produce the bricks.

The first brickyard was established near the southern edge of what was to be Brickton near a small lake (Fog Lake). A man named Duncan opened the first brickyard. Four others were soon to follow including the A.W. Woodcock brickyard in 1889. William S. Oakes, who had learned brick-making from his father and grandfather in Nova Scotia, Canada, worked at the Oakes brickyard as did William's brother, Charles, who was an expert brick-burner.

Ownership of the brick-yards switched hands often with original owners moving on and new investors coming on. For many years, the brick industry and its payrolls were essential to the area and nearby Princeton's economy.

Brick-making is hard, laborious work. The hours are long and the work arduous. Men often worked day and night for seven or eight days before the brick was burnt. Wages were $1.50 to $1.75 a day. Bricks could be purchased for approximately $9.00 to $12.00 per thousand bricks.

Piece-work was available, and the more one worked, the more money one made. Wages for piece-work were seventeen cents per thousand, and in 1920 approximately forty-two cents per thousand. Most workers preferred not to endure the back-breaking work of wheeling the brick into the kiln, and then loading them onto railroad cars.

Mr. Oakes emphasized in a personal letter that not only was the work hard for the men, the horses deserved extra mention. Not only did they provide the power for the brickyards during brick season, but they were sent north to the logging camps in the winter all for a few oats and hay.

In conjunction with the brick industry, a residential/retail community was developed. The Brickton post office was established on May 6, 1901, and was discontinued on August 15, 1928.

Brickton had approximately 300 to 400 residents. The town boasted a potato warehouse, two stores, a railroad depot, sawmill, three boarding houses for the single-workers, and over thirty homes. The two stores were company stores, owned by the brickyards, and they sold nearly everything. At one time there was even a dance hall. It was common for the halls to host bands most weekends. Not only were the men hard workers, many were hard drinking rowdies. It was even possible to purchase liquor and moonshine from local residents.

Brickton also had a two-room schoolhouse serving up through sixth grade. Seventh and eighth graders were expected to go to Princeton. There were no school buses so transportation was by any method they could devise.

According to Agnes Leuck, who attended the Brickton school from 1912 to 1918, the school had stationary desks, a wood-burning stove, water dipper, and an outhouse. There was a gravel playground with no equipment. The school day was from nine o'clock to four o'clock. Agnes recalled that the teachers were kindly, patient and dedicated. One teacher, a Miss James, suggested the students bring wrapped potatoes to school. They would place them in the ashes of the stove and by lunch-time, the students had a school "hot lunch."

Construction trends and economic conditions would affect the brick industry and would eventually cause the demise of Brickton. Clay deposits near Minneapolis/St. Paul, prohibitive transportation costs, the Great Depression, and the trend towards concrete blocks, which are cheaper to produce and to lay would all contribute to the town's end. Brickton's last bricks were produced in 1929.

The bricks produced in Brickton throughout its heyday and for years afterward were the Minnesota Architects gold standard. They were often designated as "the brick" to use in architectural drawings, plans, and specificiations.

Many public businesses and finer homes in the area were built with Brickton bricks, also known as Princeton cream bricks. The Princeton Railroad Depot, now the home of the Mille Lacs County Historical Society, is a prime example of the bricks produced in Brickton.

After the brick production ceased, so did Brickton. Residents moved on, buildings were packed up and moved, razed, or burned. The school house was moved and became a private residence. Farming replaced brick-making.

Oakes and Kuhn, brickyard owners, had long suggested that a Brickton historical marker be erected. Oakes made the first donation and soon other donations came in. Six-hundred-fifty dollars were raised, and a firm in Ohio was awarded the contract. Erection was completed in November of 1976. The marker was dedicated on May 29, 1977.

The marker is made of Brickton brick and reads:

BRICKTON
MINNESOTA
1889-1929

WITHIN A QUARTER MILE RADIUS THRIVED A VILLAGE OF 400 PEOPLE. BRICKTON HAD TWO STORES, A TWO-ROOM SCHOOLHOUSE, POST OFFICE, RAILROAD DEPOT, SAWMILL, THREE BOARDING HOUSES, AND FIVE BRICK-YARDS WHICH MANUFACTURED 20,000,000 BRICKS AN-NUALLY. THE YARDS WERE OPERATED BY FARNHAM BROTHERS, KUHN BROTHERS, WOODCOCK AND OAKES, AND RUFUS MORTON AND CLARENCE YOUNG.

ERECTED BY
THE MILLE LACS COUNTY HISTORICAL SOCIETY
1976.

Inside of the marker is a metal tube containing the names of those associated with Brickton.

Brickton Historical Marker. (Courtesy of Vince http://mnbricks.com)

Morrison County

ORIGINAL HISTORIC SITE
The Village of Swan River
Site No. 1

In 1848, fur trader William Aitkin built a trading post and ran a ferry from this site, calling his settlement Aitkinsville. The Winnebago Indians traded here, crossing by ferry on their way to the Indian Agency at Long Prairie. Other businesses grew around the trading post, including a sawmill, a flour mill, a post office, the Brown Hotel and Grog Shop, an Indian cemetery, a school, and other stores. The town was renamed Swan River in 1856. With the growth of Little Falls, Swan River lost its businesses and was vacated in 1880.

MORRISON COUNTY
CELEBRATING 150 YEARS
1856-2006

Aitkinsville/Swan River. (Author's collection)

AITKINSVILLE

1848-1857
CLASS A
APPROXIMATE LOCATION:
From Little Falls:
South on Hilton Road for 1½ miles.

Noted fur-trader William Aitkin knew the spot would be the ideal location for a trading post. After all, he had established many posts throughout Minnesota including Sandy Lake and Crow Wing. So he knew what to look for. This site, one and one-half miles from the burgeoning community of Little Falls and on the east bank of the Mississippi River offered ideal geographic features. The site was situated along the Red River Oxcart trails and was along a major trade and travel route used by Native Americans. Area historian Maurice Faust writes that the Winnebago lived near Long Prairie and their trail intersected the Fort Ripley Road at Aitkin's site. Records indicate that thousands congregated at the location.

Aitkin named the post after himself, Aitkinsville. Building a ferry, which operated from 1850 until 1863, a mail drop was established. In addition to the trading post there was a hotel, a general store, and a grog shop. The alcoholic grog, Maurice writes, was never at a loss for customers.

Aitkin died in 1851, and the village became known as Swan River, which was officially platted in 1856. Area historian Harold Fisher wrote that the town site had twenty-five blocks and 179 lots. Lot owners included well-known notables such as Ojibwe historian William Warren, Governor Alexander Ramsey, and lumberman Franklin Steele. A sawmill, flour mill, hotel, stores, a warehouse, and grog shop continued in the settlement.

Fisher theorized that the town declined for the same reasons it prospered. The Red River Oxcart Trails had stopped by the Civil War, the Native Americans had been removed, and the fur-trade was dead. The town population was dwindling, and, with the Sioux Uprising of 1862, most of the remaining residents evacuated the settlement and moved elsewhere. The buildings were removed, burned or torn down and Aitkinsville/Swan River became a place of the past.

In 1959, historians visited the site in search of William Aitkin's burial site. From all records it was determined that the town's founder was buried near the town site. Today, the site is marked by a Morrison County historical plaque which summarizes the town's history. The area is rural and residential. The former town site is mostly open land along the river bank.

DARLING

1903-1911
CLASS B
APPROXIMATE LOCATION:
From Little Falls:
North on Highway 10 for 10 miles

Over the years the pines have grown so tall that it is nearly impossible to see the white church sitting on the hillside. When I first started driving Highway 10, twenty-eight years ago, the pines were just seedlings and the church dominated the countryside. As I drove by I would wonder about the church and smile at the endearing name of the area, Darling.

In 1893, residents formed the Swedish Lutheran Immanuel Church and built the white church in 1897. Fourth of July celebrations, picnics, and more were held at the church. The church and the Darling Store were the village's landmarks. The community, established in 1899, was named after an early railroad engineer. In the early twentieth century, the community consisted of the church, a store, a depot, and a potato warehouse. A post office was established in 1903.

Also in 1903, a local young woman, Annie Kintop, was brutally murdered. In April of that year, according to a newspaper article in the *Morrison County Record*, Annie took the train to visit and shop with her sister who lived in Little Falls. Two days later she made the return trip. After waiting a good amount of time for a ride, she decided to walk home. Since Annie often extended her trips to Little Falls, her family wasn't concerned when she hadn't returned home after a few days. It wasn't until

Darling Church. (Author's collection)

Darling today. (Author's collection)

the next week, when her family learned she had returned to Darling several days ago, that they became alarmed. A search ensued. Annie's body was found in a nearby swamp with a handkerchief tied around her neck. Several people were arrested, but none were indicted. To this day the murder remains unsolved. Several theories have been proposed. A 2005 book titled *Murder at the Darling Church*, by Joan Nelson-Vetsch, details the crime and the various theories.

In the 1930s the railroad operated a switching station and boxcar cleaning yard in Darling. The Darling Church membership merged with a church in Little Falls. The ensuing years were hard on the little white church. Despite the best efforts to protect and preserve it, vandals nearly destroyed the building. A group of women took on the task of restoring and preserving the historical church, raising funds and awareness.

The 1970s saw the end of an era in Darling. The Darling Store, after eighty years, closed up and was torn down. Highway 10, a major Minnesota thoroughfare, was in need of expansion and a bypass. The old landmark store was in the path of the proposed Minnesota Department of Transportation plans and had to go. Driving Highway 10 today, the grassy median still has lilacs blooming in the spring and still has the signs of a former homestead. The church still stands on the hillside next to the well-maintained cemetery. The pine trees stand tall to protect the last vestiges of a Darling community.

DIXVILLE

1895-1907
CLASS A
APPROXIMATE LOCATION:
From Buckman:
South on MN 25 for 3 miles. Turn Right on County 234/63rd Street.

Not many horses get a town named after them, but Gottlieb Schulz's horse, Dick, did. Schulz, a German peddler, a traveling merchant in the 1880s, originally operated a wagon filled with his wares and pulled by Dick. As Schulz prospered, he built a store. Area farmers urged Schulz to establish a post office, which he did. When asked for the name of the postal station, he named it after Dick—Dixville. Mary Warner, of the Morrison County Historical Society, writes that the town had a school, creamery, several stores, and a Lutheran church. The post office closed in 1907, and Dixville dwindled away. A school house stood for several years, and St. John's Lutheran Church and Union Cemetery are still active.

Granite City. (Author's collection)

GRANITE CITY

1858–1863
CLASS B
APPROXIMATE LOCATION:
From Pierz:
East on County Road 39 for 1 mile. Left on County Road 23 for ¾ mile. Junction of County Road 23 and 163rd Street—Historical Marker.

Founded, platted, and settled before the Civil War, Granite City would be abandoned before that same war ended. Platted in 1858 by Tallmadge Elwell, a distinguished daguerreotyper, the proposed community was on the Skunk River near Lastrup. According to area historian Maurice Faust, Granite City (so named for the numerous granite outcroppings in the area) was the first town east of Little Falls, predating today's Pierz by twelve years. The town had great promise as not only did the river provide power for a saw mill and flour mill, but it was also located on the heavily traveled Ojibwe trail that ran from Mille Lacs to Little Falls with a spur to Fort Ripley.

The town was thriving. However, persistent floods took their toll. The Sioux Uprising of 1862 would strike fear into the residents. Though the Ojibwe were peaceful and friendly, the townspeople were uneasy and scared. Granite City was remote, both Little Falls and Fort Ripley were miles away, and safety became a concern. Abandoned in 1862, the town was never revived. Today, the town is marked with a Morrison County 150-year historical marker that briefly summarizes the town's history.

Granite City. (Author's collection)

GRAVELVILLE

1879–1905
CLASS B
APPROXIMATE LOCATION:
From Little Falls, east on Hwy 27 - 7 miles. Left on Jeuel Road (Cty 45) - 3 miles. Right on King Road over river. Marker on right.

Lasting a quarter of a century, just twenty-five years, Gravelville had all the earmarks of a successful venture. Gravelville, founded by brothers Charless and Narcisse Gravelle in the U.S. Centennial year of 1876 was, for a time, prosperous. Alfred Johnson, who was born and raised in the village, writes that the Platte River had a waterfall with steep rocky banks, which would provide an anchor for the dam. In addition, the location was in the center of vast pine forests and rich rolling farmland. The forests would provide lumber for the region's farmers anxious to build. The lumbermen and farmers would also need a local market. The Gravelle brothers knew this was the spot to build.

In 1877, a dam was constructed to operate a flour mill. Soon a general store, school, blacksmith, and a post office would locate in the new settlement. A blind pig (illegal alcohol) saloon also operated and, according to early resident Jim LeBlanc, the saloon was the center of activity on a Saturday night. Population estimates range from eight families to a high of nearly 200 residents. A hand-sketched map (origin and date unknown), shows approximately twenty-four structures, a baseball field, and the bridge.

Within twenty-five years the timber resources would be depleted, and it was not profitable to process logs at Gravelville. As Alfred Johnson wrote, it was cheaper to build and operate a new mill in nearby Pierz. Pierz had rich farmland, but they also

Gravelville Mill foundation. (Author's collection)

Gravelville. (Author's collection)

had the new Soo Line Railroad. With implementation of Rural Free Delivery, Gravelville's general store business declined rapidly. A creamery was built in nearby Freedham, and when farmers took their cream there, they automatically shopped there as well, causing further decline of Gravelville business. The store closed shortly thereafter.

Johnson tells that June of 1906 was especially wet and rainy, and the rains caused the dam to washout, flooding most of the town within minutes. By 1957, only the school remained but that would disappear when area schools consolidated. The remaining buildings were torn down or removed.

A few months ago, I visited Gravelville. Located ten miles from Little Falls, the rural countryside gives way to a the small but scenic Platte River. Green and lush, it is hard to imagine 200 people living in the area. Cross the bridge over the river, and turn down a dirt county road, which was the town's main street, you will see a rectangular foundation of crumbling stone and concrete. That is the remains of the flour mill. Now filled with weeds, brush, and rusted metal, this is the only remaining remnants of Gravelville. A Morrison County historical marker summarizes the town's history. As I walked the village, it's easy to see why the location captivated the Grav-

elles. It still has all the earmarks of a place one would want to settle in and call home.

LINCOLN

1890-1954

CLASS C

APPROXIMATE LOCATION:
From Motley:
East on US Highway 10 for 8 miles. Left at County Road 3/320th Street for ¼ mile. Right on Azure Road for ½ mile.

Even though its beginnings were due to the railroad and the lumber, the lakes near Lincoln defined, sustained, and popularized the town and surrounding area. They still do. First inhabited by Native Americans, there were some early settlers, loggers and logging camps, and summer visitors in the region. Records indicate that an early summer resort, named Camp Lincoln, operated in the area. According to area historian Ella Hoover Topp, the Northern Pacific Rail-

Lincoln. (Courtesy of Shawn Hewitt)

road planned a cutoff line to the area. It is unclear if the summer resort operated before or after rail service to the area had been established.

Once there was rail service to Lincoln, the town and surrounding lakes area prospered. A post office was established in 1890. Elizabeth Bauman, an early settler, platted and recorded the town in 1903. There was a later addition to the town, next to and just south of Lincoln, called McKinley, but that was later vacated by court order.

An early hotel, built in 1908 boasted ten bedrooms, often used by visiting fishermen, traveling salesmen, railroad employees, and families anxious to experience the clean fresh air, the lakes, swimming, boating, and other lakeside activities. At about that same time, a steamboat offering recreational cruises on Fish Trap Lake. Later the hotel would add a third story and offer seventeen bedrooms. The hotel, later a restaurant, would be called the Lin Club. After nearly one hundred years it would close and later be torn down.

Hard to imagine now, as Ella Topp wrote, Fish Trap Lake covered most of the land (now a meadow), along Lincoln's main road, Old Highway 10 (now Azure Road). A steamboat hauled lumber from the mills, between Lake Alexander and Fish Trap Lake.

The town of Lincoln itself was thriving. It included a garage, two general stores, two hardware stores, two potato warehouses, a pool room/barbershop, a restaurant, a livestock loading yard, a bank, a depot, and engine pumphouse—water

for the steam engines was pumped from Fish Trap Lake and was always in plentiful supply. For a time, talk was to move the Staples watering facility to Lincoln. The town also had a two-story school and a church. Several nearby resorts also supported the town's businesses.

The bank, one store, and the church are still standing today. The bank and store are private residences, and the church is in a preserved status, lovingly cared for and maintained by the women of the Lincoln Ladies Aid. Built in 1912, the church is now over one hundred years old. Not in regular use, it does host special events. The old depot site is visible—vacant, but located along the tracks just across from the remaining buildings.

Though the town itself no longer exists, people still flock to the Lincoln area. Now known as Lincoln Lakes, the region is a destination for year-round visitors, residents, and lots of summer people. There are a few rural businesses, lots of resorts, campgrounds, and more. The clean fresh air, lakes, swimming, boating and other activities still captivate people, and Lincoln Lakes offers the perfect setting.

Norman County

Syre Today. (Courtesy of Andrew Filer)

SYRE

1891–1936
CLASS B
APPROXIMATE LOCATION:
From Ada:
East on MN 200 for 11 miles. Right on MN 32 for 8½ miles.
Left on MN 113.

Syre was a named for an early homesteader and was a Northern Pacific rail station. The agricultural town also consisted of an elevator, creamery, lumberyard, and a general store. The church steeple, saved from the church, was placed in the cemetery, where it still stands.

WHEATVILLE

1895–1910
CLASS A
APPROXIMATE LOCATION:
From Ada:
South on Minnesota 9 for 5½ miles. Right on County Road 33/150th Avenue for ½ mile.

At its peak in the late 1890s, Wheatville had a blacksmith, post office, store, lumberyard, a school, and two elevators. The post office was dissolved in the early 1900s when rural free delivery from Ada was established.

Syre Cemetery. (Courtesy of Andrew Filer)

Otter Tail County

CRAIGIE FLOUR MILL

NEAR THIS SPOT JAMES CRAIGIE OF ABERDEEN
SCOTLAND, WHO CAME TO OTTERTAIL COUNTY
ABOUT 1868 BUILT THE FIRST GRIST MILL IN
THE COUNTY IN 1870. THE MILL STONES AND
WHEEL WERE IMPORTED FROM SCOTLAND.
CRAIGIE AND HIS WIFE WERE DROWNED IN
OTTERTAIL LAKE IN 1872, AND AFTER LONG
LITIGATION THE MILL WAS
TORN DOWN.

Craigie Flour Mills Marker. (Courtesy of Scott Backstrom)

LEAF CITY
TRADING POST ON THE RED RIVER TRAIL
IN 1857, AND U. S. POSTOFFICE FROM 1857
TO 1860. THE SETTLEMENT WAS BROKEN UP
BY THE SIOUX OUTBREAK OF 1862

DEDICATED BY THE
OTTER TAIL COUNTY HISTORICAL SOCIETY
JUNE 26, 1938

Leaf City Marker. (Courtesy of Scott Backstrom)

Balmoral

1870-1905
CLASS A
APPROXIMATE LOCATION:
From Ottertail:
Minnesota 78 south for 6 miles. Historical marker and Balmoral Golf Course.

Arriving in Otter Tail County in 1861, the Craigies settled on the shores of Otter Tail Lake where a small creek runs into the lake. Honoring their Scottish homeland, James Craigie called their new home, Balmoral, after Queen Victoria's castle in Scotland.

Their lives were uprooted the next year, 1862, when the Sioux Uprising created an atmosphere of fear and apprehension across the Minnesota frontier. The Craigies and their daughter left, as did many settlers, for larger, more secure communities, such as Sauk Centre, which was the Craigies choice.

After their return to Balmoral, the hard-working husband and wife built a dam and gristmill. The History Museum of East Ottertail County writes that Mrs. Craigie worked as hard as any man, even traveling to St. Cloud in the frigid winter to bring back machinery for the mill. Area residents were happy to have a nearby mill and the flour, Snow Flake Flour, was reputed to be of high quality. In addition to the mill, one of the first in the county, the community included a post office that operated in three different periods from 1870 to 1905, a hotel, cheese factory, and school.

When daughter Annie Craigie turned eighteen, she fell in love and eloped with an area man and moved to Detroit.

On a gorgeous fall day in 1872, James and Mrs. Craigie, accompanied by a young Scottish woman (and wife to the Becker County auditor) went sailing. No one knows exactly what happened, but the boat capsized and all three passengers drowned. Their bodies were recovered later.

Upon the couple's death, there was an extended probate battle over ownership of the mill. James's brother and Mrs. Craigie's brother, claiming that Annie was not the Craigies' daughter, took over ownership of the mill. Annie appealed and was awarded ownership. Eventually, a new trial was ordered. The sensational trial, packed with spectators in the court room, finally ruled that Annie was the heir. She and her husband would operate the mill until 1879, when at age twenty-six, Annie died.

Today the area is a golf course and carries the village name, Balmoral. A historical marker, titled the "Craigie Flour Mill," and which incorporates the original mill stone and wheel, is located on the former town site.

Heinola

1873-1946
CLASS C
APPROXIMATE LOCATION:
From New York Mills:
County Highway 54 south for 1½ miles. Slight left onto County Highway 54/County 67. Continue to follow County 67 for 3½ miles.

An advertising campaign for a dairy products company proclaims, "It's the cows." The long-ago community of Heinola could make that same statement, for it was the cows, actually the milk, that was the mainstay of the town. The Cloverleaf Creamery Association was the principle business in the community for years.

The creamery provided a market for the local dairy farmers and with the town's central location, at the juncture of four townships, Deer Creek, Leaf Lake, Newton, and Otto, other businesses soon became part of the town. A general merchandise store, a cooperative mercantile store, grocery store, hardware store, coffee shop, two gas stations, barbershop, a blacksmith or two, shoemaker, feed store, dray (horse cart used for hauling), and also a salesman that sold insurance, windmills, and Metz cars would populate the town.

A local telephone company was established in July of 1909. Betty Lake, area historian, writes that the poles were hauled by horse, holes hand-dug, and poles erected manually. The switchboard and offices were in Heinola for twelve years until the company purchased the telephone exchange in New York Mills and moved the offices there. Service discontinued in 1953 when it was sold to Arvig's East Otter Tail County Telephone Company.

It wasn't all work. Recreational activities played a large role in the community. Heinola had its own town-sponsored baseball team. Organized in 1902, they even had their own bleachers. Other pursuits included basketball, gymnastics, dancing, and dramatics.

During the worst days of the Depression, the Workers Party, a socialistic learning political organization was active in the area. The local coffee shop was sold to the Worker's Party, and dances and meetings were held in Heinola as well as other local communities. There is no record as to how successful they were in their goals, but they did not stay long in the area.

As roads improved, residents traveled to larger towns to sell their products and to shop larger stores with more variety. The creamery closed in 1946, and the town faded. The last business in town was a gas station/convenience store. Today there are a few residences in the area.

HILLVIEW

1883-1907

CLASS C

APPROXIMATE LOCATION:
From Menahga:
Southwest on MN 87 for eight miles. Left onto County Highway 47 for 2 miles. Continue onto County Highway 19 for 2½ miles. Right onto County Highway 62.

Hillview Today. (Courtesy of Jana Timm)

Not only did Hillview have a bird's-eye view of the surrounding area and its history, it also played a prominent part in that history.

Back in the 1880s, it was the timber. A centennial supplement to the *Fergus Falls Daily Journal* reported that the area was rich in virgin forests. With trees 125 feet high and four feet across, settlers could earn twenty-five cents per railroad tie. The first settlers were Finnish, and the area has remained predominantly Finnish.

The lumber boom would keep three sawmills running for years. Hillview prospered with the logging activities and soon the town included a hotel, a livery, a blacksmith, a creamery, several stores, including the Hillview Store, as well as a service station, a car dealer, and a cheese plant. The post office, which began as Paddock in 1883 and changed to Hillview in 1907, was discontinued in 1907. The town was also known as Red Eye in its earliest days because of its location on the Red Eye River. Local country schools provided for education. Nearby halls hosted events and dances. One hall, a few miles from town was called the Red Eye Socialist Hall, it hosted meetings for area socialists. It later became the West Hall and finally a turkey barn. There was never a liquor store, though the store did sell beer for a while. Moonshine seemed to have been readily available. Temperance societies were alive and active for a few years.

Rob Ho, in the special edition of the local newspaper, writes of a Prohibition era murder in the community. Two local boys heading home from a dance in Wolf Lake hit another vehicle. Arguing over who caused the collision, the fracas turned ugly. The four men involved drove off. One, worried that the others might have been after his moonshine, took out a hunting rifle and shot the two men sitting in the rumble seat. The driver, fearing for his life, drove to nearby Hillview and called authorities. Supposedly, the alleged shooter hid out in the swamps. A few months later his decomposed body was found.

The Hillview Store was the town landmark, having been established in the early horse-and-buggy days of the community. The store was open for business for over one hundred years. Throughout its life, it also served as the Paddock Town Hall, 4-H meeting space, hosted dances, and held political rallies. The large seventy-foot-by-thirty-eight-foot, two-story building also had living quarters for the owners. Stocking a wide variety of goods, the store was a handy stop for area residents well into the twentieth century. Fresh coffee, local news, gas and oil, and candy for the kids was always available. Even today

Hillview Village. (Author's collection)

Hillview today. (Courtesy of Jana Timm)

Hillview Store Today. (Courtesy of Jana Timm)

many adults remember that candy. The store closed in the 1990s. An auction was held to dispose of the store's remnants. Those that attended recalled the unique and interesting items up for bid, especially the turn-of-the-twentieth-century brass-plated cash register.

As the timber supply was depleted and the railroads made the decision to bypass the town, Hillview slowly faded away. The store building, now a residence, still stands high on the hill overlooking the countryside. A few farms and residences and the Paddock Town Hall remain in the area.

LEAF CITY

1857-1860

CLASS A

APPROXIMATE LOCATION:
From Henning:
North on MN 108 for 6 miles. Isthmus between West and East Leaf Lake. Nearby public water access and boat ramp.

The narrow strip of land between West and East Leaf Lake has a lot of history in its past. The Otter Tail County website states that in the mid-eighteenth century, it is believed that the area was a wintering headquarters for early traders. The Northwest Trading Company had established a post there in the eighteenth century. In later years, the competing American Fur Company also built posts on the sites but the fur supply dwindled, and these posts were abandoned.

A large pink granite boulder was erected on the site by the Otter Tail County Historical Society in 1938. Attached to the boulder is a brass plaque that reads:

LEAF CITY—TRADING POST ON THE RED RIVER TRAIL IN 1857, AND U.S. POST OFFICE FROM 1857 TO 1860. THE SETTLEMENT WAS BROKEN UP BY THE SIOUX OUTBREAK OF 1862.

The marker still stands, and today the area is surrounded by resorts and lake cabins with a nearby public water access and boat launch.

The Minnesota Department of Transportation Roadside Development Structures Inventory reports that before the present day marker was erected there was a steel sign that read:

CITY—ALREADY A TRADING POST ON THE RED RIVER TRAIL IN 1857, A COLONY FROM CAMBRIDGE, MASSACHUSETTS SETTLED HERE IN THE SPRING OF 1858, AND A U.S. POST OFFICE WAS MAINTAINED FROM DEC. 2, 1857 TO APRIL 11, 1860. THE COMMUNITY DISAPPEARED WITH THE SIOUX OUTBREAK OF 1862, AND LEAF CITY BECAME ONE OF MINNESOTA'S MANY VANISHED TOWNS.

LUCE

1883-1948

CLASS C

APPROXIMATE LOCATION:
From Perham:
Highway 10 West for 3 ½ miles. Right onto County Highway 60 for 350 feet. Right on 403rd. Most of Luce is now under Highway 10. There are some remaining buildings in the area.

Gorman Township's only platted village was Luce, which was platted in 1884. The village was incorporated in 1905. Records show that the community en-

Luce Creamery. (Courtesy of the History Museum of East Ottertail)

compassed an area of 3,840 acres. In order to be granted a liquor license, a population of 600 residents was required. To meet that stipulation, the village's boundaries had to be stretched over a wide area. Upon incorporation, the liquor license was obtained and immediately a saloon called "The First and Last Chance Saloon" was built, so named because it was the first chance for travelers coming from the west to get an alcoholic drink (Frazee was on the Indian Reservation and no alcohol was sold on reservations). It was also the last chance for travelers from the east to get a drink before entering the reservation. The saloon would operate until the 1920s after which time there are no records of any saloons in the village.

Luce would grow quickly. A town band and the saloon brought many to the town on Fridays. During the day they would shop, and at night there would be dances. Luce had a livery barn, blacksmith, potato warehouse, general store, farm implement dealer, auto repair garage, creamery, hotel, and two restaurants, where it was advertised meals could be had at all times. A bank was also started but was abandoned in the 1920s. The auto mechanic would later become an electrician, and when the REA (Rural Electrification Administration) came to the area, he wired many area farmsteads.

Being a railroad town, Luce also had a depot that handled both freight and passengers. The depot was moved to Syre in Norman County in 1930, and moved again in 1970 to Ada, where it became part of the area's pioneer village. A large elevator, the Monarch, later the Peavey operated until 1931, when it was moved to North Dakota. In 1916, the History Museum of East Otter Tail County estimates that Luce had a population of 180. The post office was discontinued in 1931. The Luce Concrete Products Company began making septic tanks and cement blocks in 1945, operating until 1970. The school district closed in 1957.

Active, though declining, Luce was never the same after the "First and Last Chance Saloon" closed. Since a liquor license was no longer needed, the village opted to dissolve the incorpo-

ration. Highway 10 was being built and the village would be assessed, by the mile, for their share of the road construction costs. Records indicate that the books and the dissolution papers never reached Fergus Falls, the county seat, so Luce is still on the maps.

When Highway 10 was widened and made into a four-lane in the mid-1970s, the last of the town, including the buildings, half a dozen homes, and the Luce Concrete Products Company was moved.

Although most of Luce is under the highway, a few buildings remain in the vicinity.

OTTER TAIL CITY

1850-1894
CLASS C

APPROXIMATE LOCATION:
From Ottertail:
Highway 78 south to edge of town. Left on Highway 108 for one-fourth mile. Ottertail is just east of the old town site—Historical marker.

It can be confusing. Otter Tail is the county, the lake, and the river, and Ottertail the present-day city. At one time there was another, earlier town by the same name. Present-day Ottertail began in 1903, when the Soo Line Railroad came through the county. The other, Otter Tail City (two words) was a thriving village on the east side of Otter Tail Lake, just west of the present-day city.

John Crandall, in his history of the first town, *Boom and Bust*, writes that the 1858 platted town was six hundred acres stretching from Lake Buchanan to Otter Tail Lake and then south. That same year Otter Tail City would be designated the county seat. The 1860 census lists more than 200 inhabitants of the town. A post office was established in 1858 and was discontinued in 1863. It would reopen in 1874 and last until 1894. The Sioux Uprising saw the land office raided, and the town was nearly abandoned for the next six years. In 1868, R.L. Frazee would choose the town as the site of his new sawmill and new life would flow into the community.

Designated as a supply depot for the expanding Northern Pacific Railroad, the town burgeoned. By 1871, it was estimated that there were over 2,000 people in the town. With the railroad's construction headquarters based in Otter Tail as well, business flourished. Hotels, stores, and saloons seemingly appeared overnight. Saloons seemed to be the best business venture, estimates range on the number of saloons in the village, from a low of twenty-seven to a high of forty. The town also included a

Luce Station. (Courtesy of the History Museum of East Ottertail)

154

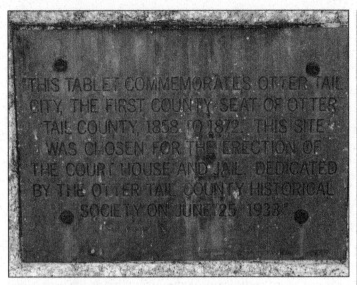

Otter Tail City Marker. (Courtesy of Scott Backstrom)

Given a second chance in 1904, history would repeat itself. Otter Tail City was surveyed by the Soo Line Railroad as a possible station town. Incorporated in 1904, and again unable to come to terms with landowners, the rail line was resurveyed, missing the town by a mile. The new town of Ottertail was platted just to the east of the old town site.

There is a historical marker at the old town site, and the St. Paul House, a former hotel and today a residence, still stands.

RICHDALE

1900-1916
CLASS A
APPROXIMATE LOCATION:
From Perham:
Highway 10 East for 3½ miles. Left of Haberham Street for 200 feet. Most of Richdale is now under Highway 10.

wholesale liquor store, hardware, brewery, blacksmith, carpenter, and all manner of gambling. It is said times were wild in the town and often catered to the shadier elements of society.

In 1871, the railroad wanted to purchase land for their depot, sidetrack, and other facilities. The owner of the land and the railroad could not agree on a price for the property. At an impasse, the railroad opted to run a new line from Wadena by way of Perham. It was the beginning of the end for Otter Tail City. Overnight the migration of businesses and customers began, saloons dried up due to lack of customers, and houses and businesses were moved. Fergus Falls became the new county seat. The land owner who could not make a deal with the railroad sold his land for one dollar an acre and was not heard from again.

Even though Richdale is still on some maps, you will be hard pressed to find any remnants of the town today. Platted as Richland in the early 1870s, it was later learned that a town by that name already existed so the name was changed to Richdale. Promptly upon its recording, there was a depot, wheat elevator, general store, and post office. The store operated until 1917 when it, and the store-keeper's home, were destroyed by fire. Two miles south of town was a country school. The community also had a Lutheran church, though it was later moved to New York Mills.

For many years, news briefs from Richdale appeared in the local newspapers, reporting events such as cattle being struck by lightning, hard luck stories during the Depression, and the comings and goings of residents.

In 1975, Highway 10 was expanded into a four-lane expressway with an overpass above the railroad tracks. Most of that overpass sits on the former town site.

Otter Tail City Marker. (Courtesy of Scott Backstrom)

STOD

1888–1906
CLASS C
APPROXIMATE LOCATION:
From Rothsay:
East on County Highway 24 for 3/12 miles. Left on County Highway 21 for 2 miles. Left on County 28—South Immanuel Church.

Northwestern Otter Tail County is farm country. The rich, fertile soil and the level land produces bumper harvests year after year. In the heart of this agricultural region stands South Immanuel Church, and cemetery, the only visible remnants of the town of Stod.

As a 1989 article in the *Pelican Rapids Press* reported, Stod, meaning "to stand still," was settled by Norwegian immigrants in the late 1880s and named for a village in their homeland. That same article, one of the few resources available, also summarized the village.

Stod, just a few miles from Rothsay, consisted of a creamery, store, and the church. The creamery operated year-round. Ice for the ice-house was cut from a nearby lake, Midboe. Cut into eighteen-inch square blocks and packed in sawdust, the ice lasted until late summer.

The store had a post office, the first in Trondhjem Township. It operated until 1906 when rural free delivery became available. The store-keeper, after many years, moved back to Norway, and the store had a succession of owners until its closure in 1913. The building was then used for community events. During World War I the Red Cross members and supporters met there to make sweaters and mittens for the troops.

The *Pelican Rapids Press* article states that before cars, a trip from Stod to Rothsay took half a day and to Pelican Rapids it took a full day. When cars became popular, it was easier to travel to larger towns, and the small businesses in smaller towns declined.

South Immanuel Church and the cemetery are still being used today.

TOPELIUS

1901–1916
CLASS A
APPROXIMATE LOCATION:
From New York Mills:
East on Highway 10 for 4 miles. Near intersection of Highway 10 and Topelius Drive.

A few years ago I visited Topelius, not even aware of its existence at the time. Heading from Bluffton to New York Mills, I had car trouble and sat on the shoulder of the road at the intersection of Highway 10 and Topelius Road while waiting for roadside assistance. The rural landscape gave no indication of the once vibrant town that had occupied the site. It was only when I was researching Otter Tail County's places of the past that I learned of Topelius. If I had known, I would have paid more attention.

Topelius, once known as Amboy and Benton's Crossing was lastly named by the Finnish settler to honor their homeland's nineteenth-century writer, educator, and editor Zachris Topelius. A fire had leveled the area in the late 1890s but as re-growth occurred, the village grew as well. Primarily a farmer's trading town and a station town on the Northern Pacific Railroad, the depot was busy twenty-four hours a day. Businesses in the community included two stores, a post office, two blacksmiths, a potato warehouse, garage, and a co-op creamery. Country schools provided education. Two churches were established, one with a cemetery

As transportation methods improved, Topelius declined. The History Museum of East Otter Tail County writes that a few remains and remnants (sidewalk pieces and block foundations) were visible as late as 1975. Since that time they have been cleaned up, and fields plowed. The cemetery remains just a short distance off Highway 10 along Topelius Road.

Pennington County

Erie Today. (Courtesy of Andrew Filer)

ERIE

1905–1938

CLASS B

APPROXIMATE LOCATION:
From Thief River Falls:
East on MN 1 for 21miles. Right on 350th Avenue NE for 3½ miles.

Owner and editor of the Eleven Towns newspaper, a publication that covered eleven townships, Alexander Lattimore named the town after his native Erie, Pennsylvania. A post office was established in 1905 and a settlement soon followed. The town, though declining, operated until the late twentieth century when the town's store closed.

HAZEL

1904–1954

CLASS B

APPROXIMATE LOCATION:
From Thief River Falls:
East on US 59 for 9½ miles. Right on County Road 3 for 2.8 miles.

The small settlement, once an agricultural town, now houses the Cenex Harvest States shipping facility.

Hazel today. (Courtesy of Andrew Filer)

Hazel Postcard. (Author's collection)

MAVIE

1907–1944

CLASS C

APPROXIMATE LOCATION:
From Thief River Falls:
East on MN 1 for 11 miles. Left on 250th Avenue for 1½ miles.

As settlers began arriving in 1904, they soon needed a place to purchase supplies and goods. By 1910, the town of Mavie, named after an early postmaster's daughter, and platted in 1914 on eleven acres, grew to meet those needs. Consisting of a creamery, blacksmith, dance hall, bank, hardware store, elevator, rail depot, livery, general stores, and a school and church, the town was thriving. Those early years, from 1910 to 1914 were Mavie's boom years. By 1921, the boom was over. In 1945, the grocery store and the school closed. Little remains of the community today.

Mavie. (Courtesy of the Pennington County Historical Society)

Mavie Today. (Courtesy of Andrew Filer)

Mavie Today. (Courtesy of Andrew Filer)

Pine County

Banning. (Courtesy of the Sandstone History and Art Center/Amy Troolin. Pine County History blog)

Banning. (Author's collection)

BANNING

1896–1912

CLASS F

APPROXIMATE LOCATION:
From Sandstone:
MN 23 East for 2 miles. Right for state park access road.

The Hinckley area's pink sandstone was so distinctive that architects called for it by name, "Hinckley Sandstone." It was the building material of choice in the early twentieth century. The stone was used throughout the Midwest and can still be seen in Minneapolis and St. Paul in such landmarks as the Minneapolis Courthouse and Pillsbury Hall on the campus of the University of Minnesota. Paver stones were used in the streets of the Twin Cities as well as other locations.

The stone was quarried along the Kettle River in Sandstone and a few miles upstream at a site first called Quarry and later renamed Banning, in honor of Civil War veteran and railroad contractor William Banning. The Banning Quarry was owned by Martin Ring, who had earlier been associated with the Sandstone Quarry. The Banning Quarry was smaller, with fewer employees, shipping out less product, and, as park naturalist Megan Johnsen wrote, "with fairly modern and impressive equipment." The quarry operated from 1892 until 1912. The Great Hinckley Fire of 1894 destroyed the quarry and the town and several lives were lost.

In 1896, with big plans for the quarry and big orders coming in, Ring platted a village large enough to house several hundred people. A spur line from Groningen was built, and business boomed. The quarry employed about 300 to 500 workers. Platted with six streets, Banning included a school, two hotels, a saloon, general stores, post office, several houses, and the two quarries. James Taylor Dunn, Banning historian,

wrote that there were community baseball games, dances, wrestling matches, and cribbage tournaments. Soon, an asphalt company joined the settlement. A 1911 election resulted in the building of a new water tower and pumping station.

Things looked prosperous for Banning, but it didn't last. Demand for the stone dropped dramatically. In July of 1911, a fire leveled most of the town. Many residents left, the store closed, and by 1912, only four families lived in Banning. A post office was no longer needed, and it was discontinued. The railroad tracks were pulled up in 1918. As Megan Johnsen wrote, the increased use of structural steel for building, repeated area fires, and the building pressures of World War I were the reasons for the quarry's closing. With the quarry closed, the settlement declined. Eventually the town was abandoned. The town site property was transfered to private ownership.

Efforts to preserve the town site, quarry, and scenic beauty of the Kettle River had been ongoing for years. First proposed as a park in 1934, it wasn't until nearly thirty years later, in 1963 that the Banning State Park bill was passed by the Minnesota Legislature, and the nearly 6,000-acre park was a reality. The quarry site and ten miles of the newly-designated Wild and Scenic River, the Kettle River, were encompassed in the park. Unfortunately, the town site, though surrounded by the park, remains in private ownership.

Banning State Park is a Minnesota treasure. Kayakers, canoeists, and nature lovers frequent the park and the river. Caution is noted as parts of the river are wild, with chutes, rapids and cascades that challenge even the most skilled water enthusiasts. For the rest of us, the scenery is breathtaking from the shore. A park trail parallels the river frontage.

The trail is also a self-guided walking trail through the old quarry. The two-mile trek is detailed on a park map/brochure with informational markers along the trail. A copy can be obtained at the park office. The brochure gives a brief history of

Banning. (Courtesy of the Sandstone History and Art Center/Amy Troolin)

Banning. (Courtesy of the Sandstone History and Art Center/Amy Troolin)

Banning Quarry Remains. (Author's collection)

the quarry and each point of interest is numbered, correlating with more information on the brochure and map. I can say, from first-hand experience, that the Quarry Trail is a must do activity—scenic, quiet, and a living history lesson for everyone, young and old. Sandstone remnants are visible along the trails, as are steep walls of granite with the drill bit marks. Massive stone walls from the power house appear as if from the mist.

Look closely inside the four walls, an artesian well is still flowing. The park brochure states that bottling water from the well was big business back in the day and was sold as far away as Chicago. Big boulders and benches provide rest on along the trail. A campground allows visitors the option of a longer visit.

Unfortunately, visitors are not allowed to visit the old town site. Surrounded by park land, the town site is on private property. If visiting, please respect the property owners and stay on state land. The town was not preserved and is now a hay field.

Banning Quarry Remains. (Author's collection)

Banning Quarry Remains. (Author's collection)

CHENGWATANA

1856-1873
CLASS G
APPROXIMATE LOCATION:
From Pine City:
East of Pine City on the Southeast Shore of Cross Lake and at the beginning of the lower course of the Snake River Dam.

First an Ojibwe village, Chengwatana, was, in 1856, designated the Pine County seat. At that time it was renamed Alhambra, but that name was not accepted and thus short-lived. The post office, established in 1856 kept the name Alhambra for just one year, and, in 1857, the name was again Chengwatana. The post office existed until 1873 when it was discontinued. The settlement was a frontier military post from 1862 to 1863.

When the railroad was constructed on the west shore of Cross Lake, a new village, Pine City (Chengwatana loosely translated is White Pine Town) became the thriving location. As Pine City flourished, Chengwatana declined. In 1870, Pine City became the new county seat of Pine County.

A historical marker is at the former town site with a more detailed marker along the railroad bridge crossing the Snake River in Pine City.

FORTUNA

1857-1887
CLASS G
APPROXIMATE LOCATION:
Originally north of Sandstone, it has been mostly absorbed by Sandstone.

Fortuna seemed to have everything it needed to be a success. Platted in 1857 and designated as a county seat, the settlement had an established stage relay station, water power, and vast forests of timber surrounding the town. In 1857, Fortuna was considered part of Buchanan County. The Sandstone History Club in its book on Sandstone history writes that the north, east, and west boundaries of Buchanan County were the same as present day Pine County.

The plat map shows a town one mile east and west and one-half mile north and south. Fortuna included a hotel and two parks. Later surveys showed foundations of a few buildings, one a thirty-five-foot-by-sixty-foot rectangle. A road bed was also visible.

By 1887, the population was estimated at 200. Speculation was that the financial panic of 1887 may have been a factor in the abandonment of the town and its further development. In 1860, the Minnesota Legislature dissolved Buchanan County and merged it with Pine County.

FRIESLAND

1896-1917
CLASS A
APPROXIMATE LOCATION
From Hinckley:
North on County Highway 61/Old Highway 61 for 5½ miles. Left on Friesland Road.

The advertisements touted the area's fertile soil and good farmland. No mention was made of the rocks. Still, the 1895 Theodore Koch Land Company ads, targeted at Koch's fellow Ducthmen, attracted many to the new development four miles north of Hinckley. By 1896, Friesland, named for a town in the Netherlands, was home to 400 people, most of them from the Netherlands. Friesland had a depot, hotel, boarding house, general store, post office, and land office. A town newspaper, *The Friesland Journal*, written primarily in Dutch lasted just a few weeks.

The rocky soil was difficult to farm. Without funds to improve the land and techniques, many Frieslanders moved on to other jobs and locations. By 1910, only the depot and one general store remained. A new school, built in Friesland's declining days lasted until consolidation with Sandstone in 1968. Primarily rural, the area is dotted with farms and private residences.

Friesland. (Courtesy of the Sandstone History and Art Center/Amy Troolin)

The Great Hinckley Fire of 1894 destroyed most of the early town. Residents were able to save the section house by hauling muddy water from a nearby slough. The depot burned, but no lives were lost. In 1918, Groningen had two general stores, three cream buyers, a potato warehouse, a few blacksmiths, a hotel, barber shop, bank, and school.

The little town lasted until the 1950s when the post office, general store, and bank closed. The area today is rural with the streets still bearing the village's name. Folks still arrive in Groningen via the old rail line. The rail tracks are long gone—the new path is a hiking and biking trail.

Friesland railroad. (Courtesy of the Sandstone History and Art Center/Amy Troolin)

Groningen today. The hiking/biking trail. (Author's collection)

GRONINGEN

1896/1954

CLASS A

APPROXIMATE LOCATION
From Sandstone:
MN 123 South for 1 mile. MN 123 South turns slightly left and becomes MN 23 West for ½ mile. Continue onto County Highway 28 for ½ mile. Right on Groningen Road for 3 miles. Right on Groningen Loop.

Groningen had its own version of New York City's New Year's Eve crystal ball. As Amy Troolin posted in her Pine County History blog, at the turn of the century, residents of Groningen celebrated the arrival of 1900 at the schoolhouse. Building a bonfire out of straw barrels soaked in kerosene, they made a sign with 1899 on one side and 1900 on the other. As the clock struck midnight the bales were lit, and revelers, residents, and train passengers saluted the New Year.

Begun as a railroad station, Groningen, originally called Miller Station, was renamed for the residents' Dutch homeland. Attracted by a fellow Dutchman's land sales advertisements, the town grew quickly.

MISSION CREEK

1876/1909

CLASS A
APPROXIMATE LOCATION:
From Hinckley:
I-35 South for 2½ miles. Exit Ramp 180 for MN 23 West. Left on MN 23 East for ½ mile. Third left on T-181.

By September of 1894 most of the timber had been cleared from the surrounding area. The logging company had shut down most of its operations and was ready to move on to new locations and new timber resources. The timber in the region near the small village of Mission Creek had been profitable for years. The first mill had been built in 1878. At its peak, one hundred men and nearly one hundred oxen had processed 75,000 feet of lumber a day. The company town, built to support the logging industry had a mill, a general store, hotel, blacksmith, school, and twenty-six homes.

The spring and summer of 1894 had been exceptionally dry. For several days, residents had been battling small fires through-

Groningen Store. (Shawn Hewitt Collection)

Groningen today. (Author's collection)

out the region. Even though it was windy and dry, mill workers burned a huge pile of stumps near town. That decision would prove to be life-saving.

Later that day near Hinckley, just three miles north of Mission Creek, the scattered fires fed off the wind. A temperature inversion with the cool air fueling the flames and a land covered with timber slashings, stumps, and brush prompted the fire to rage. Growing too big too fast, the flames flared forty to eighty feet high. It was impossible to stop or to outrun.

Daniel James Brown in his history of the Great Hinckley Fire, *Under a Flaming Sky*, writes that by mid-afternoon fighting the fire was futile. He describes that broiling heat, the cinders falling, the blazing branches falling all around, and the air so hot it cooked the ground. Residents of Mission Creek covered their bodies with wet blankets and buried their faces in the warm soil of the potato patch. The intensity of the flames destroyed everything in its path.

For nearly an hour, the fire roared through Mission Creek. All of the town's residents did survive the fire, and none were seriously injured. The town itself did not survive. Every building but one was leveled. Had those stumps not been burned

that morning, the heat would have intensified and most likely many lives would have been lost. Brown relates that, after the fire, residents dug the potatoes out of the still warm ground, finding them already roasted. A large deer, trapped in a barbed wire fence and badly burned, was killed. That evening, in the one remaining building, the residents ate potatoes and venison.

Mission Creek was destroyed. Except for the general store, the town was not rebuilt. The store operated until the 1920s or 1930s. After the fire, the area was settled by farmers. Amy Troolin in her Pine County History blog tells of one farmer saying there were 400 stumps on an acre. They were so close together he had trouble walking among them.

Today, the only remnant of Mission Creek is the cemetery and a memorial marker.

Mission Creek School. (Courtesy of the Sandstone History and Art Center/Amy Troolin)

Polk County

Dugdale (Tilden Junction) today. (Courtesy of Andrew Filer)

DUGDALE

1884-1940s

CLASS A

Approximate Location:
From Red Lake Falls:
Highway 32 South towards Fertile. Just south of MN 32/2
Junction.

During World War II, women stepped up to take the place of men deployed in the war effort. Employed in jobs traditionally reserved for men, women embraced the opportunity and proved well-suited for any task and challenge. Dugdale, also going by the name of Tilden Junction, saw two such enterprising women manage the rail depot in the 1940s. Deftly handling all of the tasks—throwing switches, operating the telegraph, selling tickets, and handling freight—the women were vital to the operation of the depot.

Founded in the late 1880s, Dugdale was a rail station. Soon after the depot was built, a hotel, store with post office (1888 to 1927), gas station, and a two-story brick school were added. The Polk County Historical Society writes that the school was unique for its time, the early 1900s, in that it was a consolidated school.

The school had three teachers, one of whom lived in a spare room on the second floor. Modern for its time, it had running water and steam heat. There were even horse-drawn school buses.

Records do not indicate anything about the decline and demise of the town.

MALLORY

1880-1916

CLASS A

APPROXIMATE LOCATION:
From East Grand Forks, east on Highway 2 approximately 7
miles.

Aye! The Scottish are a proud people, proud of their heritage, their homeland and their national poet, Robert Burns.

Settling on land not yet surveyed, the Scottish immigrants from Canada, were called squatters. In 1874, once the land was recorded, they were able to make their claims legal. One of the first things they did was organize a Burns Club. Each January, the Scottsmen would celebrate with a dinner and

Tilden Junction (Dugdale) today. (Courtesy of Andrew Filer)

dancing until dawn. The festivities drew people from all corners of the region, some bringing the train to partake in the event. The evening was a family affair. The Polk County Historical Society writes that when the children would tire, they would put the sleeping children on shelves in the cloak room and soon they would be nestled beneath the latecomers' wraps. Often the activities would end just in time to start early morning chores.

Upon arriving, the hard-working settlers set about building a community, with a depot, post office, store, church, school, and a town hall.

In 1978, hoping to be included in a planned heritage center, three of Mallory's original log buildings were dismantled, piece by piece, and rebuilt in East Grand Forks. There are still a few families in the area.

Mallory today (above and top). (Courtesy of Andrew Filer)

Red Lake County

Dorothy church. (Common use)

Dorothy. (Common use)

Dorothy. (Courtesy of Andrew Filer)

DOROTHY

1898-1908/1920-1945

CLASS C

APPROXIMATE LOCATION:
From Red Lake Falls:
East on County 13 for 11½ miles. Left on County 3 for 3½ miles.

Father and son, Reme and Louis Hance settled on adjoining tracts of land in Red Lake County. Arriving in the 1870s, from Austin, Minnesota, they set out to homestead their quarter sections. The provisions of the Homestead Act required the building of a dwelling on each claim, and the pair complied. Building one cabin, half on Reme's section and half on Louis's, the two shared their homes and their work.

When the Northern Pacific Railroad extended their line with a spur through Red Lake County, the town of Dorothy developed along the tracks. A much-needed grain elevator was among the first businesses established. Louis's son James operated the elevator and was a major force in the growth of the community. In time, James would build a large mercantile, establish a post office and form the Hance Oil Company. He would also be one of the founding fathers in the creation of St. Dorothy's Catholic Church.

Amateur theater was very popular in Dorothy. The Red Lake County Historical Society writes that the Dorothy Dramatic Club would host theatrical plays and presentations on an on-going basis for over twenty years. People from all over the region would attend.

Another mainstay of the community was St. Dorothy's Catholic Church. In the early days of the township, Mass was held in private homes. A parish was organized in 1918. Funds were raised, and in 1919 construction began on the church. Sixty-five families made up parish membership. One of the early priests, Father Bossus, arrived in Dorothy in 1926. Times were not easy for Father Bossus as the Depression hit the area hard. Yet the church grew to about eighty families during those years.

During Father Bossus's last years at St. Dorothy's, the priest's eyesight began to fail. When his eyesight was restored by cataract surgery, he was so grateful that he built a shrine to the Blessed Virgin Mary on a knoll a short way from Dorothy, near Huot and the state (now county) park.

A succession of priests ministered to the church over the years. A fire in 1962 destroyed the bell tower and steeple. The steeple was removed, and the church continued on until its closure in 2000. It is a private residence today.

John Thibert, Red Lake County Historical Society president, a descendant of early settlers, writes that today Dorothy has about half a dozen homes. The school house is used as the township hall. The store and elevator closed in the 1970s. The elevator is still a landmark of the region. As transportation improved, the need for local businesses declined and the town faded away.

GARNES

1896-1910

CLASS A

APPROXIMATE LOCATION:
From Oklee:
MN 222 North for ½ mile. Continue onto County Road 5 for 4 miles. Left on County 1 for one mile. Two farmsteads mark the old town site.

Railroad towns were few and sparsely located in the early years of Red Lake County. Without roads and only rudimentary, burdensomely slow transportation methods, it was extremely difficult, if not impossible, for settlers to get necessities and supplies. Stores and businesses had to be centrally located and within easy distance to the homesteaders. Garnes was one of the early centers in Red Lake County.

The first store in Garnes was built in the late 1890s. Before long, a post office (from 1896 to 1910), a blacksmith, feed mill, town hall, schools, and a cheese factory would make up the business district of the town. Residents welcomed the cheese factory as most had cows, and the cheese factory provided a much-needed source of income. A church was built three miles east of Garnes. Destroyed by fire, it would be rebuilt in 1936. The church and cemetery still remain.

When the Soo Line Railroad extended to Oklee and better transportation methods became an option, Garnes, the town, would cease to exist. Two farmsteads mark the old town site. The township still retains the name.

GRIT

1898-1913

CLASS A

APPROXIMATE LOCATION:
SE Quarter of Section 19—Equality Township

I've heard the tale of and seen the movies, never realizing that Minnesota had its own version of a land rush. As the *Red Lake Falls* reported in December of 1902, on May 15th,

1896, at the stroke of 9:00 A.M., the rush was on! The reporter observed that all manner of men, of all nationalities, and every conceivable form of transportation from foot to horse and buggy, were poised to rush off, all with hopes of laying claim to their own piece of land. Previously part of the Red Lake Reservation, the millions of acres of land were open for the taking. Equality Township would be established out the new territory. It was also reported that those that had traveled lightly had a distinct advantage. The area had been inundated with torrential rains for a month or more, and the soil was literally waterlogged.

The first settlement in the new township was in Section 19. Appropriately named Grit, as it took a lot of it to carve a life out of the wilderness. The settlement included a the township's first store and post office. Even though getting supplies over the nearly twenty miles of impassable roads was difficult, it was said that the store was never out of supplies, especially the necessities.

Today, Grit is a field.

HUOT

1881-1937
CLASS C

APPROXIMATE LOCATION:
From Red Lake Falls:
County Road 11 for 7 miles. Right on County Highway 3 for 1 mile. Second right for 1/3 mile. Straight on County 104 for ½ mile. To the Northeast is the Old Crossing Treaty Wayside Park and Huot Cemetery.

Few places in Minnesota are as historically significant as Huot. In the mid-1800s, the heavily-traveled Red River Oxcart Trail was the highway of its time. Stretching over 400 miles, the system of trails traversed western Minnesota to Pembina, North Dakota, and on to the Hudson Bay Company's post at Fort Garry (now Winnipeg) Canada. The carts, piled high with furs, trade goods, and supplies, were the main link between St. Paul and Canada. Along the routes, rivers and creeks had to be crossed and one of the most important fords was at the Red Lake River, known as Old Crossing.

Near the crossing stood a large cottonwood tree with a wood box nailed to the trunk that served as an early post office. Oxcart drivers would pick up or drop off letters as they passed through. In 2000, lightning struck the tree leaving only a stump remaining.

Perhaps one of the most significant events in Minnesota history took place at the Crossing in 1863. It was then that the Ojibwe/Chippewa signed a treaty with the U.S. government, ceding nearly twelve-million acres of land, roughly 180

Huot. (Courtesy of Andrew Filer)

miles in length by 127 miles in width. The Ojibwe received $510,000 and a few trade goods and gifts. Today the area is a county (former state) park, Old Crossing State Wayside Park. Within the park stands a life-sized bronze statue of an Ojibwe man holding a peace pipe.

By the time the township was created in 1879, a rich historical legacy belonged to the area. The new township was given the name Louisville after Louis Huot who had founded the thriving village of Huot on the banks of the Red Lake River. For years Huot had been a local center of activity and included a general store, creamery, blacksmith, and a Catholic Church. The Huot store would operate well into the late twentieth century—over 100 years in business.

Several schools and a town hall were also part of the community. The town hall burned to the ground in 1940. A vote was taken to approve the construction of a new building but the vote failed. Town hall meetings were then held in the basement of St. Dorothy's Church in nearby Dorothy. John Thibert, Red Lake County Historical Society president, writes that the last remaining country school in Red Lake County was just west of Huot. It closed in 1966 and was torched by vandals that same year. The church in Huot was closed when St. Dorothy's was opened. Slowly Huot, its businesses and residents would fade away. Today there are a few private homes at the old town site, one of them the store that closed in the 1970s. The Old Crossing State Wayside Park with camping, hiking, and historical markers is nearby as is the Huot cemetery. Also near the park is the Blessed Virgin Mary Shrine erected by St. Dorothy pastor Father Brossou in thanks for his returned eyesight.

LAMBERT

1883-1912

CLASS A

APPROXIMATE LOCATION:
From Oklee:
MN 222 for 1½ mile. Left on MN 92 for 1½ mile.

E ager to take advantage of the Soo Line Railroad's extended service in northwestern Minnesota, towns began to spring up all along the new route. One of those newly founded towns was Oklee, named for Scandinavian settler Ole K. Lee.

Just a mile from the new townsite was the older, more established community of Lambert. Founded in the late 1880s by predominantly French settlers, Lambert included a hotel, blacksmith, three stores, a post office, school/town hall, several residences, a Catholic Church, and a cheese factory.

The Lambert Cheese Factory was located in a small settlement a mile southeast of Lambert known as Bucktown. Changing ownership many times, the factory would process anywhere from 1,500 to 4,700 pounds a day. The Red Lake Historical Society writes that a 1902 newspaper article estimated that area farmers averaged about thirty-five dollars a month from milk sales.

Previous to construction of the Catholic Church in the late 1890s, the region had been served by a mission priest that conducted services in private homes. Land for the new church, rectory, and cemetery was donated by an area resident.

In 1917, the majestic church was divided into two sections.

The Red Lake County Historical Society writes that the east half of the parish consisted of approximately eighty families, and the west half had ninety families. When the church was split, the east half of the building went to Brooks and the west half moved to Oklee. Moving the large church was a precarious undertaking and quite a sight to see. A city history reports that the church was lifted and set on wooden blocks while the foundation was being built. A strong wind vibrated the church so violently that the church bells rang.

The church wasn't the only building to relocate. Between 1910 and 1916, nine out of Lambert's sixteen buildings had moved to Oklee. Five were torn down. Today, the old church cemetery, used until 1915, and a few farmsteads are all that remain at the Lambert town site.

ROLAND

1910-1917

CLASS A

APPROXIMATE LOCATION:
From Oklee:
North on MN 222 for ½ mile. Continue onto County Road 5 for 4 miles. Right on County Road 1 for 4 miles. Left on County Road 10 for 2½ miles. Left to stay on County Road 10 1/5 mile. North side of river.

O ne of the first projects completed after the reservation lands had been opened up for settlement, was the building of a bridge over the Clearwater River.

Lambert. (Courtesy of the Red Lake County Historical Society)

Roland Today. (Courtesy of Andrew Filer)

It wasn't long before a store was built at the river site to accommodate the increased traffic to the area. In addition to the store, a post office existed from 1910 to 1917. Two years after the store was opened, a creamery, with butter as its chief product, was built across from the store. Limited by the creamery's small size, the farmers voted to close the facility in 1933.

Changing ownership many times, the store closed in 1954. Years later, a dance hall, the Silver Star, occupied the site for many years. In the 1970s, a boat launch operated on the grounds.

TERREBONNE

1881–1915
CLASS C

APPROXIMATE LOCATION:
From Red Lake Falls:
South on MN 32 for 3½ miles. Left on MN 92E for 6 miles.
St. Anthony of Padua Church, cemetery, and shrines are
still standing.

When the French-Canadians from Montreal arrived in Red Lake County in 1879, they were the first "white or native" settlers in the area. Christening the community Terrebonne, French for "good earth," they set about building a community, starting with the church.

In the beginning, Mass was held in the home of Louis Cadieux, his being the first home built in the town. Cadieux donated ten acres of land, and in 1882 a church and cemetery were established. The church, St. Anthony of Padua Catholic Church, was built on a rise along present Highway 92 six miles from Red Lake Falls. A succession of priests would minister the community. In 1895 a new, larger church was constructed. In 1930, two outdoor shrines, one to honor the Sacred Heart and the other the Blessed Virgin Mary and St. Bernadette were added. Improvements were made through the years until the church's closing in 2000.

St. Anthony's Terrebonne. (Courtesy of the Red Lake County Historical Society)

Growing quickly, the community soon included a general store, blacksmith, school, a physician, a lawyer, hotel, harness shop, cheese factory, an elevator, a restaurant referred to as an "eating place," a few residences, and the Terrebonne Milling Company.

The mill, built in 1884, was on the Clearwater River. Three years later it was destroyed by fire and was rebuilt one year later. The second mill, as described in a Red Lake County Historical Society article, was three-stories high. It had state-of-the-art equipment and the flour was of the highest quality. With a capacity of 400 barrels a day, the mill was so busy it operated day and night. It took three bushels of grain to make one hundred pounds of flour. In 1911, the river water level was so low that the mill was grinding grain part time until a diesel engine was installed. Again, fire would strike, burning the mill to the ground in January of 1915. By Thanksgiving of that year, the mill was operating again.

The third mill was the largest, three-stories high with an attached warehouse. In later years the warehouse was enlarged and a garage added. Roller mills replaced the grindstones. Water power was used until 1931. Electricity came in 1941.

The mill operated year-round even during the Depression and throughout World War II. Products produced were LaBelle Flour (the highest quality), Snoball Flour (second in quality), bran, wheat flour and a breakfast cereal, Buddies Breakfast Food.

Improved transportation and competition from larger, more modernized mills would end Terrebonne's obsolete and outdated milling days. On July 4th, 1954, a massive combustion explosion and raging fire would destroy the mill. It would not be rebuilt.

The town of Terrebonne had been slowly declining. In the 1970s the small superette/grocery closed followed by the church in 2000. The church, cemetery and shrines still stand on the knoll on Highway 92.

WYLIE

1883-1937

CLASS A

APPROXIMATE LOCATION:
From Red Lake Falls:
County 13 NE for seven miles. Right on County 9 for 2 miles. On left.

Generally, Minnesota townships are six miles by six miles in area. There are exceptions to that layout and Wylie Township in Red Lake County is one of them. Prior to 1910, the entire township had been part of Red Lake County. When the county lines were redrawn, to form Pen-

Wylie Today. (Courtesy of Andrew Filer)

nington County, Wylie Township was reconfigured as well.

In 1911, the two boards of supervisors, one from Polk Centre Township in Pennington County and one from Polk Centre Township in Red Lake County, met to divide the assets of the township and to form two separate entities. When the details were worked out it was decided that Pennington County would retain the Polk Centre name and Red Lake County township would be renamed Wylie, adopting the name of the region's thriving village. Also determined at the meeting was the layout of the newly formed Wylie Township. Instead of the usual six-by-six-mile layout, Wylie is two miles by six miles in area.

Wylie, located on the Great Northern Railroad mail line from Crookston to Thief River Falls, provided twice-daily rail service for passengers, freight, and mail. In addition to railroad facilities, the town included a wide array of businesses including a general store with an upper level used for dances, two grocery stores, a hardware, a lumberyard, a harness and shoe shop, a barber, three elevators, a milling company, two cream stations, a hotel, a well driller, a church, a cheese factory, and more. The cheese factory burned in 1912 and was not rebuilt. The Red Lake County Historical Society writes that the town blacksmith was considered one of the very finest, able to engineer almost anything with nothing too intricate for him. An experimental bank was started in 1901 and became a big success.

Education was important to the region's residents, and the township had three schools. One of the larger, known as the Black River School is used today as the township hall. John Thibert, president of the local historical society and descendent of early pioneers to the area, writes that after the railroad from Dorothy to St. Hilaire was taken up, Wylie faded. The church merged with one in Red Lake Falls in 1958 and the building was later torn down. Today there are a few area homes.

Wylie Today. (Courtesy of Andrew Filer)

Wylie Today. (Courtesy of Andrew Filer)

Wylie Today. (Courtesy of Andrew Filer)

Roseau County

Pelan. (Courtesy of the Roseau County Historical Society)

Pelan Park Blacksmith. (Courtesy of the Roseau County Historical Society)

Pelan Halfway House. (Courtesy of the Roseau County Historical Society)

Pelan Park Trappers Cabin. (Courtesy of the Roseau County Historical Society)

St. Pauli's Pelan Park. (Courtesy of the Roseau County Historical Society)

DUXBY

1897-1938

CLASS A

APPROXIMATE LOCATION:
From Roseau:
North on MN 310 for 1 mile. Left on County 16/330th Street for 7 miles. Right on MN 89 for 2 miles. Left on County 10/350th Street for 5 miles. Duxby/Immanuel Cemetery will be nearby.

The roads were so bad, locals called them gumbo. Thick, mucky swampland and the slough made it impossible to travel, especially during the wet seasons. Because of the difficulty in traveling long distances, smaller, inland hamlets and towns became practical. Duxby was one of those. Combining two Norwegian words, "dux" for ducks and "by" meaning town, Duxby was aptly named as the nearby river was full of ducks.

With homesteaders flocking to the area, Duxby grew quickly. A post office was established in 1897 and was first located in a home. Later it operated out of the store. The store carried a wide variety of items: dry goods, decorative and "pretty" gift items, hardware, farming supplies, and groceries. Groceries were stocked in bulk, and people purchased what they needed or could afford. A gas pump and cream stop were also part of the store. The store would purchase cream and eggs from the local residents with the cream being tested and the eggs candled on site. The store closed in the 1930s.

Music was an important part of life in Duxby. In 1916, it had a brass band. Later, the Westerners, a local music group provided music for the many barn dances in the 1930s and 1940s. Immanuel Lutheran Church had both men's and women's choir that met weekly. A mid-summer festival and picnic was held annually.

Duxby had a log school house as early as the 1890s. Well attended, the schools always had a large enrollment, fifty-two at one time. A new school was built in 1913. A well for the school was dug using a horse-powered well digger in 1914. Some say that well is still flowing. The school closed in 1946 when it consolidated with the Ross-Duxby-Pinecreek district, later that district would merge with Roseau. The school building served as a church, town hall, meeting hall, recreation center, and (as of the early 1990s) was the Pohlitz Town Hall.

FOX

1891-1937

CLASS A

APPROXIMATE LOCATION:
From Roseau:
West on MN 11 for 6 miles. Left on 330th Avenue for 160 feet. Right. Just south of MN 89/11 Intersection.

Once the center for social life and Fourth of July celebrations, the village of Fox thrived until the 1920s when most of the buildings in town burned.

Platted in 1891, a post office was established that same year and operated until it was discontinued in 1937. At its peak, Fox had an elevator, a lumberyard, a blacksmith, a livery, a railroad depot, a stockyard, a cream station, a restaurant-turned-dance hall, and two other dance halls. A body shop was built in the 1940s and was operated by several different owners over the years until it burned in the late 1980s. A gas station/convenience store occupied that site until the building was later moved to Roseau.

The Fox school was also a center of activity. Programs, town elections, and basket socials were held at the school. The building continued to be used for town business until the district consolidated with Roseau in 1946.

PELAN

1888-1938

CLASS A /CLASS F

APPROXIMATE LOCATION:
From Greenbush:
West on MN Highway 11 for approximately 10 miles. Near intersection of MN Highway 11 and 490th. Pioneer Park is a bit further west on MN Highway 11.

Today, Kittson and Roseau counties are adjacent to each other in northwestern Minnesota. Prior to 1895 they were one. In that year the eastern part of Kittson County was separated from the larger county and Roseau County was born.

Pelan, at times attributed to both counties had me perplexed as to which county to classify it under. Historical records conflict as to Pelan's lineage. Pelan, situated on the newly drawn border of both counties, was separated by the river, the western side Kittson, the eastern Roseau. Post office records provide little clarification. From 1888 to 1913 the official records state Pelan was in Kittson County. Lightning struck the early post office, burning it to the ground. From 1913 until 1938, when the post office was discontinued, the Pelan post office is listed as in Roseau County.

Dane Nordine, summarizing Ralph Johnson's earlier essay, writes that most of the community was situated on the Kittson County side of the river and was fast approaching a population of 175. Pelan voted to incorporate in 1903. The petition was approved by the county commissioners in Hallock, Kittson County, that same year. Since the historical record of Pelan is shared by and intertwined with both counties, this history of Pelan will include both counties.

When ancient glacial Lake Agassiz receded, it left a distinct impact on the land. One of the features, Campbell Beach, or as it is commonly called, the Sand Ridge, forms much of today's Highway 111, which runs through northwestern Minnesota. Where the southern branch of the Two Rivers crosses the Sand Ridge, the town of Pelan was located. The area had first been called Two Rivers Crossing or Twin Lake City.

The crossing area had long been a center of activity and an important area to Native Americans. At one time it had been part of the old Native American and fur trade trail from Lake of the Woods to Pembina. From Pembina, the fur would travel on to St. Paul via the Red River and the Red River Oxcart trail. It is said the area was once the site of a battle between the Dakota and the Ojibwe and that there were several burial mounds in the area, much more distinct in elevation than today. Agriculture, time, and erosion reduced the mounds to such an extent that they would be hard to locate today.

Prior to 1890, few white settlers were in the area. Some of the first included wealthy Englishman, Charles Pelan, for whom the community was named. Pelan started a cattle ranch, and the others didn't stay long. In 1884, Hans Olson, considered one of the founders of Pelan, took up a claim, raised cattle, and opened a blacksmith business. Another early settler was Peter Lofgren, who established the first store in the village.

Available government homesteads opened the way for settlers to come to the area and to fulfill a dream of claiming and owning their own land. The first to settle in the area were of Swedish descent, having come from North Dakota where they found the best homesteads had already been taken. A rumored Native American uprising in 1891 slowed homesteading down for a short while. When the rumors proved unfounded, settlers again flowed to the area.

In 1903, the village was incorporated, with approval granted by the Kittson County commissioners in Hallock. At one time the town included, three general stores, a bank, three saloons, a boarding house, a newspaper, a roller flour mill, a creamery, a land office, a blacksmith, two livery barns, a restaurant, a pool

hall, a meat market, doctors of varying integrity, and a few lawyers. Dane Nordine said that from 1900 to 1903 stores were so busy they employed six to nine clerks in Lofgren store alone.

Arguably the biggest and most important establishment was the Pelan Hotel and Halfway House, so named because of its distance between Stephen and Roseau, a seventy-five-mile trip. It was the stop-over place for the stage route including food and lodging. In the early days, trips were made once weekly. In later years, with two stages, the Kitty and the Medora, trips were made daily, in both directions. At the time, Nordine writes that this was Minnesota's longest stage coach route.

It was said that stage coach horses were unruly and downright dangerous at times. The stage schedule was unreliable at best, yet the coach line had a good reputation. When blizzards would stop the railroad cold, the stage always got through. In the coldest months, an enclosed caboose stage was used complete with its own wood-burning stove.

Pelan did have its wild side. Liquor and gambling were big issues. Sales were wide open and resulted in disorderliness. Blind Piggers (unlicensed alcohol vendors) enjoyed a brisk business. A Templer Lodge, anti-alcohol group, tried to eliminate the sale of liquor. In early 1903, authorities from Hallock moved in and arrested the illegal sellers. Licensing of alcohol sales began, and Pelan went from having three saloons to having five.

Most of Pelan's residents were of Swedish and Norwegian ethnicity and primarily Lutheran, though there were a few German and Polish Catholics. Disagreements did arise but for the most part the community worked together. Building the school was one of differing viewpoints but issues were worked out and the first school was held in a log hut. A twenty-four-foot-by-twelve-foot school house that was built had anywhere from twenty to fifty students attending.

The summer of 1903 saw Pelan at the peak of its growth. Its decline would begin after that year. Many reasons contributed to the town's demise. Ralph Johnson wrote of two primary causes. First the railroad bypassed Pelan. The Soo Line extended from Mahnomen to Thief River Falls. At first it was thought the line would go through Pelan on its way to Winnipeg, but in the end, it passed nine miles to the west, saving the railroad three miles of track. Johnson states that was the beginning of the end for Pelan and the start of Karlstad. James J. Hill and his Empire Builder extended through the area of Greenbush, dealing a double blow to Pelan. The community would not survive. Businesses immediately began to move to the two newer, thriving communities.

The other reason for Pelan's demise was the fact that the soil in the area was unproductive. Farming was difficult and farmers were unable to provide a living.

By 1910, little was left of Pelan.

PELAN PIONEER PARK

Known in the 1930s as Pelan Battleground Park, the park was located on the site of an 1857 battle. Summarized in the Greenbush Centennial book, the Dakota occupied Minnesota's forested areas. The Ojibwe, armed with rifles obtained from the French, drove the Dakota from the lush forests of Minnesota to the prairies of North and South Dakota and even further westward. Unhappy with this forced removal, the Dakota would periodically return to do battle over their former territory.

According to the Ojibwe, the last battle between the two tribes in the area took place at the site of the present day park. After a two-day bloody and fierce battle in terms of those engaged, the Dakota left the area. For many years the Ojibwe would celebrate their victory at the battle site.

In 1937, the Greenbush Community Band obtained the battleground site and created a park. The next year the band hosted a get-together with a powwow, theatrical performances, music, ball games, and food. It is said there were over 10,000 in attendance. The Greenbush newspaper predicted it was an attendance record that "would stand for many a day."

Efforts were made to designate the park as a state park but legislation failed. In 1939 the band approached Roseau County with the idea of a county park. Roseau County took title to the property and appointed the Community Band responsible for operation and maintenance of the grounds. A community-wide organization came together to clean and develop the area.

Governor Harold Stassen and a crowd of nearly 12,000 celebrated the pioneers of the area with a 1939 event. The following years saw a ball park created and many local presentations and programs. With the advent of World War II, the Greenbush Community Band disintegrated and the park fell into disrepair and neglect for several years.

A non-profit community corporation was formed in 1976 and took over responsibility of the park, now officially named Pelan Pioneer Park. The corporation acquired many historic buildings, including the Pauli Lutheran Church from across the street. Other buildings were also added including a one-room schoolhouse, the Soo Line depot from Karlstad, a general store, a trappers cabin, and the blacksmith business. Repairs were made by community volunteers. The Sentence to Serve crew even helped with the work. There is also a picnic shelter at the park. The cemetery still stands on the original church site.

In 2004, a centennial celebration was conducted at the Pauli Church. A turkey dinner with all the trimmings, music, self-guided tours of the buildings, wagon rides, games, and an historical presentation on Pelan were part of the activities. Throughout the years, several other events have been held at the park, including presentations, family reunions, weddings, scouting events, and more. The park board continues to improve the park and its historical legacy is strong.

Winner Town Site, (Courtesy of Andrew Filer)

PINECREEK

1896-1975

CLASS A

APPROXIMATE LOCATION:

From Rosseau:
Northwest on MN 11 for 6 miles. Slight right on MN 89 North for 10 miles. Slight right on 310th Avenue. Right on 400th Street. If you continue on MN 89, you will come to Pine Creek Wayside Park and eventually the U.S./Canadian border. Security restrictions will not allow visitor access.

Winner Silo. (Courtesy of Andrew Filer)

Farming was good and crops abundant in Pinecreek, or so the homesteaders had heard. Wanting to see if the tales were true, several Portland North Dakota neighbors traveled to the region in the spring of 1889 to have a look. The liked what they saw. Returning to North Dakota to take care of their farms, the men packed up their families and their belongings and moved to Pinecreek in the fall of that same year. Those first settlers cleared their land and started their wheat crop, a total of eight acres that first year.

The following year, 1891, the settlers feared that the Native Americans were readying for war. They hurriedly built a log stockade and several area residents sought safety in the

Axel Olson's Corner, Winner. (Courtesy of Andrew Filer)

hewn-log fort. Realizing the fear was unfounded, they returned home to find that a kindly Native American, Mickenock, had cared for their stock in their absence. The Native Americans would prove to be good friends. They often helped the women with farm chores when the men traveled to North Dakota to help with the harvest there. There the men would earn money to see them through the long cold Minnesota winters. The logs from the fort would later be used for a church and school.

Pinecreek's reputation as "the Garden of Eden" spread. Soon the community was the thriving metropolis of the region. In the 1920s the town consisted of a post office, a bank, a confectionary store, two general stores, a hardware store, a meat market, a garage, a restaurant, parsonage, a steam-powered feed mill, and a boarding house. Each store had its own hitching posts.

Improvements in transportation, cars, and roads led to Pinecreek's demise. By the early 1990s only a few residents remained. The Pinecreek Wayside Park and the Pinecreek Border Crossing, just a few miles north, carries on the name.

WINNER

1912-1937
CLASS B

APPROXIMATE LOCATION:
From Roseau:
South on MN 89 for 14½ miles. Left on County Road 4 for ½ mile. Right on County 9 for 1 mile. First left on County 19 for 100 feet. Left to stay on County 19 for 2 miles. Continue onto 500th Avenue for 1 mile. Left on County 19/Winner Forest Road 3 ½ miles. Silo is still standing. Parking Area is on the old town site, near Hayes Lake State Park in Beltrami Island Forest.

The solitary silo still stands. Once at the center of activity, it is now a lone landmark, surrounded by the pines and trees of Beltrami Island State Forest, and the only physical remnants of the used-to-be town of Winner.

The silo and a barn, were built next to Webb's store. Webb and a partner had the first store in Winner. That partnership dissolved in 1917 with Webb continuing to operate the store and his farm for many years. Winner had another store, Moen's, that would be in existence until 1939.

An area-wide fair was held at Winner in 1929. The event, held at the school, hosted displays of farm produce and household crafts. A large crowd was in attendance. The Roseau County Centennial book reports that Mrs. Moen, Winner's postmistress, took home the most ribbons.

For three years, from 1916 to 1919, Winner had its own newspaper, *The Winner Northern Minnesota Booster*. The printing press and offices were on the upper level of Webb's store.

Telephone service was installed in the early 1920s. With forty-two subscribers, a time limit of five minutes had to be observed.

The post office was closed in 1937. The Moen store would stay open for two more years until the family moved away.

Today the only remaining physical feature of the town is the silo. The old town site, as well as the cemetery, are now located within the Beltrami Island and marked on the forest's map. A parking area is at the site.

St. Louis County

Elcor. (Courtesy of the Iron Range Historical Society)

Historic Elcor Sign. (Courtesy of the Iron Range Historical Society)

Elcor School. (Courtesy of the Iron Range Historical Society)

Overlooking Embarrass Lake, Merritt. (Courtesy of the Iron Range Historical Society)

ELCOR

1898-1956

CLASS A

APPROXIMATE LOCATION:
Located between Gilbert and McKinley. No access, now part of the mine pit.

Dying a sudden death, the residents of Elcor were heart-broken at the loss of their homes and their community. Ordered off the land by the mining company in 1955, by 1956 Elcor was no more.

The Elba Mine went into operation in 1898. With the influx of workers a community soon began, first with hotels and rooming houses, later with family homes. Some homes were resident built, others company built, and some moved in from Merritt by sleigh. Regardless of the construction, all of the homes were on company land. In 1901, another mine, the Corisca began excavation and the community grew rapidly.

One of the first houses in the area was put into use as a school with the kitchen and dining room used for classrooms for the two teachers. In 1900, a larger school was built for use by students in Elba and McKinley. Grades one through eight were taught by four teachers.

The population of Elba was ethnically and religiously diverse. Churches and services were varied with Elba having a Methodist and a Presbyterian church. The Catholics attended Mass in nearby McKinley and Gilbert. The Lutherans had no building but conducted services in the parlors of family homes.

According to an article in an Elba reunion booklet, water was supplied by a community pump. Lighting was provided by kerosene lamps and heat by box stoves. Groceries and other staples had to be picked up in the neighboring communities, though delivery was available. Elba's first store opened in 1920 with a combination store and post office. When the post office was established it was learned that Minnesota already had an Elba near Rochester. The name Corsica was also taken so Elcor, a combination of the two names was chosen.

Elcor had lots of options for socializing—basket socials, baseball games, Fourth of July celebrations, winter ice-skating get-togethers, and more. At the outskirts of town there was a dance platform. A local temperance society operated for a few years.

Elcor's fortune ebbed and flowed, was boom and bust. The Elba mine closed in 1925 and things looked dim, but in 1926, the Corsica switched to open pit mining and the outlook was brighter. During the late 1930s both mines were idle, and it would take World War II to see a surge in production. The end for Elcor began in 1954 when the pit mine shut down and was allowed to flood. Announcing that the company was reclaiming the land, residents were told they had to leave. The homes and community they and their ancestors had worked so hard to build would have to be left behind. By November of 1956, every building had been torn down or moved.

Elcor is now on company land and not accessible. In fact, historian Marvin G. Lamppa advices great caution in visiting some of the old mining communities as they are unstable and dangerous. Highway 135 has been rerouted around the areas expanding mines.

MEADOW

1898-1905

CLASS A

APPROXIMATE LOCATION:
From Aurora:
North on 3rd Avenue for 1 mile out of town. Driveway is on the left.

Considered the birthplace of present day Aurora, Meadow was established in 1898. Originally called Norlander even the town was not on the railroad line and was in the wilderness, the town grew quickly. Even so, it was apparent the townsite was not ideally located. A new townsite was platted in 1905. Iron Range historian Marvin G. Lamppa writes that sellers were offering Meadow residents one hundred dollars and a free lot if they would move their house to the new townsite called Aurora. It was an offer too good to pass up. Since Aurora was on the railroad line moving was the practical choice. By 1907, only two buildings were left in Meadow. After 1970, nothing remained in Meadow.

MERRITT

1892-1893

CLASS A

APPROXIMATE LOCATION:
From Biwabik: 1 mile east on 135. Just to left across from Embarras Lake is a gravel road leading up to a hill (Herritt Hill. this is the old town site.

The lack of a railroad connection didn't hamper Merritt's growth or its optimism. In fact, with a good water supply, good drainage and a great view of Embarras Lake, Merritt was, according to area historian Marvin Lamppa, the

Trunk Found at Merritt. (Courtesy of the Iron Range Historical Society)

and Merritt lay directly in the path of the firestorm. Reports state that within twenty-five minutes, more than half of Merritt lay in ashes. A saving rain fell that night and combined with exhaustive effort, Biwabik was saved. Merritt was in ruins. Some businesses continued operating for a few months and years but Merritt would not survive. The railroad never did extend to Merritt. Within a few years, the remaining businesses and residents moved to Biwabik and other locations and Merritt became a place of the past.

NORTH HIBBING

1893-1921
CLASS B
APPROXIMATE LOCATION:
North of Hibbing at Hull Rust Mine Overview.

It was no secret that rich deposits of iron ore lay beneath the streets of early Hibbing. But then, that wasn't unusual or uncommon as most Range settlements were situated on mineral deposits. What was unusual, was Hibbing's extraordinary solution to the expanding mine and the herculean efforts to save the town.

Founded by Frank Hibbing in 1893, Hibbing cautioned that the town be built further to the south to allow for mine expansion. His admonitions were ignored. As homes and businesses were built, the mining company retained mineral rights. As the town grew, so did the mine. Eric Weber in his Mnopedia online article wrote that, by 1910, Hibbing was surrounded on three sides by the mine. Even so, mining company officials were not concerned, estimating that it would be fifteen years before the vast reserves of iron ore beneath the city would be needed. Six years later they reneged on that prediction and wanted the ore.

Hibbing wasn't the first, nor the only, town to be relocated. Some were simply abandoned when expected rail lines never materialized. Residents moved to the new track side communities such as Merritt into Biwabik. As the Minnesota Humanities website articles state, some such as Aurora and Eveleth began in one location, moved, and started again a few miles away. Others were abandoned because the ore was depleted or it was too costly to mine. Some just disappeared into the expanding mine pits after the residents packed up their homes and moved. But none had relocated on the grandiose scale of Hibbing.

In its infancy, the late nineteenth century and early twentieth century were the times of robber barons, the time of American capitalists exploiting natural resources. Iron ore was king, and the courts of the time believed it their duty to protect

fastest growing town on the Mesabi Ranger in 1892. The growth rate was unprecedented. Joan Larson, area historian writes that in February 1892 the town was forest wilderness and by July of that same year over one hundred lots had been sold in Merritt, forty buildings constructed, and a population of over 300 lived there. A post office was established and booming business district included a hotel, rooming houses, general store, restaurants, bank, clothing store, drugstore, barbershop, liquor store, sawmill, bank, and more than a few saloons. The largest building in town was a livery stable that measured ninety-six feet in length and was able to stable sixty-five horses. One hotel, The Merritt, was three stories, had sixty sleeping rooms, offices, dining room, kitchen, and bar. The Range's first newspaper, *The Mesabi Range*, was printed in Merritt. The community also had a church and plans were in process to build a school.

Without a rail connection, supplying the saloons took quite an effort. Beer kegs were transported by train from Tower to the Embarras River, dumped into the water and floated to Merritt, a trip of four days. With thirteen of Merritt's forty buildings designated as either saloons or bars, the beer was a necessity. Merritt, by all accounts, had the look and feel of a "Wild West" town.

In July of 1892 the town of Biwabik was platted just one-half mile from Merritt. Located closer to the mines, some thought Biwabik to be serious completion for Merritt. Not to worry, there were two railroads (The Duluth and Iron Range and the Duluth, Mesabe & Northern) vying for expansion to the region, surely enough for both communities.

Surrounded by wilderness and logging debris, fire was always a danger. That summer of Merritt's rapid growth had been especially dry. Recent timber cuttings and brush left the debris in tinderbox condition. Several fires had flared up and the high winds fanned the flames. Biwabik was threatened

Pines Street, Hibbing, Minn.

Pine Street, North Hibbing. (Author's collection)

property, wealth, and economic power. Lorraine DeMillo, area historian, writes that court decisions were usually decided in favor of mining interests over the rights of citizens. It was a time of public needs over private.

As it grew apparent that Hibbing would have to be moved, tensions mounted and resentment grew. Citizens sought a court injunction to stop the mining companies from destroying their property. The result—the mining companies closed the mine, putting hundreds of miners out of work. A long, contentious legal battle ensued and would last for years. Some say the underlying issue of eminent domain and citizens' rights has not been definitively answered to this day. After years of legal and political jockeying, the end result was that Hibbing would be vacated and the mine expanded.

Several options were proposed, including the development of a new community, possibly at the old Merritt town site near Biwabik. After review, it was decided that the community of Alice (two miles south of what was now referred to as North Hibbing) was the ideal spot for the relocation.

The Hibbing Historical Society writes that the bulk of the move took over two years (1919 to 1921) and involved moving

over 180 homes and over twenty businesses. Each building was moved by a system of steel cables, log rollers, horses, tractors, and a steam crawler. The massive logs were placed under the building, secured with the steel cables, and then placed on wood rails and rolled to the new locatoins at the speed of 750 feet an hour. The Historical Society estimates that the move cost in excess of sixteen million dollars during the 1920s. Eric Weber in Mnopedia writes that the larger buildings had to be cut in two or three sections.

North Hibbing. (Author's collection)

Overly tall buildings were cut down, and a worker rode on the roof using a long stick to raise electrical wires. Eyewitness accounts tell of some buildings, especially the larger ones, collapsing on the way, smoke coming out of chimneys as they were being moved and clothes hanging on a porch clothesline. Weber tells the local folklore story of a woman going into labor at the old address and the baby being born at the new address.

Funding for the new Hibbing came primarily from the Oliver Mining Company. Weber states they helped pay for the sewer and electrical lines. They also built the Andoy Hotel, City Hall, and the new high school. The high school, built at a cost of nearly four million dollars in 1923, is on the National Register of Historic Places. An 1,800-seat auditorium is nationally renowned. The school is a showcase even today.

Hibbing's relocation was national news at the time. The sheer immensity of it is mind-boggling and still captures the imagination. Hibbing's nickname is the "Town the Moved." Even a children's book has been written about the move. Historically, the move has been well documented and the Hibbing Historical Society has fascinating archives to peruse. A display at the Society's museum features a detailed scale model of the historic town. Vintage postcards show the old town site at Third Street and seeing the period city makes the move even more astonishing. After seeing the post card, I asked if it would be possible to stand at that street corner and take a current photo to compare to the old. It is not! The location shown on the postcard is now deep in the mine pit. However some of North Hibbing is accessible.

The remaining town site is now home to a BMX bike park, a model airplane field, and a dog park. Large events are held at the site, including a July festival and a car show, and it even doubles as a campground, with electric hook-ups for up to four vehicles. The premier attraction is a disc golf course. The golf course, overlooking the Hull Rust Mine, features eighteen holes, each situated on a historic site or building foundation. Signage at each hole details the history of the structure with vintage photos of the building that stood there. Two shelters at the parking lot protect and display fiberglass-embedded optic panels that further detail the history of North Hibbing. As you walk the course, you will see remnants, steps leading to nowhere, fire hydrants at the base of large trees, old rail lines, and cracked and crumbling foundations. It is a walk in the past, a walk into a lost town, a place of the past.

OLD MESABA

1887–1947
CLASS A

APPROXIMATE LOCATION:
From Hoyt Lakes:
Left at the four-way stop (Old LTV Road now Highway 666). Drive 6 miles to Cross Railroad tracks. Immediately to the right you should see a line of willow trees and an old mine dump—this is the old town site. If you get to the guard's gate, you've gone too far.

For nearly fifty years, Mesaba, just north of Hoyt Lakes, had lived a boom-and-bust existence. The discovery of large iron ore deposits in 1887 led to the establishment of the town. Built as the main outfitting point for the region's mining and logging interests, Mesaba was once the end of the railroad line.

Mesaba grew quickly to a population of nearly one thousand and with three hundred buildings including fifteen hotels, several general stores, and a school. By the end of the century, rail lines had been extended and Mesaba began to decline.

In 1907, the Spring Mine opened and Mesaba had a resurgence. Though families did live in the town, Mesaba's reputation was of a rough, crude town with saloons as the center of activity. The mine proved to be unstable and dangerous and was short-lived.

Saloon, Mesaba. (Courtesy of the Iron Range Historical Society)

City Hall, Mesaba. (Courtesy of the Iron Range Historical Society)

Restaurant, Mesaba. (Courtesy of the Iron Range Historical Society)

1914 saw Mesaba installing a lighting and water system. Many new homes were built and the town took on a modern ambience. But again, Mesaba's fortunes were short-lived. After World War I, the Oliver Mining Company pulled out of its mining interests and Mesaba began a rapid decline. In 1939, only one home was occupied. The last three voters in the village voted to dissolve Mesaba in 1947. The town hall and brick store stood until 1960 when they were demolished. And old mine dump and a willow tree line mark the old town site.

SPINA

1909–1920

CLASS G

APPROXIMATE LOCATION:
From Kinney
Just south of Kinney, now part of Kinney.

It was a real estate venture that brothers Peter and Pasqual Spina had to pursue. Within walking distance of the Kinney mine and close proximity to three others, the town site named for the brothers was four blocks long and three blocks wide. Frank Squillance, who grew up on Spina during its heyday, remembers the town as dirty with free roaming cattle and chickens, all leaving behind their droppings everywhere. Frank also recalls that Spina was a noisy town—families arguing in varied languages, drunken revelry, a house of ill repute, unsolved murders, and a Black Hand Society. The Black Hand Society terrorized the town, and history buffs will recall that the Black Hands were an extortion group that planned and implemented the assassination of Franz Ferdinand and his wife, sparking World War I.

Spina included a hotel, several saloons, a barber shop, grocery store, and a water pump on every other corner. Mine dumps were encroaching on the town from the earliest days. They were so large that Frank Squillance wrote that he never saw the sunset due to a high large dump just a few blocks from his house.

Nearby Kinney was a long-time rival of Spina and annexation of Spina by Kinney was an ongoing petition. As the mines closed, Spina declined, especially after 1920. Most residents and businesses moved to Kinney. Eventually Spina was absorbed by Kinney.

Todd County

Philbrook. (Author's collection)

KANDOTA

1856-187?
CLASS A

APPROXIMATE LOCATION:
From Sauk Centre:
Turn right on Fairy Lake Road for ½ mile. Continue on County 17 for 2 miles. Continue on County 11 for ½ miles. Left on County 95 for 1/5 mile. Near Lion's Park.

Intending to be the "ideal city," Edwin Whitefield, a Massachusetts artist, built his home south of Fairy Lake in 1856. Designing it with great care, Kandota, meaning, "here we rest," would become Todd County's first city.

Other settlers soon followed and Whitefield's vision for the community seemed to be on its way to reality. It wasn't long before the burgeoning community rivaled nearby Sauk Centre. However, Sauk Centre and its job opportunities was able to attract and lure Kandota residents.

The final blow to Kandota was that the community was located on the dividing line between Dakota and Chippewa nations. Word was out that the two tribes were preparing for war. Rumor had it that the Dakota were already destroying area homes. Though they never reached Kandota, the terrified settlers fled, never to return.

Today the area is a rural farming area, abundant in hilly land and spotted with several lakes. The name Kandota lives on in the name of the township.

PHILBROOK

1859-1956
CLASS C

APPROXIMATE LOCATION:
From Motley:
South on U.S. Highway 10 for approximately 1½ miles. Turn right on Todd County Road 28. Continue on County Road 28 for approximately 3½ miles.

Long before Philbrook was platted, it was a bustling community on the shores of the Long Prairie River, aptly called Riverside.

Back in those early days—the mid-1800s—all supplies were brought in by stage coach from Sauk Centre. With a diverse population of nearly 2,000, the community included lumbermen, farmers, and settlers of all nationalities, many of them being newly arrived immigrants.

Equally as diverse was the makeup of the town. The town consisted of two photo studios, a livery, four stores, a hotel, blacksmith, saloon, dance hall, hardware store, knitting mill, stock yard, flour mill along the river, and a post office. The community was also home to two churches, both of which are still standing, though abandoned.

One of the churches, St. James Catholic Church, was in operation from 1905 until 1961. The chapel still stands, a bit weather-beaten and forlorn, but as a testament to the early settlers and the community. The abandoned church building is adjacent to the still-active church cemetery.

There was also a school building. Ruth Pritchard remembered, that as a student in 1920, the school had such a large attendance that the upper grades went to school in the morning and the lower grades in the afternoon.

With the coming of the railroad in the late 1800s, Riverside moved a few blocks to the final location of Philbrook, alongside the railroad tracks. The new community was named by railroad officials to honor Jethro Philbrook, a lumberman who built the depot.

The post office that had been established in 1889 changed to a rural branch in 1956 and was officially discontinued in 1964.

Today, the train, from Little Falls to Staples, still travels through the hamlet but there is no stop. There are a few residences in the area.

St. James Catholic Church, Philbrook. (Author's collection)

Wadena County

Bluegrass in Early Days. (Wadena County Historical Society)

Bluegrass Today. (Author's collection)

BLUE GRASS

1880-1930s
CLASS C
APPROXIMATE LOCATION:
From Verndale:
North on County Road 23 for 9½ miles.

Having read about the grotto at St. Hubert's Catholic Church in Blue Grass, I had to see it. Set amongst the pines, built in 1931, the stone altar, with stone benches and a cross-shaped flower garden, is a welcome respite. Set next to the historic church the scene is serene. In fact, the handful of homes, the old garage with the decorative, vintage and restored gas pumps, and the two churches combine to give a sense of what Blue Grass was like in its heyday.

Early settlers called the settlement Blue Grass because Kentucky Blue Grass was so abundant. Chauncey Hills is considered the first white settler in the area and he arrived in 1880. In 1900 or thereabouts, Blue Grass's first store was built. Through the years it was bought and sold many times. Best known for its creamery and cheese factory, Blue Grass also included the store, a gas station, tavern and the two churches: St. Hubert's Catholic Church built on land donated by Chauncey Hills and the Bethany Free Church. Both are over one hundred years old.

As roads and transportation improved business in Blue Grass declined. The creamery moved, building and all, and the rest of the businesses followed suit.

CENTRAL

1897-1904
CLASS C
APPROXIMATE LOCATION:
From Verndale:
North on Highway 23 for 3 miles. Right (east) on County Highway 4 for 5 miles. Only remaining building is the church.

As one could imagine from its name, Central was the center of activity for the area dairy farmers. First called Boyd Settlement because several members of the Boyd family homesteaded in the region. As others came to the area, the Union Chapel Church was built in 1887. Since dairy farming was so prosperous, the Central Cheese Factory was established in 1900. Soon a store and post office, as well as a blacksmith were part of the community. With the coming

of the automobile, the Central Store and Post Office became a gathering place for the young men. Auto races were conducted on the road past the store and were very popular. Dances were also held at the store until people from neighboring towns started coming, getting drunk, and causing ruckuses. When the dances were discontinued, the vacant building became a feed storage area. The store operated until the 1940s when it became a private residence. Today the only remaining trace of Central is the church.

HUNTERSVILLE

1903-1919
CLASS A
APPROXIMATE LOCATION:
From Menahga:
Stocking Lake Road for 2½ miles. 370th Street 1 mile. Left on County Road 23 for 1 mile. Right on 380th Street for 6½ miles. Sharp right onto Old Bridge Road 1/5 mile. Junction of County Road 15.

So prized was the land, rich with wildlife and known as a hunter's paradise, the Ojibwe and Dakota fought over it in the earliest days. In the late 1800s, the area, now called Huntersville, was a stage stop on the Verndale to Shell Prairie route. Soon a small community grew and included a two-story, twenty-four-foot-by-thrity-two-foot general store with an upstairs dance hall, a post office, and a garage. Dancing was so popular that a second, larger thirty-foot by fifty-foot hall was built. As dancing lost its popularity, the hall became a turkey brooder. Traveling medicine shows made Huntersville a regular stop. Large Fourth of July celebrations, some with parades, were an annual event.

Hopes were high the expanding rail line would run to Huntersville. So hopeful were residents that bonds in the amount of $8,200 were approved and sold. When the railroad bypassed the community, the bonds were voided. The town declined after that.

A large forest fire, called the Huntersville Fire, scorched 23,000 acres of forest, field and marshes. Several hunting cabins, a store and abandoned buildings were destroyed. Huntersville State Forest now encompasses most of the region. Campgrounds, canoe outfitters, and horse enthusiasts now enjoy the recreational opportunities that today's Huntersville offers.

OYLEN

1906-1908
CLASS C

APPROXIMATE LOCATION:
From Staples:
Todd Line Road/Warner Road for 1/5 mile. Airport Road for 1½ miles. Right on County Road 2/County Road 30 for 9½ miles. Right on County Road 7 for 4½ miles.

For a long time folks have been coming to Oylen for fellowship and faith. Beginning in 1904, and incorporated in 1914, Oylen Camps has outlasted the town of the same name. Originally held under a tent in the brush, and in various locations within the town, the camp in later years established permanent buildings, a tabernacle, dining hall, parsonage, and several cabins to house the summer campers. For two weeks each summer, in mid-June, campers enjoy fun, friends, and faith along the shores of the Crow Wing River and at the outskirts of what used to be a bustling town, Oylen.

Anna Pederson, in her memoirs, wrote that in 1900 the Olson's bought five acres of property along the river upon which they built a store and home. With the store came a post office and the official beginning of Oylen, named for Olson's father's homeland in Norway. Multiple owners bought and sold the store with additions of feed, hardware, more grocery variety, and dry goods over the years. At one time, a service station operated in the town as did many area sawmills.

Oylen did not have a school building, but classes were offered in the kitchens and homes of the settlers. Rural electric came to Oylen in 1949.

There are still a few area homes and residents and the camp still operates for two weeks in June. Many past campers, as well as area volunteers, come together to create a memorable time for the young campers. Though the town is no more, the old service station, though in decrepit condition still stands surrounded by vehicles. There are heaps of old lumber, including the remains of the old store.

Oylen today. (Author's collection)

Main Street Oylen. (Courtesy of the Wadena County Historical Society)

Oylen today. (Author's collection)

SHELL CITY

1879–1901

CLASS A

APPROXIMATE LOCATION:
From Menahga:
Stocking Lake Road for 4 miles. Left on County Road 23 for 1 mile. Right on 380th Street for 3 miles. Left on 199th Avenue for one mile.

When you get to the campground, I've been told, keep going and you'll be in Shell City. That's the advice. I was so close but didn't go far enough. Shell City, located near the Wadena/Hubbard County line, began in 1879 and was named Kindred for the founder. Originally a stop on the stage coach route from Verndale, forty miles south, wheat was also shipped that same route to Verndale. A small community by today's standards, seventy-five residents, it was quite large for the times. A store or two, a hotel, post office from 1879 to 1901, stage coach barn, and a button factory that supposedly made buttons out of the clams in the river were some of the businesses in the community. Hopes for the town's prosperity were dashed when the Great Northern Railroad bypassed Shell City for a route seven miles to the west.

Teacher and author John Crandell wrote a detailed history of Shell City. Using the information unearthed in his research, he and area historian Frank J. Mitchell erected information signs in the old town site. The wooded signs were crafted in Crandell's classroom. The signs mark the locations where the businesses and other buildings were situated in the town. Some depressions can still be seen and if you look closely, marks and ruts made by the coaches. It is said that now the city streets are lined with large pine trees.

Wilkin County

Tenney today. (Common Use)

TENNEY

1887-2011
CLASS C

APPROXIMATE LOCATION:
From Breckenridge:
US 75S for 16½ miles. Left on MN 55E for 2 miles.

Once Minnesota's tiniest town, Tenney is now, officially, a lost town. Residents voted to dissolve the town by a two-to-one margin. Quite literally, it was two to one, for the town had only three voters to cast votes in that election. A few years back, the town had six residents, up from the previous count of four. As Tenney resident Heidi Haagenson wrote, many joked about the demographic numbers for the small community. When two residents moved to the town, the population increased by fifty percent. When a murder occurred in the town of four, Tenney had the highest murder rate per capita in the nation. Kidding and joking aside, Tenney, at one time home to nearly 200 people, was a thriving town, with a hardware store, butcher shop, pool hall, hotel, general store, town hall, school, church, bank, and a town water pump. Tenney was founded by hard-working German and Scandinavian immigrants and named for Minneapolis lumberman and owner of Tenney, who donated land to the Soo Railroad.

The town population peaked in 1910 at 200, but by 1970 it had dwindled to twenty-four and down to five in 2001. For years, according to a *Minneapolis Star Tribune* article, City Clerk Oscar Guenther tried to recruit new people to the town. Deeming it in the middle of nowhere, there weren't any takers.

In 1928, the town hall needed a new cookstove. Getting a stove meant that meals could be prepared and made on site rather than in individual kitchens and transported to the town hall. There were no funds available to purchase a stove so the close-knit community, the women of the community, came up with a plan—a quilt.

The Tenney Quilt, as it would be known, was a dual money maker. First, people would pay ten cents to have their name embroidered on the quilt. After signatures were sold and stitched, the quilt was raffled off, raising more funds. Seven hundred names were bought, some fictional, some historical and some duplicates. Heidi Haagenson, whose mother, grandmother, and great-grandmother grew up in Tenney wrote a remarkable book on the quilt—*The Tenney Quilt: Celebrating the Women of Minnesota's Tiniest Town*. The book tells the story of the quilt, itself a historical document, as well as of the women of Tenney and Tenney the town.

Large corporate farms began to buy up the land. As the population dwindled, the school closed in 1956 and the post office was discontinued in 1980. In the summer of 2010, a 125th anniversary celebration was hosted by the town. Live music, lawnmower races, and other events were held. The recently arrived and newly elected Mayor Kristen Schwaub hoped the celebration would raise enough funds to repair the roof of the church turned City Hall.

Most buildings in Tenney have been demolished. The Tenney Fire Hall, razed in the early 2010s, had been on the National Register of Historic Places. Today, the Canadian Pacific Railroad has a grain terminal in Tenney. Trains roll through the town frequently and pick up shipments from the grain terminal and elevator.

Tenney today. (Common Use)

Bibliography

AITKIN COUNTY

"$40,000 Own the Entire Town of Solana, MN" (Aitkin County), Craigslist, 13 January 2013 Web. 31, January 2013.

Aitkin County Historical Society. "Aitkin County Communities." Aitkin County Historical Society. N.d. Web. November 2012.

Aitkin County Historical Society, *Aitkin County Heritage*, Dallas: Taylor Publishing, 1991.

"The Great Fires of 1918" MN150. Minnesota Historical Society. 30 October 2007. Web. 8, January 2013.

Megarry, Mary Bain., "Memoirs of Bygone Days." Aitkin County Historical Society. 2012. Web. November 2012.

Minnesota Department of Natural Resouces. "Grayling Marsh WMA." Minnesota DNR. N.d. Web. 7, January 2013.

Minnesota Department of Natural Resources. "Hill River State Forest" Minnesota DNR. N.d. Web. 7, January 2013.

Minnesota Department of Natural Resources. "Solana State Forest" Minnesota DNR. N.d. Web. 7, January 2013.

Minnesota Department of Natural Resources. "Soo Line North ATV Trail." Minnesota DNR. N.d. Web. 7, January 2013.

Minnesota Historical Society. "Arthyde Stone House." Minnesota Historical Society. 2009. Web. November 2012.

Trunt, Leo. "The Town of Bain, Minnesota." Rootsweb. Ancestry.com. N.d. Web. November 2012.

Trunt, Leo. "The Town of Shovel Lake, Minnesota." Rootsweb. Ancestry.com. N.d. Web. November 2012.

Trunt, Leo. *Beyond the Circle*. Baltimore. 1998.

Upham, Warren. "A Geographical Encyclopedia." Minnesota Historical Society. 2009. Web. November 2012.

Vellas, Stacy (transcribed). "Cornered in the North." Aitkin Age N.d. Rootsweb.Ancestry.com. Web, November 2012.

BECKER COUNTY

"A Pioneer History of Becker County, Minnesota." Rootsweb. Ancestry.com, N.d. 12, December 2012.

People's History of Becker County. Lake Park Area Historical Society. Dallas: Taylor Publishing, 1976.

Teague, G.E., Prentice, Ken. *Horse and Buggy Days at Detroit Lakes*. Detroit Lakes: Becker County Historical Society, 1949.

Upham, Warren. "A Geographical Encyclopedia." Minnesota Historical Society. 2009. Web. November 2012.

Images of America: Detroit Lakes. Becker County Historical Society. Charleston: Arcadia Publishing. 2012.

BELTRAMI COUNTY

"Bemidji-Opoly." Patchwork Press. Bemidji: 2012.

Borden, William, "Looking for Farley," *The American Scholar*, Vol 69, No. 4, Autumn 2000.

Buena Vista Ski Area, Web. December 6, 2012.

Carlson, Elmer, "Foy," North Country History, Vol. 2, #4, Beltrami County Historical Society, 1981.

Dickenson, Dianne, "Buena Vista: Gone But Not Forgotten." North Central Minnesota Historical Society, Bemidji, 1974.

Eggers, John R. "Have You Heard the Spirits Whisper on Buena Vista?" *Bemidji Pioneer*, October 26, 2012.

"Fowlds." North Country History, Vol. 1, #4, Beltrami County Historical Society.

Hagg, Harold T. "The Beltrami County Logging Frontier," *Minnesota History*, Vol. 29, June 1948.

Hagg, Harold T., "The Mississippi Headwaters Region: Scenes from the Past." Beltrami County Historical Society, 1986.

Halseth, Lloyd, WPA Historical Project No. 3769, following an interview of Mr. Dickinson, June 9th, 1938.

"History of Old Shotley" Rogerscg.net, Rogers Campground and Marina, N.d. Web, 12, July 2012.

"A Little History of Early Shotley" taken from *Bemidji Pioneer*, 1937, N.d.

Hoyum, Wanda. "Lake Julia Sanatorium" KAXE Radio Interview, April 8, 2010.

"Lake Julia Sanatorium." Common Ground, Lakeland Public Television, December 23, 2010, Web. March 1, 2013. (Scott Knudson)

Martin, Mrs. Frank, "Fowlds: Then and Now." Beltrami County Historical Society, 1958.

McClellan, Ralph, "Fowlds." North Country History, Vol. 1, #4. Beltrami County Historical Society.

"Mrs. Julius Nyren Celebrates her 94th Birthday November 1963" N.d Web, July 15, 2012.

Muncy, Bert, personal writing, LaVonne Peterson, N.d.

Nyren, Julius, taped recording transcript, November 9, 1963.

Russell, Carol. "In Our Own Backyard: A Look at Beltrami, Cass and Itasca Counties at the Turn of the Century." North Central Minnesota Historical Society, Bemidji, 1979.

Sandberg, Mrs. Gust, personal letter, September 19. 1960.

Thomas, Suzanne. Personal letter, December 2012.

Thomas, Suzanne, Personal interview, August 2012.

Vandersluis, Charles. "Mainly Logging." Mineota Clinic, Mineota 1974.

Williams, Anne "Stepping Back in Time with Buena Vista Logging Days, honors heritage of lumberjacks, early logging." Agweek.com, February 8, 2005, Web. December 6, 2012.

CARLTON COUNTY

"1900" aaca.org. Antique Automobile Club of America, Web. 20 February 2013.

Beck, Bill, "A Visit to Almost Forgotten Forbay." *Minnesota Power*, May 1982.

Beck, Bill, "Northern Lights—An Illustrated History of Minnesota Power," *Minnesota Power*: Eden Prairie, 1985.

Carroll, Francis M., *Crossroads in Time: A History of Carlton County Minnesota*. Carlton County Historical Society; Cloquet N.d.

Gerber, Robert F., "They Named It Carlton." Carlton County Historical Society, N.d.

Hiller, Kris. "Forbay." Personal email (February 12, 2013)

Iverson, Juella Sandwick, "Iverson, 2nd edition." Bicentennial Celebration at the Iverson Inn June 1994.

Martin, Greg, Memories that began at Fond du Lac Duluth, MN. Hydro Electric, 2008.

CASS COUNTY

"About the Cass County Pioneer." Chronicling America, Library of Congress N.d. Web. March 4, 2013.

Brunson, Bill. "The Town of Mildred Vanishes From Scene." Cass County Historical Society files, 1989.

Cass County Heritage. Cass County Historical Society, Dallas 1999.

Cass County Ordinances, Cass County Recorder, Cass County Historical Society files, May 28, 1896.

"Christmas at Lothrop." *Cass County Pioneer*, January 5, 1899.

"City of Ellis." *Cass County Pioneer*. September 18, 1894.

Croff, G.R. "Early Days." Cass County Historical Society files. N.d.

Eickenberry, Dan. Early Logging Around Ten Mile Lake. Ten Mile Lake History: 200 Years, 2005

Erickson, Mrs. M.G. Weekly Scratch Pad, Cass County Historical Society files, N.d.

Geving, Peter (Tuck). Ten Mile Lake History: 200 years. Birch Lake Association, June 2002.

Geving, Renee. Personal interview. August 2012.

"Gull River." *Brainerd Tribune*. September 11, 1880.

Gull River Lumber Mill Map. Text. Unknown. September 5, 1983, Crow Wing County Historical Society files.

Larson, Alice Dade. Personal letter. March 14, 1977.

"Lothrop" *Cass County Pioneer* Walker. Dec. 19, 1896, Reprint from 25 January 1895.

Lothrop Map, Cass County Historical Society files, N.d.

Lund, Duane. Tale of Four Lakes: Leech Lake, Gull Lake, Mille Lacs Lake, the Red Lakes and the Crow Wing River. Staples. 1977.

Macklin, Bill. "Lothrop: Reminiscenses of Early Days." *Walker Pilot Independent*, Walker August 22, 1985.

McCormick, Carol. Mustache Liz. Ten Mile Lake History: 200 years. Birch Lake Association, June 2002.

McCormick, Carol. "Mustache Liz." Celebrating 100 Years, Hackensack, Minnesota.

McDowell, Elizabeth, Minnesota Death Index, January 11, 1937.

Melgaard, Ross. Mary Norton Oral History Interview. Ten Mile Lake History: 200 Years. September 18, 1987.

"Mildred." Photo and caption, *Brainerd Daily Dispatch*. October 17, 1970.

"Mildred Store Burns to the Ground Friday, December 13." *Walker Pilot Independent*. December 20, 1946.

"Mildred Store Takes Change to New Ownership." *Walker Pilot Independent*. May 22, 1930.

"Mildred Town Getting Out of a Rut on No. 19", *Walker Pilot Independent*. March 13, 1930.

"New Town of Wilkenson." *Cass Lake Voice*. June 11, 1904.

Norton, Mary Ann, "Cyphers." Cass County Heritage. Cass County Historical Society, Dallas 1999.

Pederson, Thomas H. "Memoirs." *Cass County Independent*. November 20, 1936.

Plat of Lothrop, Cass County Historical Society files N.d.

Plattner, Clem "Weekly Scratch Pad." Unknown, Cass County Historical Society files, April 23, 1970.

"Roadbuilders of Pine Lake: And also a few remarks about the Dead City of Lothrop." Cass County Historical Society files, October 20, 1916.

Robinson, Robby. "Wilkenson Store plans to close after 55+ Years." *Cass Lake Times*. July 23, 1998.

Thomas, Hattie. "A Brief History of Lothrop, Minnesota." Cass County Historical Society files, N.d.

Houchins. Elwood. Tobique, Minnesota. Cass County Historical Society files. February 23, 1998.

Topp, Ella Hoover. Personal Writing. Cass County Historical Society files, ca. 1997.

Upham, Warren. "A Geographical Encyclopedia." Minnesota Historical Society. 2009. Web. November 2012.

Wickmann, Richard. Between Then and Now: A Story about Southern Cass County, Sylvan Lake and the Village of Pillager. Brainerd. 2004.

Vandersluis, Charles. "Mainly Logging." Mineota Clinic, Mineota 1974.

Zapffe, Carl. A. Indian Days in Minnesota's Lake Region: A History of the Great Sioux-Ojibwe Revolution. Brainerd. 1991.

CLAY COUNTY

Peihl, Mark. Personal email. August 30, 2012.

Peihl, Mark. "Ghost Towns of Clay County." Powerpoint Presentation. Undated.

"Construction of the Stockwood Fill." North Dakota State University. www.ndsu.edu August 30, 2012.

Upham, Warren. Minnesota Geographic Names. http://mnplaces. mnhs.org/up ham/ November 10, 2012.

CLEARWATER COUNTY

Hayes, David M. "Mallard Minnesota 1902-1915: A Boom/Ghost Town Revisited. University of Minnesota Graduate School. December 1992.

"History of Clearwater County: Headwaters of the Mississippi. Clearwater County Historical Society. 1984.

Holland, Ren. "The Edge of Itasca: Life at the Mississippi Headwaters and in Early Itasca Park Communities. Little Falls. 2004

"Mallard." Clearwater County Historical Society files. N.d.

"Moose Musings." Shvelin Advocate. Ca 1908

Palm, Birdie McCollum. "How Moose Began." Clearwater County Historical Society files. N.d.

Sandin, Olka Bakke. Ressler, Norma Bakke. "The Mallard Area." 1996.

Vandersluis, Charles. "Mainly Logging." Mineota Clinic, Mineota 1974.

COOK COUNTY

"Authentic North Shore: Ryden's Café." http://www.northshore-hwy61.com/bm/features/dining/authentic-north-shorerydens-caf‾print.shtml April 5, 2013.

"Chippewa City Community and Church." Unknown. N.d. handwritten letter, Cook County Historical Society files.

Cordes, Jim. "The Treasures of Minnesota's North Shore and Gunflint Trail: A Lake Superior Journey." 2008.

Drouillard, Staci G. "Turn of the Century Visitors to Chippewa City." Unknown N.d. Cook County Historical Society files.

Drouillard, Staci G. "The Village of Chippewa City." Cook County Historical Society brochure. N.d.

Fawcett, Lois. M., Minnesota Historical Society letter June 14, 1955.

"History Recalls Forgotten Island Town." Cook County News Herald. November 2, 1992.

Johnson, Barbara Jean. "Moments in Time: Growing Up in Mineral Center." WTIP Radio Program. Web. November 1, 2011.

Linehan, Roger. WTIP Radio, personal email. October 16, 2012.

Linnell, Gertrude. "Birchwood School, Mineral Center." Cook County Historical Society files, N.d.

Mayo, Kathryn. Mayo, William. "61 Gems on Highway 61." Cambridge, 2009.

"The Mineral Center Store." Cook County Historical Society files. N.d.

Morrison, Mike. "19th Century Towns." Unknown newspaper N.d. Cook County Historical Society files.

Moore, Max. M. "Outlaw Bridge." Rotarian, June 1971.

Mineral Center Map. Unknown. N.d Cook County Historical Society files.

Munsch, Andrew. "Mineral Center Road." www.deadpioneer.com Web. November 20, 2012.

Munsch, Andrew. "Old Border Road. Old Highway 61." www.deadpioneer.com Web. January 12, 2013.

"Outlaw Bridge." Rotary Club. Rotaryfirst11.org.

"Parkersville." www.nps.gov/history/history/online_books/story/chap 6.htm March 12, 2013.

Soderberg, Olga N. "Ghost Towns of Cook County." Ca 1950, Cass County Historical Society.

Wilkinson, E.J. Works Progress Administration letter. April 2, 1936.

Works Progress Administration, N.d. Cook County Historical Society files.

Wurzer, Cathy. "Tales of Highway 61." Minnesota Historical Society Press. St. Paul, 2008.

CROW WING COUNTY

"Barrows." Unknown. audio tape transcript. June 1981.

"Barrows. Big for Its Age." Brainerd Dispatch. May 13, 1915.

"Barrows Enjoys Building Boom." Brainerd Dispatch. May 9, 1913.

"The Barrows Fire: The Tale of Friday's Raging Wildfire Could Have Been Much Worse." June 6, 2006.

"Borezak." Crow Wing County Historical Society files.

Coleman, Sister Bernard. Labud, Sister Verona. Humphrey, John. Old Crow Wing: History of a Village. Baxter 1967/2000.

"Crow Wing County Genealogy and History: From the 1856 Stage Coach Travel Diary of C.C. Andrews." http://genealogytrails.com/minn/crowwing/crow wing.html October 29, 2012.

Crow Wing County Historical Society. Personal letter March 8, 1989.

"Crow Wing State Park.(Crow Wing County) Brainerd, Minnesota. Minnesota Treasures. www.mntreasures.com December 10, 2012.

"Crow Wing State Park." Minnesota Department of Natural Recources Brochure.

"Crow Wing State Park Management Plan." Minnesota Department of Natural Resouces, Division of Parks and Recreation. June 2002.

"Crow Wing Village." www.brainerd-mn.info/crowwing.html January 4, 2013.

"Crow Wing Was Most Important in Central Minnesota." www. brainerdhistory.com October 29, 2012.

Foote, Gene. "The Church of Manganese Village." Cuyuna Communities. Date unknown.

Foote, Gene. "Manganese School Picnic." Cuyuna Communities. Date Unknown.

Hansen, Avery. "Farmer's Wife Chooses Her Own Way of Life." *Brainerd Daily Dispatch.* December 1969.

"Gorst's Mill." Crow Wing County Historical Society files.

"Gorst's Mill Site." Minnesota Archeological Society Site File. Crow Wing County 1981.

Heald, Sarah Thorp. "History of Old Crow Wing." Crow Wing County Historical Society files.

"Honing in on History for the '99 Permits: The Story of Crow Wing." Minnesota State Parks Traveler. Minnesota Department of Natural Resources. 1998.

Laporte, Mary. "Crow Wing State Park." www.brainerd.com June 26, 2006.

"Manganese: Life and Death of a Busy Mining Town." Cuyana Communities.

Meyer, Roy W. "Everyone's County Estate: A History of Minnesota's State Parks. St. Paul, 1991."

"Mrs. Dullum's Life Tied Closely to Town History." *Brainerd Daily Dispatch.* December 13, 1969.

"Mr. Barrows works on the South Range." *Brainerd Daily Dispatch.* Date unknown.

Nagorski, Kathi. "Barrows Wildfire." *Brainerd Daily Dispatch.* June 2006.

Nichols-Anderson, Gladys. "The Forgotten Town of Barrows." *Brainerd Daily Dispatch.* June 29, 1989.

Richardson, Renee. "History of Wilson School." *Brainerd Daily Dispatch.* October 27, 2000.

Sloan. Jim. "Cuyuna Range Mining City Survives in Memories." Unknown. Crow Wing County Historical Society files.

Sloan, Jim. "Manganese Revisited." *Brainerd Daily Dispatch.* May 8, 1985.

Schwendt, Trudy. Unpublished memoir, Crow Wing County Historical Society files. Date unknown.

"Townsite Co. at Barrows." *Brainerd Daily Dispatch.* May 21, 1915.

Zander, Jack. "Lennox Still on State Maps but Actually Doesn't Exist." *Brainerd Daily Dispatch.* August 12, 1963.

Zapffe, Carl A. Indian Days. 1990.

Zapffe, Carl A. Personal letter to Charles Vandersluis. April 5, 1974.

"Town of Crow Wing." Crow Wing County Historical Society files.

DOUGLAS COUNTY

"Belle River Township." Douglas County Historical Society files. N.d.

Dahl, Mildred Anderson. Spruce Hill Remembered. Douglas County Historical Society, 1996.

"Early Village – Brandon." Douglas County Historical Society files. N.d.

"Joy – Section 4." Douglas County Historical Society files. N.d.

Lieffort, Al. "Spruce Hill County Park Pavilion" Douglas County Historical Society files. N.d.

Peterson, Duane V. "Chippewa." Ghosttowns.com. Web. September 9, 2012.

Peterson, Duane V. "Belle River." Ghosttowns.com, Web. September 9, 2012.

Sibell, Gene. "The Saga of Spruce Hill, Part II." *Lake Region Press.* July 18, 1984.

Lake Region Press. Plat Map Spruce Hill. Platbook of Douglas County. Douglas County Historical Society. July 1, 1984.

Rosenquist, Bernard. "Rose City." Douglas County Heritage. Douglas County Historical Society. N.d.

"Spruce Center." Douglas County Historical Society files. N.d.

"Scriven, Later Called Spruce Center." Douglas County Historical Society files. N.d.

GRANT COUNTY

Benson, Patty. Personal email. November 28, 2012.

Grant County Minnesota History. Rootsweb. Ancestry.com. November 11, 2012.

Goetzinger, William M. "Pomme de Terre. A Frontier Outpost in Grant County." *Minnesota History.* June 1962.

Simar, Candace. *Pomme de Terre: A Novel of the Minnesota Uprising.* St. Cloud. 2010.

Upham, Warren. *Minnesota Place Names.* http://mnplaces.mnhs. org/upham/. November 9, 2012.

HUBBARD COUNTY

Holland, Ren. "The Edge of Itasca: Life at the Mississippi Headwaters and in Early Itasca Park Communities. Little Falls. 2004.

Mitchell, Frank J. "Farris and Graceland." Hubbard County Historical Society files. N.d.

Mitchell, Frank J. "Latona-Horton." *Lakes Country Scenic Byway Newsletter,* March 2007.

Mitchell, Frank J. "Yola." Hubbard County Historical Society files. N.d.

Upham, Warren. "A Geographical Encyclopedia." Minnesota Historical Society. 2009. Web. November 2012.

ITASCA COUNTY

Bergan, Kathy. Personal email. September 18, 2012.

Stone, Alan. Loren, Buescher, Vergal. "Cooley, MN." *Range Reminiscing* March 2007 Iron Range Historical Society, Gilbert.

Trunt, Leo. "The Village of Cooley." *Beyond the Circle*. 1998.

Upham, Warren. *Minnesota Place Names*. http://mnplaces.mnhs. org/upham/ November 9, 2012.

KANABEC COUNTY

"Brunswick, Three Locations." Kanabec County History Center

"Coin." Kanabec County History Center.

Cole, Edna "Warman Creek and North Mora." *Kanabec Kontact* Kanabec County History Center, March 10, 1999.

"Grass Lake." Kababec County History Center summary.

"The Grass Lake Mission Church." Kanabec County History Center.

"Groundhouse City." Kanabec County History Center.

"Hillman." Kanabec County History Center.

"Hedin." Kanabec County History Center.

Ken-A-Big, *The Story of Kanabec County* Kanabec County History Center.

"Kroschel." Kanabec County History Center.

"Lewis Lake." Kanabec County History Center.

"The Lost Towns of Kababec County." Kanabec County History Center summary.

"Preserving the Memory of Grass Lake." News article, Kanabec History Center.

"Raritan." Kanabec County History Center.

"Riverdale." Kanabec County History Center.

"Riverdale." *Kanabec County Times*. 1908 Kanabec County History Center.

Warman. B.D. "A Short History About and Around Warman Minnesota." Audio tape transcript. July 1982, Kanabec County History Center.

"Warman Store to Close: Served Area for 60 Years." Unknown, December 8, 1966 Kanabec County History Center.

"Warman" Unknown, Kanabec County History Center.

"Warman Consolidated School." Unknown, Kanabec County History Center.

Upham, Warren. *Minnesota Place Names*. http://mnplaces.mnhs. org/upham/ November 9, 2012.

KITTSON COUNTY

Adams, Cindy. "Enok." Kittson County Historical Society Newsletter, Fall, 1992.

Adams, Cindy. Personal phone call May 10, 2013.

Bergh, John. "Ownership of a Great Farm." Ancestry.com www.roots web.ance stry.com Web. May 13, 2013.

Browne, Glenn. Personal email, October 10, 2012.

Browne, Glenn, Personal email, October 19, 2012.

Browne, Glenn, Personal email, April 26, 2013.

"Caribou, Minnesota." Kittson County Historical Society Newsletter, Spring 1992.

Clow, Scott. "Walter Hill Farm." Ancestry.com www.rootsweb.an-cestry.com Web. May 13, 2013.

Giffen, Renee. "Northcote: The Industrious Center." Ancestry.com www.rootsweb.ancestry.com Web. May 13, 2013.

Larson, Gladys. Schwenzfeier Hattie. "Orleans." Our Northwest Corner, Kittson County Historical Society, 1976.

Lewis, Trish Short. "Hill Farms." St. Vincent Memories, blog, www. 56755.blog spot.com.

Lundell, Phil. G. "Enok, an Inland Hamlet."

Lundell, Phil G. "UpNorth, Memories and Reflections of a Lundell Farm Boy." 2005.

"Noyes Roadside Parking Area" Minnesota Department of Transportation Historic Roadside Development Inventory. www.dot. state.mn.us.

"Our Northwest Corner." Kittson County Historical Society, 1976.

Reese, Vanessa. "The Birth of Northcote." Ancestry.com www. rootsweb.ancestry .com Web. October 22, 2012.

"Robbin Store 1938." Kittson Historian, http://kittson historian. ning.com.

"St. Michael's Church, Caribou." www.hobbydog.net/caribou-church. htm.

Youngren, Mrs., MacFarlane, Mrs. "Northcote." Our Northwest Corner, Kittson County Historical Society, 1976.

KOOCHICHING COUNTY

Census of Rainy Lake City, September 18, 1894.

Drach, Hiram M. *Koochiching, Pioneering Along the Rainy River Frontier*. 1983.

Gemmell, Minnesota History, Gemmell Minnesota Community Guide, www.lakesnwoods.com.

Henricksson, John. *A Wild Neighborhood*. Minneapolis, 1997.

Northome Bicentennial Book. Koochiching County Historical Society. International Falls, 1977.

Perry, David. E. *Gold Town to Ghost Town: Boom and Bust on Rainy Lake*. International Falls, Minnesota. 1993.

"Proctor Man Tells Romantic Story of Rainy Lake City." *Duluth Herald*. November 13, 1915.

Rainy Lake City Council Meeting Minutes, Book of Minutes, Koochiching County Historical Society Museum.

Rainy Lake City Incorporation Papers and Plat Map, Recorder's Office, St. Louis County, Minnesota.

Rainy Lake Gold Rush. National Park Service, Department of the Interior, Voyageurs National Park brochure.

Rajala, Benhart. *TIM-BERRR! Pine Logging in the Big Fork River Valley*. St. Cloud, 1992.

"Reminisces of Rainy Lake City." Writers Project No. 1400, Koochiching County.

Salmonson, Jamie. "Gemmell." Jmc.northome.k12.mn.us/history/ Jamie.htm November 20, 2012.

Siats, Roxann. Sweatt, Helen. Thomas, Dolly. Albrecht, Lorraine. Olson, Peggy. Northome-Mizpah-Gemmell Minnesota History 1903-1977 Northome Bicentennial Book Committee.

Visitor Destinations. National Park Service, Department of the Interior, Voyageurs National Park brochure.

LAKE COUNTY

Mayo, Kathryn. Mayo, William. *61 Gems on Highway 61*. Cambridge. 2009.

Bishop, Hugh E. *By Water and Rail: A History of Lake County, Minnesota*. Lake County Historical Society.

Cordes, Jim. *The Treasures of Minnesota's North Shore & Gunflint Trail: A Lake Superior Journey*. Duluth. 2008.

Gangi, Kim. Lake County Historical Society. Personal email. December 5, 2012.

Gilson, Agnes. "Sawbill Landing." Personal letter. May 2013.

Kess, David. "The Town That Disappeared into the Forest." Ely-Winton Historical Society. Date unknown.

Kraker, Don. "In Wake of Pagami Fire, Forest Recovery Is Swift. Minnesota Public Radio. *Brainerd Daily Dispatch*. September 12, 2012.

"Illgen City No. 1." *St. Paul Sunday Pioneer Press*. August 10, 1924.

Lamb, Linda. "Sawbill Landing: A Lumberjack School." *Schroeder Area Historical Society Newsletter*. September 2011.

Monthei, Heather. Personal email. September 3, 2012.

Monthei, Heather. Personal email. October 17, 2012.

Nikula, Dale. Personal letter. November 26, 2012.

Riebe, Angie. "Section 20 Mine: I wouldn't have wanted to live anywhere else growing up." *Mesabi Daily News Online*. March 18, 2008.

"Rudolph and Mary Illgen, Pioneers Who Saw Some of Their Dreams Come True." *Silver Bay Times*. June 10, 1958.

Sando, Mel. Lake County Historical Society, Phone. November 9, 2012.

Schauland, Honor. Personal email. January 17, 2013.

"Section 30: 2180 Acres of Claims and a Quarter Century of Court Battles." Unknown.

Silver, Robert H. "Memories of Cramer." Unpublished memoirs. 1989.

Slade, Andrew. *Camping the North Shore: A guide to the 23 best campgrounds in Minnesota's spectacular Lake Superior region*. Duluth. 2008.

Stenlund, Milt. *Section 30: The Mine and the Community*. Ely-Winton Historical Society. Grand Rapids. 1992.

Suota, Matt. "Landmark Burns in Illgen City." *Lake County News Chronicle*. November 12, 2009.

Sweet, Margaret. Personal email. July 17, 2012.

Sweet, Margaret. Personal email. July 25, 2012.

Sweet, Margaret. Personal email. September 25, 2012.

Wurzer, Cathy. *Tales of the Road*. Minnesota Historical Society. St. Paul. 2008.

LAKE OF THE WOODS COUNTY

"Beltrami Island State Forest." Minnesota DNR http://www.dnr. state.mn.us/ state_forests/sft00005/index.html April 22, 2013.

Hagen, Carla. *Hand Me Down My Walking Cane*. St. Cloud 2011.

"*Hand Me Down My Walking Cane* now in its third printing" www.baudetteregion.com April 23, 2013.

Hirst, Marlys. Mason, Wally. "The Cedar Spur Area." Lake of the Woods County: A History of the People, Places and Events. Lake of the Woods Historical Society 1997.

Hirst, Marlys. Johnson, Alice. Olson, Roy. Peterson, Ernie. "The Forest Area." *Lake of the Woods County: A History of the People, Places and Events*. Lake of the Woods Historical Society 1997.

Lake of the Woods County: A History of the People, Places and Events. Lake of the Woods Historical Society 1997.

Olds, Larry. "Investigating the Resettlement of My People." Guest Blog. www.carlahagen.com April 24, 2013.

"Peppermint Creek and Waganica." *Lake of the Woods County: A History of the People, Places and Events*. Lake of the Woods Historical Society 1997.

Peterson, Ernie. "The Faunce Ridge Story." *Lake of the Woods County: A History of the People, Places and Events*. Lake of the Woods Historical Society 1997.

"Rako." *Lake of the Woods County: A History of the People, Places and Events*. Lake of the Woods Historical Society 1997.

LIFE CYCLE

Conlin, Michael V., Lee Joliffe, ed. *Mining Heritage and Tourism: A Global Synthesis*. UK, Routledge, 2010.

"Ghost Towns of Newaygo." E-Press Chronograph Number II. Big Prairie Press. Winter 2007. Web. 16, November 2012.

MAHNOMEN COUNTY

"Forefolk—Duane F. Porter." Comcast.net, N.d. 6 February 2013.

"Rev. D, F. Porter Notebook." *Family images*, Comcast.net N.d. 6 November 2012.

Kramer, J., "Abandoned Communities." Personal email, (December 31, 2012).

MILLE LACS COUNTY

A Short Account of Brickton, Princeton, MN. May 29, 1977, Printed by Princeton Union-Eagle, May 1977.

"Brickton School Remembered." Baldwin Township. N.d. Web. November 2012.

From a Ribbon of Clay. Brickton, MN, Kathy Becker, August 31, 1979.

Minnesota Bricks "Brickton Marker" Personal email (Dec. 3, 2010).

William S. Oakes. "William S. Oakes Brickton History." Minnesota Bricks, n.d. Web. November 2012.

MORRISON COUNTY

"3 Buildings at Lincoln Wiped Out by Flames." *Little Falls Daily Transcript*. November 23, 1935.

Arntzen, Mary. "Darling Store, Landmark, Goes into Oblivion." *Little Falls Daily Transcript*. November 20, 1975.

Brown, Steve. Brown, Marilyn. Email/Mary Warner. November 2, 2010.

"Dixville—A Town That Was." Unknown. Undated.

"Driver Jumps to Safety in Train Crash, "North Coast Plows into Stalled Auto at Darling." Unknown. September 1928.

Dubois, Gene. "The End of An Era, 80-year-old Darling Store Closes for Last Time." *St. Cloud Times*. January 17, 1975.

Dubois, John. "Darling's Landmarks Replaced." *St. Cloud Times*. October 7, 1985.

Faust, Maurice. *Aitkinsville to Zerf*. Pierz. 2002.

Fisher, Harold L. *The Land Called Morrison*." St.Cloud. 1976.

Fuller, Clara K. *History of Morrison and Todd Counties: Their People, Industries and Institutions*. Indianapolis. 1915.

"Gravelville." Unknown. Undated.

"Gravelville Once Scene of Activity, Mill Foundation, House Remains." *Little Falls Daily Transcript*. July 22, 1949.

"Gravelville Mill." *Little Falls Daily Transcript*. October 4, 1967.

"History of the Lin Club." Lin Club Menu. Undated.

Ingersoll, William. Hart, Evan A. "Burial Place of Pioneer William A. Aitkin, Site of Forgotten Village Located South of Town." *Little Falls Daily Transcript*. 1959.

Johnson, Alfred. "History of Gravelville Morrison County." September 1967 Rev. 1969.

Kasperek, Valentine E. "Swan River Indian Cemetery. Abandoned Cemetery and Private Burial History Form D." April 24, 1942.

Kay, Larry. Interview by James LeBlanc. "There Was Once a Gravelville." *Morrison County Shopper*. April 12, 1977.

"Lincoln/Cushing Makes Visitors Feel Welcome." *Morrison County Record, Visitors Guide*. May 18, 2003.

"Lincoln Twp. (Morrison) Minnesota." http://mntreasures.com December 2012. February 21, 2013.

Long, Dave. "Gravelville Fades into Historic Past." Unknown. Ocober 3, 1967.

Mares, Mrs. Peter interview by Ermyle Goodrich. "Early Days of Lincoln Minnesota." Undated.

"New Hotel at Lincoln." *Little Falls Daily Transcript*. August 17, 1903.

Nelson, Joan-Vetsch. *Murder at the Darling Church*. 2005.

"New Sawmill." *Little Falls Daily Transcript*. May 27, 1896.

Phillips, Mary. "Community Pride Key to Church Restoration." *Little Falls Daily Transcript*. July 2, 1979.

Richardson, Nathan. "The History of Morrison County." *Little Falls Daily Transcript*. November 17, 1880.

Rutz, Lenny. Rutz, Betty. "What Life Was Like at Gregory Depot." Undated.

"Sites and Tours. Morrison County." Unknown. Undated.

Topp, Ella. A Chosen Place, Land of Lake, Pine and Prairie. Lincoln, Scandia Valley, Rail Prairie. Staples. 1994.

Topp, Ella Topp. Personal Letter. July 27, 1989.

"Turn of the Century Farm House." Bermel-Smaby Realtors as. 1982.

Upham, Warren. *Minnesota Place Names*. http://mnplaces.mnhs.org/upham.

"Vawter, Minnesota (Morrison) Ghost Town." http://www.mntreasures.com April 12, 2012. February 21, 2013.

"Vawter—On the Soo Line." Unknown. Undated.

Warner, Jan. "KLTF—Yesterday, Part of Tomorrow" May 1, 1983.

Warner, Mary. "Ghost Towns in Morrison County." http://morrisoncountyhistory.org. July 18, 2012. November 9, 1952.

"Young Woman Murdered Near Randall—100 Years Ago." *Morrison County Record*. April 1, 2005.

NORMAN COUNTY

Nelson, Nancy. Personal letter. June 15, 2013.

Our Towns of Western Norman County. Unknown. Hendrum. Undated.

Upham, Warren. http://mnplaces.mnhs.org/upham/ June 21, 2013.

The Very Best of Norman County Trivia and Fascinating Facts. Unknown.

OTTER TAIL COUNTY

Belar, Linda. History Museum of East Ottertail County. Personal email. July 2, 2012.

"Craigie Flour Mill." Otter Tail County Minnesota website. www.ottertail.com.mn.us May 5, 2013.

Crandall, John M. Boom and Bust: Reflections Chronicling Ottertail City 1858-1875. Wadena 2003.

Drechsel, Bob. "Almora Vanishing as County Town." *Fergus Falls Daily Journal*. August 21, 1968.

East Otter Tail Historical Society Book Committee, *East Otter Tail History*, Vol 1 1977.

"Forgotton Towns. Muse-ings. www.museings.areavoices.com June 7, 2012. July 2012.

"Forgotten Towns: Luce." Muse-ings. www.museings.areavoices.com January 12, 2012. July 2012.

"Forgotten Towns: Topelius." Muse-ings. www.museings.areavoices.com February 2, 2102. July 2012.

"Ghost Towns of this County." *Fergus Falls Daily Journal*. October 8, 1938.

"Heinola." History Museum of East Ottertail County. www. Historymuseumeot.org, September 13, 2012.

Hotokainen, Rob. "Hillview: The Town that Might Have Been." Fergus Falls Daily Journal December 16, 1982.

"Joy." History Museum of East Ottertail County. www. Historymuseumeot.org, September 13, 2012.

Lake, Betty. "Village of Heinola." History Museum of East Ottertail County. www. Historymuseumeot.org, September 13, 2012.

Leaf City Historical Marker, Minnesota Department of Transportation, http://www.dot.state.mn.us/roadsides/historic/files/iforms/OT-LLT-001.pdf May 7, 2013.

"Lost or Nearly Vanished Towns in East Otter Tail." Perham Enterprises Bulletin. January 4, 2007.

"The Lost Town of Topelius: Little Remains of Proud Village." Perham Enterprises Bulletin January 4, 2007.

"Luce Village." History Museum of East Ottertail County. www. Historymuseumeot.org, September 13, 2012.

"Memories of Butler." History Museum of East Ottertail County. www. Historymuseumeot.org, September 13, 2012.

Myhre, Joel. "Ghost Towns Still Abound in Otter Tail County, depending on definition." Fergus Falls Daily Journal. February 24, 1996.

Newsbrief." Perham Enterprises Bulletin. December 1, 1898.

"Otter Tail or Ottertail." Muse-ings. www.museings.areavoices.com February 16, 2012. July 2012.

"Ottertail City." History Museum of East Ottertail County. www. Historymuseumeot.org, September 13, 2012.

"Ottertail Had 36" History Museum of East Ottertail County. www. Historymuseumeot.org, September 13, 2012.

"Richdale: Gone but Still on the Map." Muse-ings. www.museings.areavoices.com June 7, 2012. July 2012.

"Richdale Village." History Museum of East Ottertail County. www. Historymuseumeot.org, September 13, 2012.

"South Immanuel Church All That Remains of Early Town." Pelican Rapids Press. August 23, 1989.

"Topelius" History Museum of East Ottertail County. www. Historymuseumeot.org, September 13, 2012.

Upham, Warren. "Minnesota Place Names" Minnesota Historical Society. http://mnplaces.mnhs.org/upham/ April 20, 2013.

PENNINGTON COUNTY

Svensgaard, Bill. Mavie–A Ghost Town Lives On. www.blurb.com 2010.

Upham, Warren. Minnesota Place Names. Minnesota Historical Society. http://mnplaces.mnhs.org/upham.

PINE COUNTY

"Banning Quarry–Self-Guided Trail." Banning State Park brochure. Minnesota Department of Natural Resources, Division of Parks and Recreation.

Banning State Park brochure. Minnesota Department of Natural Resources, Division of Parks and Recreation.

Brown, Daniel James. Under a Flaming Sky: The Great Hinckley Firestorm of 1894. Guilford, 2006.

Cordes, Jim. Personal email. September 8, 2012.

Cordes, Jim. Pine County . . . and its Memories.

Dunn, James Taylor. "Banning Minnesota." Gopher Reader. Minnesota Historical Society Press, St. Paul 1975.

"The Great Hinckley Fire of 1894." City of Hinckley website. http://www.hinckley. govoffice2.com/index.asp?Type=B_BASIC&SEC=%7BFD8DC19D-5036-4403-8C87-061FFE2E781A%7D January 2, 2013.

Johnson, Megan. Personal email. September 7, 2012.

Johnson, Megan. Personal email. September 12, 2012.

Langseth, Muriel. Editor Sandstone, the Quarry City. Sandstone History Club. Dallas 1989.

Meyer, Roy W. Everyone's Country Estate: A History of Minnesota's State Parks. Minnesota Historical Society Press. St. Paul 1991.

One Hundred Years in Pine County. Pine County Historical Society. Askov. 1949.

Troolin, Amy. "Fun Facts. Banning." Pine County History Blog. http://pinecountyhistory.blogspot.com/ April 20, 2012.

Troolin, Amy. "Fun Facts. Friesland." Pine County History Blog. http://pinecountyhistory.blogspot.com/ July 15, 2012

Troolin, Amy. "Fun Facts. Groningen." Pine County History Blog. http://pinecountyhistory.blogspot.com/ May 13, 2012

Troolin, Amy. "Fun Facts. Mission Creek." Pine County History Blog. http://pinecountyhistory.blogspot.com/ May 13, 2012

Troolin, Amy. Personal email. July 6, 2012

Troolin, Amy. Personal email. September 10, 2012

VanDerWerf, Richard. Sandstone in Bygone Days.

POLK COUNTY

"Dugdale." Polk County Historical files. November 2012.

"Mallory." Polk County Historical Society files, November 2012.

Polk County Historical Society. Personal letters, November 2012.

RED LAKE COUNTY

"Equaility Township." Red Lake County Historical Society. www.redlakecountyhistory.org April 24, 2013.

"Garnes Township." Red Lake County Historical Society. www.redlakecountyhis tory.org April 24, 2013.

"Ghost Towns." Red Lake County Economic Development Corporation. www.prairieag.comm April 24, 2013.

"Lambert Township." Red Lake County Historical Society. www.redlakecountyhistory.org April 24, 2013.

"Louisville Township." Red Lake County Historical Society.

www.redlakecountyhistory.org April 24, 2013.

"Polke Center Township." Red Lake County Historical Society. www.redlakecountyhistory.org April 24, 2013.

"Red Lake County History Tour." Red Lake County History. www.harpercollege.edu April 25, 2013.

"Tennebonne Milling Company." Red Lake County Economic Development Corporation. www.prairieag.comm April 24, 2013.

Thibert, John. Personal email. April 28, 2013.

Upham, Warren. "Minnesota Place Names" Minnesota Historical Society. http://mnplaces.mnhs.org/upham/ April 20, 2013.

"Wylie Township." Red Lake County Historical Society. www.redlakecounty history.org April 24, 2013.

ROSEAU COUNTY

City of Greenbush, Minnesota. www.greenbushmn.gov April 4, 2013.

County of Roseau Centennial 1895-1995. Roseau County Historical Society N.d.

Dahl, Britt. Roseau County Historical Society. Personal email. April 4, 2013.

Dahl, Britt. Roseau County Historical Society. Telephone converstation. April 4, 2013.

Greenbush, Minnesota 1905-2005. Greenbush Centennial Committee. Roseau County Historical Society.

ST. LOUIS COUNTY

Abrahamson, Julius. "Rise of Elba." Personal letter. Elba-Elcor Reunion brochure January 28, 1955,

Alanen, Arnold R. "From Tower to Soudan: Townsites & Locations on the Vermillion Iron Range. www.minnesotahumanites.org October 12, 2012.

Alanen, Arnold R. "The Locations: Company Communities on Minnesota's Iron Ranges." Minnesota History. Fall 1982.

Anderson, Elizabeth. "Photographing a Ghost Town. Part I, Researching and Understanding Your Location." www.photable.com June 4, 2010 September 14, 2012.

Breining, Greg. "Mesabi Ghosts." Minnesota Volunteer. Minnesota Department of Natural Resources. July-August 1992.

Chinn, Marion J. "Childhood Memories." Elba-Elcor Reunion brochure

DeMillo, Lorraine. "The Moving of North Hibbing." Range History 1978.

"Elba-Elcor Reunion 1897-1956" brochure. 1982.

Eldot, Walter. "Death of a Mining Towns" Duluth News Tribune. July 17, 1955.

Eldot, Walter. "Range Reminiscing, Those Were the Days." Iron Range Historical Society Newsletter. June 1993.

Finsand, Mary Jane. The Town that Moved. Minneapolis 1983.

"From Pickax to Pellets: Touring the Ghost Towns & Growing Towns of the Eastern Mesabi Range." St. Louis County Historical Society. Duluth. October 12, 1963.

Glaven, Gregory S. "The Elcor Smokestack." "Range Reminiscing, Those Were the Days." Iron Range Historical Society Newsletter. September 1999.

"Ghost Towns Along the Mesabi." www.minnesotahumanities.org October 15, 2012.

Grinsgteinner, Kelly. "Building Protectors of the Past." www.hibbing.mn.us August 28, 2012.

Halunen, Rod. Ghost Towns and Locations of the Mesabi Iron Range. Virginia. 1992.

"Hibbing Minnesota on the Move." Hibbing Booklet Committee.

Hibbing Historical Society. Personal email. September 27, 2012.

"Homesteading Iron Range Country." www.minnesotahuman ities. org October 15, 2012.

Krier, John G. Krier, Jonelle J. "North Hibbing: Reminisces of a Ghost Town." Hibbing Historical Society. Hibbing. 1976.

Kuzma, Scott. Republic of Kinney. Fargo. 2007.

Hibbing Historical Society. Personal email. Septmber 24, 2012.

LaFreniere, Connie. City of Hibbing. Email. September 25, 2012.

Lamppa, Marvin G. "Ghost Towns & Locations of the Vermillion and East Mesabi Mining Districts" Master's Thesis. University of Minnesota June 1962.

Lamppa, Marvin G. "Merrit, A Ghost Town." Range History. March 1976.

Lamppa, Marvin. G. Minnesota's Iron Country: Rich Ore, Rich Lives. Duluth 2004.

Lamppa, Marvin G. "Old Mesaba." Range History.

Lamppa, Marvin G. Personal letter. October 24, 2012.

Larson, Joan. "Merrit, A Ghost Town." "Range Reminiscing, Those Were the Days." Iron Range Historical Society Newsletter. Fall 1981.

"Lindsley Moving Syracuse Professional House Movers Doing the Work." The Biwabik Times. November 29, 2012.

"Location Houses Go to Mesaba." www.minnesotahumanities.org October 15, 2012.

Lynch, Daniel. To Tipple a Prince. St. Cloud. 2010.

"Mesabi Range Towns and Cities at a Glance." www.minnesotahumanities.org October 4, 2012.

"The Mesabi Range." www.minnesotahumanities.org October 12, 2012.

"Minnesota Mine." www.miningartifacts.org September 18, 2012.

"Moving the Range Towns." www.minnesotahumanities.org January 12, 2012.

"North Hibbing—Hull Rust Mahoning Mine Walking Tour". City of Hibbing. www.hibbing.mn.us.

Pagnucco, Ann Shuster. "I Remember." Elba-Elcor Reunion brochure.

Potocnik, Joseph. "The Tale of the Elcor Mercantile." Elba-Elcor Reunion brochure.

Sowers, Susan. Personal email. October 11, 2012.

Squillace, Frank. "Spina Location." *Great Scott Township Centennial Book.*

Tilsen, Peggy Nicolas. "Elcor and Berry Picking Time." Elba-Elcor Reunion brochure. June 1981.

"The Vermillion Range." www.minnesotahumanities.org October 15, 2012.

"The Village of Merrit." Zenith City Online. http://zenithcity.com January 2013.

Weber, Eric. "The Relocation of Hibbing 1919-1921." *Minnesota Encyclopedia.* www.mnopedia.org August 27 2012.

"Welcome to Hibbing Area Disc Golf." Hibbing Disc Golf Association. www.hibbingdiscgolf.org November 9, 2012.

Wolff, Julius F. "Some Vanished Settlements of the Arrowhead Country." *Minnesota History.* Spring 1955.

TODD COUNTY

"Todd County: Then and Now." Todd County Historical Society. Dallas, 1998.

Upham, Warren. "A Geographical Encyclopedia." Minnesota Historical Society. 2009. Web. November 2012.

WADENA COUNTY

Bakke, Rose. Personal email. November 13, 2012.

"Blue Grass." *Wadena Pioneer Journal.* November 27, 1958.

"Blue Grass Farmers Buy Cheese Factory." *Wadena Pioneer Journal.* January 29, 1914.

"Blue Grass, Minnesota." *Minneapolis Star Tribune.* August 11, 1996.

"Blue Grass Pioneer is Hale and Hearty at 95." Unknown. Wadena County Historical Society files.

Boen, Harold E. "Original Store at Blue Grass Built About 1900." *Wadena Pioneer Journal.* September 8, 1966.

"Central: Our Sister to the Northeast." Unknown. Wadena County Historical Society files.

Crandall, John. *Shell City: Silhouettes of Time.* Nimrod. 1984.

"An Early History of Wadena County." Unknown. Wadena County Historical Society files.

Komppa, Rebecca. "Who Can Forget the Huntersville Fire of 1976?" *Review Messenger.* May 7, 2008.

Ladelle, Neal. "The Central Store and Post Office." Unknown. Wadena County Historical Society files.

Mitchell, Frank J. Personal Letter. April 30, 2013.

Pederson, Anna. "Oylen." Unpublished memoirs. Wadena County Historical Society files.

"Pioneer." Unknown. Wadena County Historical Society files.

"Sawmill Operations." *Wadena Pioneer Journal.* July 9, 1985.

"Shell City." www.ghosttowns.com October 15, 2012.

"Some of Fitzsimmons Family walked from Iowa." Unknown. Wadena County Historical Society files.

Timbs, Dawn. "Oylen's Camp Doors Open to All for over 100 Years." *Staples World.* July 26, 2012.

Zosel, Bob. "Kern Family Knew Early Days of Blue Grass." *Wadena Pioneer Journal.* April 16, 2011.

WILKIN COUNTY

Haagenson, Heidi. http://www.tenneyquilt.blogspot.com/ October 15, 2012.

Haagenson, Heidi. *The Tenney Quilt: Celebrating the Women of Minnesota's Tiniest Town.* Minneapolis. 2007.

Johnson, Jill A. *Little Minnesota: 100 Towns Around 100.* Cambridge. 2011.

Peters, Dave. "Going, going, . . . " *MPR News* June 21, 2011.

Smith, Mary Lynn. "Tenney says tata; Residents Vote 2-1 to Dissolve Town." *Minneapolis Star Tribune.* www.startribune.com June 22, 2011.

Tevlin, Jon. "Living Inside a Snow Globe: Tiny Tenney, Minnesota." *Minneapolis Star Tribune.* www.Startribune.com May 25, 2010.

Index